BEYOND SPORTS

From the huddle, from the locker room, and from the heart of this great quarterback comes a powerful story of living, loving, losing, and winning.

"One is left with the impression that Roger Staubach is not only a tremendous quarterback but also a devout and dedicated Christian gentleman. This comes through very vividly in this interesting book."

Best Sellers

"So refreshing after the endless series of critical books that pictured players as mindless creatures unable or unwilling to direct their own destinies."

Dallas Morning News

STAUBACH
First Down, Lifetime To Go

**Roger Staubach
with Sam Blair
and Bob St. John**

 AVON
|PUBLISHERS OF BARD, CAMELOT, DISCUS, EQUINOX AND FLARE BOOKS

AVON BOOKS
A division of
The Hearst Corporation
959 Eighth Avenue
New York, New York 10019

ISBN: 0-380-00806-8

First Avon Printing, October, 1976

AVON TRADEMARK REG. U.S. PAT. OFF. AND IN
OTHER COUNTRIES, MARCA REGISTRADA,
HECHO EN U.S.A.

Printed in the U.S.A.

To my wife, Marianne,
and our daughters
Jennifer, Michelle, and Stephanie,
who are the heart of my life.
And to my parents,
Bob and Betty Staubach
who gave me this life.

Contents

Acknowledgment

To my teammates, coaches,
and good friends throughout my career
on and off the field,
I offer my thanks and gratitude.
Life has been comforting,
fulfilling and satisfying
because of the people
I have played with and shared with.

Preface

Many books have been written about the negative aspects of professional football, some of which I found to be greatly exaggerated and even imagined to a certain degree. This is a different type of book. I have tried to approach controversial subjects in a more objective or constructive manner. I think there is too much negative thinking in this world.

I'm afraid I haven't been to any dope parties, and do not feel football has dehumanized me and taken away my individuality without giving me a choice in the matter. Certainly, there are rules and regimentation but a man isn't forced to play. He chooses to play of his own free will. If a person went to work for the Xerox Corporation, for instance, he would undoubtedly be expected to abide by rules set down by that organization. Football has been good to me and I believe I have contributed something to it.

Don't get me wrong. Football has its problems. On the dark side of the game there are such things as drugs, racial problems, and exploitation to a degree, but I believe that in most instances the extent of the problems is less than in society as a whole. Some players take pep pills and speed, just as some stock brokers and people in other walks of life do. But I think these players are in the vast minority.

In this book I don't believe I've looked at football, or life, through rose-colored glasses. I found that you tend to lose some innocence and idealism in Vietnam. Football is my vocation, my hobby, one of my passions, so naturally there is a lot of football in this book. But it also is a book about my life—the love, compassion, happiness, heartbreak, success, and failure I've encountered which I hope reflect not just my life but life as a whole. I have run the gamut of human emotions, both on and off the field, and have attempted to tell these experiences with the feeling that most people can identify with them.

—*Roger Staubach, 1974*

We chose to begin this book with a chapter on the final days of Elizabeth Staubach's life because we feel as you read of the great courage, compassion, and faith she showed until the very end, you'll see these traits reflected in her son.

—Sam Blair and Bob St. John

1

A Champion's Heart

Few things hurt more inside than watching someone you love die. It is a helpless, deeply sad, gnawing feeling for which there is nothing you can do and it diminishes everything else. Throughout the 1973 season Roger Staubach watched his mother, Elizabeth (Betty) Staubach, die of cancer.

Sometimes away from the field he would be himself again, laughing and joking as he will about his reputation of being square. But the sadness and hurt were always near, just a thought away.

"Roger earned the respect of everybody on this team with the courageous way he played that season," said Dallas Cowboy middle linebacker Lee Roy Jordan. "The guy is so mentally tough. He did a great job for us under conditions I don't believe another man could have handled."

"Oh Honey, can you see the agony in Roger's face?" Betty Staubach told a friend, Honey Rank. "I hate this so very much. It's hard to watch someone you love suffer. You'd so much rather have that suffering yourself."

The time I most like to remember during mother's last years was after we won the Super Bowl in January of 1972. I had been fortunate enough to win the Most Valuable Player award and she attended the award luncheon, sitting right there at the head table. Once when I looked over at her she had a big smile on her face and her green eyes were just shining, which gave me a happy, warm feeling inside. She was over sixty then but looked so young and healthy, with only a few streaks of gray in her dark hair. Mom was a large, robust woman then, about 5–7, perhaps 140 pounds. . . . And that's how I like to remember her.

When she died in December of 1973 her weight had dropped to sixty pounds, her skin was drawn and her voice, once so strong and clear, had become soft, sometimes only a whisper. But inside she never changed, keeping up her courage until the very end. I dedicated everything I did on the football field that season to her. Some days didn't work out as I had hoped but she was an inspiration to me throughout her last autumn, and I was always aware how strong and positive she was. I always will be.

Her sickness had come as a surprise to us. She had been so active and enthusiastic about life that it was difficult to imagine her being seriously ill. We weren't poor when I was growing up but we didn't have a lot of extras either. Mom had worked for twenty-nine years but was retiring and planning to open her own antique shop. She was going to take golf lessons, travel, and live an independent life. After my father died she had taken an apartment in Cincinnati, near the small town of Silverton where I was raised. I hate it that she didn't live to enjoy what could have been the easiest part of her life.

"In one of my weak moments I bought a fur," Betty Staubach told Honey Rank. "I had myself a ball that day. As a single you live differently and don't have much cause to have a fur. But I sure enjoyed getting it."

Her friends told me she hadn't been feeling well, which was evident when she visited us early that summer in Dallas.

"Your mother just isn't eating anything at all," my wife, Marianne, told me. "I'm worried about her."

"Oh it's nothing," mother said when I asked her about

2

her appetite. "It's just that I don't feel so good sometimes but it'll all pass." I was later to find out she had been to the doctor and was taking medicine. I insisted she go again, which she did after returning to Cincinnati. Doctors conducted more tests but couldn't locate the problem.

Finally, they put her into the hospital while I was on vacation with my family in New Mexico. Dr. Robert Hummel was going to perform exploratory surgery, though he felt reasonably sure she only had gall bladder problems. "Don't worry," she said when I phoned her. "I feel good. There isn't much to this." I immediately went to Cincinnati and brought in another specialist. He agreed she probably had gall bladder trouble. She looked terrible—jaundiced and very sick, but the doctors didn't expect it to be anything serious.

Dr. Hummel took a long time before coming to talk to me after surgery. I felt if everything had gone all right he'd have come right down. When I finally saw him he was shaking his head slowly as he walked toward me. "It's the very worst," he said. "I'm sorry. We found a huge tumor, the size of a softball, behind the pancreas. It can't be removed. We did a by-pass of the bowel so the jaundice should go away. And actually, she could feel pretty good for, oh, six to eight months. But no. I can't be sure how long she'll last. . . ."

I broke down. I didn't know what to do. Dr. Hummel advised me not to tell her, feeling it would only depress her more. He didn't know her very well and, looking back, I know we should have told her right away. We convinced her we only wanted her to come to Dallas to recuperate from the operation. Otherwise, we'd have had a difficult time keeping her from staying in Cincinnati.

By the time she was able to fly to Dallas I had gone to training camp in Thousand Oaks, California. Camp was especially important to me that year. I missed most of the 1972 season with a shoulder separation and faced a tremendous challenge from Craig Morton as I tried to reestablish myself as the No. 1 quarterback.

Dr. Dale Rank, a friend of mine who's a top surgeon in Arlington, a small city near Dallas, examined mother and

3

advised us she should be told immediately she had terminal cancer. Dale and his wife, Honey, were extremely kind to mother during her illness. The eldest of their three sons died of cancer when he was fifteen. Dale had written a book about the disease and spent a great deal of his time researching and studying the most advanced treatments. I left camp and returned to Dallas to be with her when she found out.

I arrived after she had gone into Dr. Rank's office. She did not know I was in the waiting room. When she came out and saw me tears immediately came into her eyes. I couldn't stand it. I hugged her and we were both crying. But her tears were gone almost as quickly as they had come and she acted as though nothing was wrong on our drive back home. She wasn't crying for herself. She was afraid she would become a burden on me and my family.

Mother had taken care of my grandmother, who was bedridden, during her last years and also nursed my father for a number of years before he died. She was determined not to burden us. "Roger, I'm going back to Cincinnati just as soon as I'm well enough to travel," she insisted. I knew she would never go back. But there's always a chance for a miracle so we never gave up hope completely. We wanted her to have no feeling of finality and kept her apartment and car waiting for her in Cincinnati. Except for the few weeks she spent in the hospital she stayed at our house during those final months of her life.

Marianne, who's a registered nurse, was just incredible during that time. She took extremely good care of mom, giving her shots at all hours, turning her over when she couldn't move, and doing everything for her. My wife is quite a woman. During all that time she still cared for our three daughters and tried to take all the strain possible off my mind, which allowed me to concentrate as much as I could on football. Not once did Marianne complain and she always seemed to have a smile on her face.

Marianne had had a lot of experience with cancer patients and told me, "I've never seen anybody hold up so well. She's such a brave woman." Mom had always been tough. Once when she was getting out of a car, somebody

4

slammed the door on her finger. She didn't yell or cry but only said, "Will you please open the door? My finger's caught." Another time her car started rolling down an embankment. She ran to stop it. Somehow the car went right over her ankles. They were swollen something awful yet she just went on about her business. Friends finally talked her into going to the doctor, who was amazed she could go so long without getting treatment.

She showed that same kind of courage in the biggest and last battle of her life. When I got back from training camp in mid-August I couldn't believe how much weight she had lost. But, as always, she kept up a good front. "Oh, don't worry yourself about me," she said. "I'll be fine. In a few days I'll have my strength back and be up and around again in no time."

Oh Honey, can you see the agony in Roger's face? I hate this so much. It's hard to watch someone you love suffer. You'd so much rather have that suffering yourself.

We had originally planned to take her to our exhibition game against New Orleans in Texas Stadium. Mrs. Landry had invited her to sit in their box, which was air-conditioned and much more comfortable than seats in the stadium. But the more I thought about this, the more I worried about how it might look. Craig and I were locked in a battle for the starting quarterback job. Some stupid things were being said about coach Landry favoring me because we shared many religious convictions. This couldn't have been farther from the truth. Coach Landry would never let something like that become a factor in selecting a quarterback. Actually, Craig was his kind of quarterback. Craig ran a game just as Landry wanted. I was sometimes wild and unpredictable, going against his philosophy. But I didn't want anybody who saw my mother in his box to think favoritism was involved. I discussed this with her and she decided not to go. It was a completely selfish thing on my part and made me feel terrible afterwards.

5

The last time mother saw me play football was our third game of the regular season against St. Louis. Coach Landry had picked me as the No. 1 quarterback but in our victories over Chicago and New Orleans I hadn't done much. As you'll learn, the Cardinals have played a more important role in my career than any other team. They came to Texas Stadium undefeated, fresh from an upset over Washington. The game was for first place in the NFC East. Mother was very excited. A friend of mine, Joe McKinney, invited her and Marianne to watch the game from his box. I kept telling myself the morning of the the game, you must do well. . . . You must do well. You must make her proud of you.

On a hot, sultry day Roger Staubach had one of his best games, completing seventeen of twenty-two passes for 276 yards and two touchdowns as he led the Dallas Cowboy offense to 578 net yards, second highest total in the team's history.

Dallas won 45–10, reminding followers of the awesomeness of the Super Bowl championship team.

In retrospect I don't know if it was that important to mother that I was the starter or not. She had told me she felt sympathy for Craig, too, when he didn't get to play. Games excited her but she was always praying that I wouldn't get hurt.

That St. Louis game straightened me out and was a big factor in the season. I felt great about it. Our first draft choice, tight end Billy Joe DuPree, had caught three touchdown passes, two from me and another from Craig, and this excited the whole team. I worked out with him during the summer and felt he could be outstanding. He was proving it. The team was great. Everything was working again.

The sun and heat had taken its toll when I met Marianne and mother in the parking lot after the game. Mother's coloring was bad, her face was drawn and tired. So I realized again just how sick she was. Sometimes a person can get caught up in the excitement of life and forget, for a moment, that someone you love is dying. Then when it hits, it shatters everything. You see the suffering they're going through and feel so helpless and it tears your insides out.

Oh Honey, can you see the agony in Roger's face? I hate this so much. It's hard to watch someone you love suffer. You'd so much rather have that suffering yourself.

The season dragged through October. The team had its ups and downs and mother became weaker. We were all worried. She wasn't responding well to the treatments. We had to put her into the hospital and just before she left she said, "I don't feel so bad, actually. I'll be back on my feet soon. You'll see."

This pain can really wear a person down.
—*Betty Staubach*
to Honey Rank

You can tell a person and the people who love them that they're going to die but they'll never really give up hope, not completely. Life is hope and as long as a person is alive, hope is never completely lost. I'm sure my mother told her friend, Honey Rank, things that she didn't tell us. And, despite how awful she was feeling she would sometimes seem at peace and even a little lighthearted.

Once Betty Staubach told Honey Rank, "You know, I feel so peaceful. God is very near."
And another time she said, "Honey, I'll buy the doughnuts for everybody here if somebody will go get them. That way, maybe I can sneak one myself."

We lost to the Eagles in Philadelphia, which was our worst performance of the season and left us with a 4–3 record. I went to see mother in the hospital after I got back. I felt terrible about her, the team, everything. "Roger, you've got to pull yourself out of this depression," she said. She talked to me a long time. To see her, like she was, trying to improve my spirits, made me feel ashamed.

Oh Honey, can you see the agony in Roger's face? I hate this so much. It's hard to watch someone you love suffer. You'd so much rather have that suffering yourself.

Mother's closest friends came down to see her the next week when we played Cincinnati in Dallas. She had grown up with these people and she and dad had had a lot of good times with them. She got out of bed and we had a dinner for her. She smiled and laughed and seemed happy, despite her pain.

John the Baptist lived on locusts and wild honey. Hmmm. Wonder how he fixed those locusts?
—*Betty Staubach*

Her friends naturally were Cincinnati Bengal boosters but they pulled for me that day. I especially wanted to play well against my hometown team, before many of the people who had watched me grow up. Mother, of course, was far too weak to attend the game.

Paul Brown had a fine team at Cincinnati, as the Bengals later proved by making the playoffs. But we got a big jump on them when Lee Roy Jordan intercepted three of Ken Anderson's passes in the first quarter, returning one for a touchdown and setting up a touchdown with another.

Roger Staubach was near perfect, hitting fourteen of eighteen passes for 209 yards and three touchdowns. The Bengals had hoped to blitz Staubach, keeping him off balance. Once Roger anticipated the blitz, calling an audible which sent Bobby Hayes streaking straight downfield. Hayes caught Staubach's pass on his fingertips in the end zone, a thirty-one-yard scoring play.

8

Mother had no more good days after her friends left. We had to put her in the hospital again for intravenous feeding before Thanksgiving. The doctor felt a few days in the hospital might make her feel a little better. I hated to see her go but she told Marianne that it might be better because everyone would be having turkey, the kids would be laughing, and it would be difficult not being able to take part.

We lost to the Dolphins on Thanksgiving and I went right to the hospital to visit her after the game. As I entered her room it all hit me so strongly. . . . She was making no progress. Her life was slipping away. I tried to stop myself but the tears just came. It was such a stupid thing to do in front of her, but she straightened me out.

"Please don't do that," she said, calling me over to her. "I'll be fine. Look at it this way. You'll always have a friend in heaven."

Oh Honey, can you see the agony in Roger's face? I hate this so much. It's hard to watch someone you love suffer. You'd so much rather have that suffering yourself.

"Honey," Betty Staubach whispered, "I'll . . . I'll be seeing you later."

While mother was still at our house, the kindness and compassion she was shown by our neighbors and friends was overwhelming. My teammates' wives, for example, brought dinner to our family frequently during her final days. Not long before she died, our parish priest, Father Claude Smith, came to say Mass for the sick. Mother was nothing but skin and bones then and could hardly move. Yet she tried to get up and sing Psalms during the Mass. I will never forget that.

Also, Father Smith and another close friend, Father Henry McGill, gave mother Holy Communion on numerous occasions.

Her faith had been the focal point of her life. She had

9

been a good Christian and I don't believe she worried about dying. She was prepared to be with God and see my father again. She was more concerned about us . . . about other people . . . than herself.

I'm not afraid of dying. But I do so hate to leave Roger, Marianne, and the girls. If I only had three weeks left I'd want to enjoy it with them. . . . And I'd much rather go from the bridge table than from this bed.

—*Betty Staubach*

"Betty was one of the dearest, sweetest people I've ever known," said Honey Rank. "She was such a kind person. When you said something she liked, she would reach both arms out to hug you. She used to say, 'I'm just a sentimental old Irish woman.'

"Nurses at the hospital would come to Betty with their problems. She welcomed them and never hurried over anyone. . . . It was like going home to know Betty Staubach."

We beat Denver and won our showdown game with Washington. Father Joseph Ryan, a navy chaplain and one of my best friends since my Annapolis days, had come to be with us then. When I came home from the Washington victory he was in the room with mother. I went over to her and said, "Well mom, we won." She smiled and grabbed my hand. She went into a coma that night and we never communicated again.

Roger was so good to his mother. He easily could have kept her in the hospital and visited her once a day but he and Marianne had her with them. This had to mean so much to her in those final months.

When I visited them in her last days I said Mass every morning. Roger was holding her hand, tears streaming down his face. He loved her so much.

—*Father Joseph Ryan*

On Thursday, December 13, mother passed away. I arranged for the funeral that morning and went to practice in the afternoon. I flew to Cincinnati on Friday and her services were held on Saturday. All her friends came and there was a feeling of great sadness. But she would have wanted us to be happy. The pain was over for her.

When I delivered her eulogy at graveside I said she was so proud of Roger, not so much because he was such a great football player but because he was a fine man, a fine husband, and a fine father.

—*Father Ryan*

I flew on to St. Louis to join the team on Sunday. We needed a victory to clinch the division title. I had missed a couple of days practice and had no idea how I'd perform physically. But then I became very determined. I know when you say you're going to do this or that it just doesn't always work out. But somehow, some way I would play well for her that day.

Winter had hit St. Louis, turning it into a Christmas card. Snow surrounded Busch Stadium. Tom Landry was worried that his club might face a natural letdown after the big victory over Washington. The Cardinals were limping with many injuries but were still capable.

The letdown never came. Roger Staubach, taking charge, completed fourteen of nineteen passes for 256 yards and three touchdowns. He not only led the Cowboys to a 30-3 victory but also won his second National Football League individual passing championship.

"Considering what he went through this week, the game he played was remarkable," said Tom Landry.

Remarkable.

I know I didn't experience anything different than a lot of people go through everyday. Death strikes close to us all at some time or other. People wanted to talk to me about it because I was an athlete. I'm sure I learned what others have found out at such a time. You must keep a positive attitude about life and what you have to do. I was emotionally ready to play that game in St. Louis.

Craig stood up at a team meeting the next week and said, "After what Roger's been through he should have a game ball for the St. Louis victory." I'll cherish that game ball always.

Sometimes it was difficult to concentrate on my job that season. But when Sundays came and the games started I played with everything I had. Standing on the sideline, listening to the National Anthem, I'd get the same old butterflies. I'd feel the same excitement of anticipation and then I would think of mother's tremendous strength and this, in turn, would give me strength as I went on the field.

She was an inspiration for me then and, as I think back on my life, I can see the positive influence she had ... the boyhood years, the sandlots, high school, when I was learning discipline at New Mexico Military Institute, at the Naval Academy, in Vietnam, and when I found a career in professional football after being away for four years. She always has been an influence. She always will be.

2

First Plateaus

Roger's parents had a tremendous influence on him. A lot of times kids complain about coaches or teachers or something else and parents side with the kid. Rog's always sided with authority and didn't offer him an outlet of rationalization. I think that helped him become a man.

> —*Vince Eysoldt*
> Roger's lifetime friend

It may surprise you that I was once a budding Van Cliburn. Circumstances, however, conspired to end my career—lack of talent. However, my mother was very conscious of opening up a variety of areas for me and then letting me choose what I wanted to do. So, she saw to it that I took piano lessons.

I must have been ten or eleven at the time, and didn't like it very much. Kids were always banging on the door while I practiced, wanting me to play ball. As soon as the lesson was over, I'd grab my glove and bat and run to the park. My lessons lasted for about three years. I really didn't have a musical ear, but my music teacher, Helen Rudolph, kept telling mother what a great pianist I was going to be.

The turning point of my musical career came during a recital at a big music hall in Cincinnati, just a few miles from the small suburban town of Silverton where I was raised.

It was my first recital, and I was all pinched up in a little tuxedo. One piece I had memorized and worked on for hours was the "William Tell Overture"—the Lone Ranger theme. My time came, and I went up on the stage. Suddenly, I forgot the whole thing. I knew I had to do something, so I just started pounding on the piano. Sometimes I'd remember a part of the piece and swing into it, then forget again and start pounding. Everybody was laughing.

Finally it ended and I sat down. Some people were still laughing, so I forced a grin and looked over at my dad. He just held his head down in his hands and didn't say a word. I think that convinced them that I should go back to my first love, sports. But today, looking back, I do regret, as my mother warned, quitting the piano lessons. I would give anything to have the ability to play.

I was born February 5, 1942, in Silverton, Ohio. Silverton is a small place with a shopping area in the center of town, a few churches, and a grade school. The main street leads into Cincinnati, actually making Silverton part of Cincinnati. When anybody asked where you were from, you'd say, Cincinnati. It was a town straight out of "American Graffiti." Silverton had all the ingredients of a small town, including the closeness and concern people felt for each other. I was an only child, but I never felt lonely. The neighborhood was so close that the other kids seemed like my brothers and sisters.

I had no special athletic heritage. My father, Bob Staubach, was a big man of German ancestry, about 6–2 and 195 pounds. He was born and raised in South Gate, Kentucky, right across the river from Cincinnati. A good baseball player, he did well in a semipro league in his youth, but that was about his only experience in athletics. He was a manufacturer's representative in the shoe, leather, and thread business. It was a good, honest, hard-working business, but I guess he only made $50 or $55 a week and was provided a car. Money wasn't his main objective, though. His family was.

My mother, Betty, was a tall, stately woman. She was Irish, very determined and outspoken, but had a great warmth and love about her. She was from Cincinnati and had always enjoyed watching sports. Her brother, Harry

Smyth, apparently had tremendous potential as an athlete, but it seems he never took it seriously.

My parents never forced me into sports but when they saw my interest and talent, they helped me all they could. My environment was also conducive to sports. The Brannens, who lived across the street, put up a basketball court and we played there a lot. We had a fairly big backyard where we played baseball. The Biens, whose kids were sports enthusiasts, had a big lot that became our football field. I developed a love for sports and competition, right there in my own neighborhood.

Looking back, it's probably a good thing I used up a lot of my energies in sports because I was prone to get into fights and mischief.

I remember one time when I was scared to death. They had just poured concrete next door to us and I sneaked over and scribbled all over it. A man who had done the work saw me and I took off. He chased me to our backyard and I ran crying into the kitchen. My dad was there. Yes . . . I would say I learned a lesson that day.

I used to get into a lot of mischief with a good friend named Vince Eysoldt. I was a server or altar boy at Mass. Vince was new at the job and didn't know when to ring the bell during Mass. So I told him to just look at me and I'd nod when it was time to ring the bell. I couldn't resist. I nodded at all the wrong times and it nearly broke up Mass. Vince would start ringing that bell like crazy. All the nuns got mad at him. He never did trust me much after that.

Like most boys, I got into trouble occasionally but I committed only one major crime, and I still remember it. I hadn't started to grade school yet, and we were visiting friends when I saw some change on the table. I picked it up when nobody was looking and put it into my pocket. A little later I realized I was a thief. It really tore me up. I told my mother and, after talking to me a long time, she made me return the money. That ended my career in crime, but not in mischief, which I'm afraid carried over into my adult life.

My religious convictions started with my parents. Many

parents lecture children on religious thoughts and philosophy but if a child doesn't see these things practiced by his parents, he realizes the hypocrisy of the whole thing. And the parents actually do him a disservice. My parents were excellent examples of Christianity. They didn't bring me up in the overly religious, fire-and-brimstone-type atmosphere, but rather with a solid foundation that enabled me to determine for myself which direction I wanted to go.

One example I'll never forget. I must have been about twelve. Some black people from Cincinnati had started to move into Silverton. People were saying things like, "Gee, it looks like the blacks are going to come in and take over Silverton. They'll run us out of our own neighborhood." My mother was a good neighbor and they respected her, but she really chewed them out. I was there when she did it and it left a lasting impression on me.

"These are good people, too," she told them. "You're church-going, God-fearing people who love God and try to live a good life and yet, just look at you! You're worrying because a man with a different colored skin is moving into the neighborhood. It makes me ashamed."

She told them they were hypocrites. When I think of the feeling at the time—the great prejudice so many people felt—it was really something for her to be speaking out like that.

My parents also taught me responsibility and the true meaning of love—by their actions. When I was about ten, my grandmother (my mother's mother), who had lived with us since I was born, became very ill and senile. Nana was seventy-five then and almost bedridden with hardening of the arteries. Because of her condition, she required a great deal of care. But my mother refused to put her in a nursing home.

We had two bedrooms and I shared one with Nana. It was terrible seeing her so ill. I wanted to do something to help her, to make her all right, but there was nothing that could be done.

Although mother had gone back to work to help make ends meet when I was about nine, she'd work all day, then spend all evening caring for my grandmother. We would

16

all help. The greatest part of the work fell to mother, but she never complained. This was just another example of her great capacity for love.

I had been involved in sports almost since the time I could walk and played on my first organized team when I was about six or seven. A man named John Fink organized a Pee Wee Baseball League in Silverton. I played about every position. In the fourth, fifth, and sixth grades we got into the Knothole League and I played catcher on one team that won thirty-nine games in a row and the state championship.

I got into other organized sports for the first time in the seventh grade. I went to St. John The Evangelist grade school, a Catholic school for kids from Silverton and Deer Park. The Catholic Youth Organization was organizing sports for kids our age in the Cincinnati area. The public schools hadn't gotten into organized athletic programs then and this later gave us an advantage when we went to high school. I played baseball, guard in basketball and halfback in football.

It's a very significant time as I look back at sports in grade school. That's when you start getting your first impressions of athletics. You're very young but your whole world revolves around those your own age. A touchdown for you is just as important as one in the Army-Navy game or in the Super Bowl.

In the eighth grade I realized a guy could be somewhat of a hero playing football. That idea appealed to me. We hadn't won a game in the seventh grade, but we turned things around and won all of our games in the eighth grade. We were very proud of ourselves. Randy Shoemaker and I switched back and forth between halfback and fullback and we each scored seventeen touchdowns.

Being a hero seemed like a big deal. But my parents kept telling me that I was just on one plateau, that if I thought I was so great on this plateau, I wasn't going to achieve another level. It was the old adage about not letting something go to your head, but it sank in. I think I

17

kept my head because they kept stressing that plateau analogy.

I had begun to notice this certain cheerleader in grade school. We called her Pidge and she lived near our neighborhood. I saw her at some parties and later on we dated on and off during high school. Her real name was Marianne.

Some strange and disappointing things happened when I was in the eighth grade, but they taught me some valuable lessons. There were rules about weighing in at the beginning of football season because there was a weight limit. Randy had been sick and nobody ever told him to weigh in. One of our opponents protested saying he was overweight. Grant weighed in and was fine, but they found out he hadn't weighed in earlier and we had to forfeit our first seven games. St. Agnes was in second place and so they were moved to the top. Oddly enough, we played St. Agnes that eighth game and beat them 39-7. It got so bad that a priest came down and told us to take it easy. We won the rest of our games but instead of being 10–0, it went into the books as 3–7.

Something disappointing also happened in baseball. We were in the semifinals of the city championships, ready to play a team by the name of the Guardian Angels. If we beat the Angels we'd get to play for the championship in Crosley Field. That was unbelievable to a bunch of eighth graders. Crosley Field was the home of all our heroes— Ted Kluzewski, Johnny Temple, Jim Greengrass, Gus Bell, and Roy McMillan. We were getting ready to leave for the game when our coach discovered he had gotten the time mixed up. We were supposed to play at one, and he thought the game started at three. We lost on a forfeit. Just incredible! We lost without ever playing. We appealed to the League, begging for a chance to play the game. But they said, "That's tough."

The eighth grade was also one of the most frustrating times of my life. We lost the basketball championship in the final game of the season. But at least we were actually beaten. Losing on a rules violation or because of a forfeit makes it doubly hard to accept defeat. But I've always found defeat extremely difficult to accept anyway.

It's a popular story in Cincinnati that when you enter Purcell High School the first thing you see is a huge color portrait of Roger Staubach. Then you walk down the hall and there's an eight-by-ten-inch photo of the Pope.

"Am I surprised Rog has done so well? Not at all," said Jerry Momper, co-captain with Roger at Purcell. "Everybody in high school felt he'd do well. No success he ever achieves surprises me. He's just a damn sharp guy. He's dedicated, competitive. When he gets out of sports he'll do well, too. The more I'm in the business world the more I appreciate the attributes Rog has to be a success at anything."

"Rog was everything in high school," recalled Vince Eysoldt. "He was prom king, president of the student body, and starred in football, basketball, and baseball. He was and is a super friend, though I doubt you could trust him to tell a server in Mass when to ring the bell."

Purcell was an all-boys Catholic high school. Without girls around I guess we could concentrate on sports more. The Roman Catholic high schools were very strong in athletics then. When I went to high school, Catholic schools such as Purcell, Elder, St. Xavier, and Roger Bacon had outstanding football teams.

I had done most of my growing between the eighth grade and my freshman year at Purcell. I'd grown to about six-feet tall and gained over forty pounds to about 160. Over 100 kids went out for the freshman football team. I knew there were two things I could do—catch the ball and run with it. Since everybody wanted to carry the ball, the halfback line was the longest. I picked end, because it was the shortest line. After a couple of weeks, I moved up to the starting job.

The freshman coach was a dynamic guy named Bernie

19

Sinchek. He certainly helped me learn discipline. One day I was late for practice.

"Staubach, you're late and now you're on the last string," Bernie told me. It took a week for me to work my way back up.

It was a good year. I caught as many touchdown passes as any other freshman end had at Purcell. I also played basketball and baseball.

I coached Roger in the Municipal Baseball League where he played catcher and hit .422. I continued to coach him in the Muny league the next few years and he was a fine prospect, though I personally felt basketball was his second best sport. I do recall one incident while he was playing baseball for me. We were losing 3–2 in the eighth inning with two on.

Roger had gone 0–for–4 and I gave him the take sign. He called time, walked over to me and said, "Coach, I can hit this guy. Give me the hit sign." He went back and hit the ball twenty yards over the centerfielder's head. The runs scored. We won. That's what you call good coaching.

—*Bernie Sinchek*

I just knew I was going to be an end in those days. Sophomores were on the reserve team and I was anticipating all the passes I was going to catch. But one day the reserve team coaches told me Jim McCarthy, the head coach, wanted me to play quarterback. I fought it, saying I wanted to be an end. It did me a lot of good to protest. They put me at quarterback.

I had seen that particular group as freshmen and sophomores. The quarterbacks were too short and were not able to throw the ball very well. I told my assistants that I didn't think any of the three quarterbacks could make it on the varsity. I asked them who was their best athlete. Roger's name came up. I told them Roger Staubach was now a quarterback.

—*Jim McCarthy*
Purcell head coach

I did okay at quarterback and we won the first game, although we lost the second game. Jim McQuade and Bob Krueger, the reserve coaches, were really mad. They knew football and certainly helped me learn the game, but they were like a couple of drill sergeants at Parris Island. They got us out to practice the next day and killed us. They put me on defense for a while and I broke my hand. This finished my sophomore year except for the final game.

Jim McCarthy was somewhat the Tom Landry type. He stayed pretty aloof from the players. You would walk down the hall at school and he'd just go right past you without even speaking. He treated everybody the same. His rules were strict, and I remember he kicked a guy off the team for smoking. But when you graduated and weren't part of the team anymore he'd do anything for you. He would go all out to help you get a scholarship.

In McCarthy's system, juniors played on defense and served as backups to the seniors, who played offense. I was a defensive halfback and a backup quarterback. So it wasn't until my senior year that I really learned about quarterbacking—running when I was supposed to pass.

His approach was to have a good, strong, running game, stressing fundamentals. Nothing fancy. We didn't have one quarterback running play, not even a quarterback sneak. So I just started taking off after I'd drop back to pass. It just came naturally to me. I'd go back to pass and . . . I'd just want to take off. We didn't have many passing plays called but I think I gained over 500 yards running the ball.

"We never let our quarterbacks run," said Jim McCarthy. "We spent too much time training them to let them get hurt carrying the ball. We had three other backs to do that. Roger changed all that. If the

21

receiver wasn't open, he'd more or less panic and take off."

"We called him Roger the Dodger and also Ostrich because he had those long legs and that three-quarter gait," said Jerry Momper. "I was the center when he moved to quarterback, so you might say I gave him his start."

Dad was in the hospital and missed our big game with Elder, our crosstown rival. Steve Tensi, Elder's big quarterback who also went into pro ball, and I were battling to be the best quarterback in the city and our teams were battling for the championship. Dad had seen all the games but something had happened to him. He had a blister on his foot and it wouldn't go away. I didn't realize diabetes was a factor at that time. Gangrene had set in and the doctors decided to amputate part of his foot. Mom knew the history of diabetes, since both my uncle and grandfather had gone through it. The amputation was part of the diabetes syndrome.

It was during this time that life became very real for me. You grow up in a warm environment, your parents are good to you, and you take their health for granted. In grade school you learn a little about life, but it's an automatic thing with your parents. You go home and they're there. You forget about the things that they're going through. They don't tell you their troubles and you don't see them as just living day-to-day through their own problems and troubles. You look at them, love them, and they're like rocks. You just can't believe it when they're any other way. I played the Elder game for dad. It was probably the best high school game I ever played.

"A victory over Elder would give us the championship, or the co-championship the way it turned out because we lost our final game," Vince Eysoldt recalled. "Very late in the game a power sweep was called, with me carrying the ball and the guards pulling.

22

"As we broke the huddle, Rog told me to act like I had the ball. He faked to me and kept the ball himself on a naked reverse. He fooled everybody, including coach McCarthy. Rog ran sixty-two yards for a touchdown and won the game for us, 20-14."

I had planned to use that play during the game, and was just waiting for the right time. It worked! I took films of the game to dad's hospital ward and showed them to him. It really picked him up. Here he was bedridden in the hospital for the first time and losing part of his foot, and he was still showing how proud he was of me.

I grew up a lot that last year in high school. Dad's illness was a great awakening for me, a realization about his sickness. It really tore me up. He got progressively worse as the years went by. He had been such a strong, healthy man, and now the illness was eating away at him. My mother urged him to take care of himself, but he was very stubborn about it. He tried to ignore the diabetes. It was as if he thought that if he hung in there long enough he would beat the disease. He'd go away on trips and when he'd come back, the insulin kit wouldn't even have been used.

I had a big decision to make as far as my future was concerned. There were a lot of offers from colleges. My mother didn't want me tied to her apron strings, though it certainly would have been easier to choose Cincinnati or Xavier.

"Don't worry about your dad," she told me. "Everything's going to be fine with us. It's time for you to get away and find out what life is all about outside our home."

I had some ideas where I wanted to go to college, but it certainly didn't turn out the way I expected.

3

Finding the Right Road

Some forty colleges tried to recruit Roger Staubach to play football for them when he finished his senior season at Purcell High. You might think Notre Dame was one of those trying the hardest to land him. After all, he not only was an outstanding quarterback, he was an outstanding Roman Catholic quarterback. Maybe that's how the story would go in a movie, but that's not how it went in the spring of 1960.

While all these other schools were after me I never heard from Notre Dame. Naturally, being a Catholic from Cincinnati and knowing all about the Gipper and Knute Rockne since boyhood, I always had been aware of Notre Dame and would have strongly considered going there. But Joe Kuharich was the coach then and had a recruiting program which was suspect.

I'm not saying that just because of myself. There were a number of good prospects in Cincinnati, including several right at Purcell, but Notre Dame didn't contact any of them. Chuck Lima, a reserve fullback at Notre Dame who had gone to Purcell, took some film of my games and told the coaches, "I think you ought to talk to this guy." They just told Chuck, "Our quarterback quota is full."

I was feeling plenty of pressure from other schools, though, particularly right in my hometown. The two local universities, Cincinnati and Xavier, were after me all the time.

I was caught in a bind there. Since they were nearby, their coaches came by school to visit frequently and, of course, they had close associations with some of the Purcell coaches. That made it even more difficult for me to say no.

I couldn't tell a coach, "No, I don't want to go to your school." I would just say, "Well, I've just got to think about it." Instead of narrowing the schools down to the few which really interested me, I'm afraid I led some others on thinking they might get me. The pressure was building up through all those months and I increased it by not making my feelings clear.

I never really wanted to go to college in Cincinnati, although a lot of my teammates did. Both Cincinnati and Xavier had good football programs then but I wanted to get away. Mother made it clear that the path was wide open for me despite dad's health problems. Still, the Cincinnati-Xavier situation was a tough one and I kept putting off telling them to forget about me.

It really erupted one day just before a baseball game with Roger Bacon. Paul Misali, a tremendous guy, who was varsity baseball coach and also an assistant football coach, was very upset with me. He grabbed my arm, pulled me into a room and said, "You've got to make a decision! You're just leading these Cincinnati people on."

I couldn't believe it. We were close friends and I really respected him. But there he was raging at me. I just broke down and almost started crying. I was in sad shape. He wasn't even going to let me play that day.

Paul had some good friends at the University of Cincinnati, where he later served as an assistant coach, but he wasn't trying to get me to pick it over Xavier. It was just a matter of my indecision and he felt I was being unfair to a lot of people.

I'll never forget that day. That's how tough the pressure of recruiting was for me. I told him I didn't know what I wanted to do. When I settled down and walked out of that room I really got mad. I was mad at myself, mad at him, and I went out and played in the game. I think I hit the longest home run of my career. I just stepped up to the plate my first time at bat and whacked one over some garages out beyond centerfield.

When I rounded third base, Paul came out, grabbed my

hand and put his arm around me as I ran toward home plate. We were friends again. But I made my decision right there I was going to tell both schools that I wasn't staying in Cincinnati.

Five Big Ten schools contacted me and I was heavily recruited by Ohio State and Purdue. I flew to Michigan for a visit but decided against the school right away. Many of these schools have athletes show you around, and at Michigan I was with the wrong guy. He just wanted to go to bars and burlesque shows. He said, "Yeah, this is what we do all the time. It's great being a jock here!"

Those things just didn't interest me. I loved to have a good time but to go out and drink with a bunch of guys wasn't how I wanted to spend my time. That was a wasted trip.

Next, I flew to Purdue. I became interested in the school because of a Purdue alumnus in Cincinnati named Carl Bimal. He was a great guy and never really high-pressured me. He would just come by to talk and maybe take me out for a milkshake after school. He also got my parents interested in Purdue. And I liked the idea that Purdue was also after Jim Higgins, one of my Purcell teammates.

Bob DeMoss, who later became head coach, was quarterback coach at Purdue then and I was very impressed with him. He was a good man and I knew he would be the coach who worked closely with me. His approach was just the opposite of what I had encountered at Michigan. The first thing he did was take me over to the Newman Club at the Catholic church. He introduced me to the people there and told me what a great club it was. Now that was something that appealed to me. He tried to show me something about college life other than football and parties.

I liked Purdue and eventually signed a tender there, which meant I would go to Purdue if I went to a Big Ten school. But before I signed I had quite an experience with Woody Hayes at Ohio State.

Moody had compiled his great coaching record with

tremendous ground teams and he was excited about me because he had seen some of my high school films. He knew I was a running quarterback and that really triggered him. He personally stayed after me, calling me often and making sure his recruiter in Cincinnati stayed in contact.

He had me up to Columbus, about 100 miles from Cincinnati, for one visit and when I came home my mother was very outspoken against Ohio State.

"That school is too big," she said. "That is one place you are not going."

Well, that didn't slow Woody down. Next time he called I told him I wasn't interested, but he said, "How about bringing your mother up for a visit?"

I was agreeable but mother was very reluctant to go. I finally talked her into it and we drove up there one weekend. We were given a tour of the campus and had lunch. Then Woody took us to his office.

We walked in and sat down. Immediately he took off his coat and rolled up his sleeves, just like he does on the sideline during a big game. He's very impressive, a jut-jaw-type who communicates great strength and determination. When he talks, you listen, and he really started talking.

He went to a blackboard and started listing all the advantages of going to Ohio State: scholastically, morally, socially. You name it, he had a pitch for it. The whole presentation was for my mother. He didn't mention once that her son was going to play football there. He made it clear how he and his people took care of the boys who come to his school.

As we were leaving mother said, "Roger, you make your own decision. If you want to go to Ohio State, you can go."

What a sales job! That's Woody Hayes for you, a real professional. He believes in and loves the school and he can sell it to young Ohioans.

Just before I signed the tender with Purdue, Woody was on the phone with me seven straight nights trying to swing me over to Ohio State. But never once did he offer me anything other than the normal scholarship. I know there are a lot of violations in college recruiting—under-the-table cash, cars, clothes—but in all my experiences with different schools I saw very little of that.

I signed the tender with Purdue during the spring, and when I graduated in June I thought I would probably go there. But I was never certain. I had visited the Naval Academy and really liked it, although I had no interest in the navy and there was no navy background in my family. The school had a great atmosphere about it and I also became good friends with Rick Forzano, the Navy assistant coach who recruited in the Cincinnati area.

I made so many trips to Cincinnati to see Roger that the other Navy coaches thought maybe I had found the Messiah there. I had had my eye on him since his junior year, when I dropped by Purcell High to look at some game films. I kept noticing this kid playing defensive back and back-up quarterback who just looked like a good athlete.

His coach, Jim McCarthy, told me Roger would be the starting quarterback the next fall and he thought he might be a great one. I wanted to learn more about him so I watched him play baseball. He went three-for-five at bat that day. I met Roger afterward and learned that on top of being a fine athlete he was a great young man. It was too early to be serious about recruiting him then, but I wrote him a few letters through the months just to keep his interest.

When I went back to Purcell and looked at films after his senior season, I really got excited. I'll never forget one play. Roger dropped back to pass and was trapped, but he rolled out and ran fifty or fifty-five yards for a touchdown. By then Jim McCarthy was sure he would be a great college player.

Roger really wanted to go to Notre Dame and I figured Notre Dame would grab him, but I kept calling and dropping by to visit. A couple of men in Cincinnati offered valuable help. One was Dick Kleinfeldt, a "bird dog" for the Navy recruiting program who took

28

Roger and a number of other prospects to visit the academy. The other was Bill Clark, who had been a great Navy player and now worked for Chevrolet, where Roger's mother worked. Between us we kept him conscious of the Naval Academy, plus the fact we had a great product to sell in the school itself. Roger was really impressed with it when he visited.

—*Rick Forzano*

The whole atmosphere at the Naval Academy was better than what I had seen at some other schools. I went out with some midshipmen. They took me to a movie and a sporting event and talked about the importance of studies and education.

I knew I was going to have a tough time in college playing sports and getting an education because I had not formed good study habits in high school. I made good grades, but I had a difficult time studying. I believed the Naval Academy would, at least, teach me to study and make my college years worthwhile. At some of the schools I was shown around by goof-offs—guys who would never graduate. I was afraid of that happening to me.

Then I learned I couldn't get into the Naval Academy. I took the College Board exams and scored very high in math but very low in English. The entrance requirements then said you had to qualify with a certain score in each. If they had combined the two scores, as the academy does now, I would have made it. But that did me no good then. I figured the Naval Academy was out. They talked to me about attending prep school for a year, saying I would have no trouble with the entrance requirements after that. I didn't want to, though. It looked like a wasted year. So I began thinking strongly about Purdue.

All along I kept thinking something would work out for Roger at Notre Dame. Still I kept in touch. His parents were great people. They wouldn't turn you off just because you were talking about a school their son probably wouldn't go to. I kept hoping we could change Roger's mind about waiting a year to enter the Naval Academy. Then one day he called me.

"Coach, I'm not going to Notre Dame," he said. "Now I want to go to a school that plays Notre Dame. I'm going to Purdue."

"Purdue!" I screamed. I never thought he was serious about Purdue. I grabbed a plane to Cincinnati for one more talk with Roger.

He still had doubts about the four-year service commitment which followed graduation from the Naval Academy. And he was dead set against a year at prep school. So out of the blue I said, "Roger, how about going to New Mexico Military Institute? It's a junior college and a fine school academically. You can go there on a football scholarship with no obligation to the Naval Academy. If you decide after a year you want to attend another school, you can transfer all of your credits. Meanwhile, you'll be starting your college education and getting a sense of direction."

The idea seemed to appeal to Roger. "Let me think about it," he said. I really felt encouraged. I called Bob Shaw, an old friend who had just taken over as head coach at NMMI and was taking a number of other players interested in the Naval Academy.

I said, "Bob, I've got a player for you who'll make you a great coach." He said, "I'm out of scholarships." I said, "Well, dig up another one somehow. If you don't take Roger Staubach you'll always be sorry."

Well, Bob agreed to find a scholarship and then Roger told me that he liked the idea of a year at NMMI and would go. Suddenly everything fell into place and I was delighted. I felt if he went that far, he eventually would be playing for Navy.

—*Rick Forzano*

By the end of June I still was confused. The Purdue people had been nice to me and I had signed that tender, but still it seemed too big—like some of the other schools I had seen. Suddenly, the idea of going to New Mexico Military Institute really seemed right.

By the time I played in the Ohio High School All-Star game later that summer, I was definitely set on NMMI. I had prayed very hard to make the right decision and finally I knew I had. I was going to the Naval Academy after a year in junior college. Mom said, "Fine, if that is your decision."

Naturally, there were a lot of college scouts at the All-Star game. I played for the South, which was coached by Pete Ankney of Dayton. His nephew, Mo Ankney, was also on the team and played most of the game at quarterback. I played regularly on defense at safety and wound up tackling Paul Warfield ten or eleven times. Warfield was the game's outstanding player and spent the night breaking into our secondary. I also played wide receiver some and got in about a quarter at quarterback. Overall I had a good game.

Roger was tremendous in that game. He had all those unassisted tackles on Warfield. He made some great catches. As a quarterback he was two-for-two passing and got loose on a long run which excited everybody.

In the locker room after the game all those college scouts, including Notre Dame's, were mobbing him. I said, "Uh, oh." He already had his plane ticket to New Mexico but I was afraid he would never use it.

Finally I caught his eye. He came over to me and said, "Coach, I told you I'd try NMMI. I'll be on that plane."

—*Rick Forzano*

The next day Notre Dame called me and said if I wanted to go to school there, I had a four-year scholarship. If I had heard that back in the spring it really would have influenced me. But it was too late.

Mom and dad wished me the best. It was a big decision for them to let me go off to school so far away. But, it was the beginning of my future—the key decision which would determine the course of my life.

4

Oh, New Mexico

We had a quarterback coming in with more fanfare named Tim Van Galder, who later went on to star at Iowa State and play pro ball, too. Tim was highly recommended. But after I looked at Staubach for a while, I moved Van Galder to defensive halfback.

—Bob Shaw
head coach, NMMI, 1960

My control of the English language is not enough to tell you all the good things about Roger, so I'll just say you have a most wonderful young man for a son.

—Bob Shaw
in a letter to Mr. and Mrs. Robert Staubach,
May 1961

The most amazing thing about Roger was that he never changed. He was one of those young men born to lead without fanfare or bragging. I've never met a person who didn't think Roger was a great guy.

—Bob Shaw
recently

Roger a straight guy? You kiddin' me! Rog was one of the biggest cut-ups, one of the craziest guys I've ever known.

—Bob Henry
friend and teammate

33

When I landed in Roswell, New Mexico, I was about as sick as I've ever been in my life. I had never made a long cross-country flight before and so the 1,500-mile trip from Cincinnati to New Mexico seemed to take forever. I had to change flights in Dallas, and board a small prop job in order to get to Roswell. I think the pilot had once been a crop-duster. It was a hot August day. We made a few stops on the way and just seemed to be bobbing around in the sky, like we were being held up by a loose cable or rope. I got so sick at my stomach I didn't even care whether we crashed.

I was met at the airport and must have made a great impression. Here I was this sick, green-looking, hunched-over soul that they almost had to roll off the airplane, and they had given me a scholarship.

"Are *you* Roger Staubach?"

"Hi, (burp), yes."

It was about 100 degrees and as far as I could see there were tumbleweeds dancing around in the wind and sand was blowing all over the place. Roswell was a fairly large city but the area was barren and desolate. I was ready to go back home—but not on *that* plane. And I had no earthly idea what to expect at New Mexico Military Institute. The superintendent was Lt. Gen. Hobart Gay, one of our foremost officers during the Korean War. I believe he had also served under Gen. Patton.

NMMI was a very strict military school with a fine academic program, excellent teachers and a lot of tradition. Unfortunately, NMMI also had a three-year high school, where I suppose wealthy families sent their kids. High school kids were integrated into the brigade and so, after they'd been there two or three years, they had rank. It was a difficult adjustment! You even had to call these high school kids, "sir." I never had any disciplinary problems in high school but suddenly I was in a strict military routine and I just couldn't adjust. I found it very, very difficult to brace up to high school students who wanted to harass me.

It was a bunch of garbage. We hated it. You should have seen Rog bracing up.

—*Bob Henry*

We'd brace up in this exaggerated way—rod-stiff backs, eyes bulging, and looking as if we'd just swallowed a lemon or jumped straight up after sitting on a tack. Naturally, I got into serious trouble right away. A high school senior was giving out laundry. I went over to get mine, gave him my tag and said, "I'd like to get my laundry."

"What did you say!"

"Well, I said I'd like to get my laundry."

"Don't you say, *sir*, to me?"

"Yessss surrrrrrr."

He really got mad about my sarcasm but I just didn't think to call him, "sir." He was a little guy but he grabbed my laundry bag and threw it at me. I caught it and slung it back at him, knocking him right over. I was really mad and told him if he wanted any more trouble to come on outside. He wanted some trouble, but not outside. This incident got me a lot of demerits but, fortunately, I was an athlete so they worked things out and I didn't get thrown out of school. However, demerits were tough, I can vouch for that. If you got twenty demerits, that meant you had to walk twenty hours of tours with a rifle on your shoulder on weekends. I think I became more famous for walking tours on the quadrangle than I did for athletics.

That laundry bag caper branded me a trouble-maker so I tried to be especially nice to everybody. But it was difficult.

Athletes had to be waiters to help earn our scholarships. We wore white aprons and served the guys in the dining hall. We did everything to irritate them—putting peas in their applesauce, things like that. Or we'd go on strike and do everything in slow motion. About twenty of us would come in with the food trays and, all of a sudden, we'd start moving in exaggerated slow motion. Some of them didn't particularly like us.

35

I'm thankful, though, for all that discipline at NMMI because if I hadn't gone through it, I don't think I'd ever have made it at the Naval Academy. I had enough trouble there anyway. But I sure learned some discipline plus some domestic chores like how to spit-shine shoes, polish brass and things that took a lot of getting used to.

Staubach didn't spit-shine his shoes. He used Windex.

—*Bob Henry*

I threw the football only five or six times a game in high school but worked hard on my passing during the summer before college. I knew I could throw because I always had a very strong arm in baseball. I worked and sometimes I'd zip the football right in there and other times it would take off nowhere. So I practiced like mad. I was told I could develop as a quarterback and I really got to liking the position. Even in high school I liked the idea of going out and taking charge. Things fell into place at NMMI and I threw a lot.

Bob Shaw had taken over as head coach and athletic director the summer before I came to Roswell. He was a big man, about 6-4 or 6-5 and very impressive. He wore glasses that actually steamed up at times. He had a strong temper and insisted on having everything exactly his way. Bob had been all-America end at Ohio State under Paul Brown. He later played end for the Rams and Cardinals and made all-pro. He once set an NFL record by catching five touchdown passes in one game. He was a fine coach and introduced me to the wide-open, pro-set offense.

Roger was like a sponge because he grasped things so quickly. He was very enthusiastic and knowledgeable. He always had an uncanny ability to gauge receivers. We worked with him on Unitas' technique for the bomb, the up-and-over motion, getting the ball over the defensive back's head into the receiver's arms.

36

That 1960 team was a good one. Eight or nine went on to play first string at Navy and four others played for the Air Force.

—Bob Shaw

Coach Shaw helped me in other ways too. He knew I was homesick so he used some reverse psychology. He started telling me I had to help the other guys on the team who were homesick. It worked. I relaxed. Shaw took a bunch of guys who had never played together and put together a 9-1 record. I hit over 60 percent of my passes. I had finally become a passer.

We played top competition such as the Air Force Academy junior varsity, Cameron, Oklahoma; and San Angelo, Texas. We were ranked the fourth or fifth team in the country and just missed going to the Junior Rose Bowl. Tyler Junior College was 12-0 and got the bid, though naturally I thought our schedule was tougher and that we should have gone.

That Staubach. He was always into something. One night we stole two pies out of the mess hall. These other guys tried to get a piece and we ended up having a fight. Pie was scattered all over Rog's room. He stayed up all night getting it ready for inspection.

Something else about him. He loved to sleep.

—Bob Henry

A beautiful thing about NMMI was the small band that marched into the quadrangle every morning to wake us up. The band consisted of twelve guys and they'd be out early beating the drums and playing bugles, which I guess was better than an alarm clock. There were trash barrels all over the place. One night we sneaked out and rolled all those barrels to the main entrance and stacked them, one on top of the other. The band couldn't get in the next morning and it upset the school's timing all day.

I was just making the best of things and having a good

time—under the circumstances. After the third game of the season there was some bad news from home and I was ready to quit again. We had beaten Trinidad, Colorado, in a close, exciting game, and when I phoned home I found out Dad was going into the hospital again. They were going to amputate more of his toes. Then I got on the bus for the all-night ride back to Roswell and just broke down. I was thinking about dad and also what mother was going through by herself and I couldn't hold it back. I decided I had to quit and go back home where I could help.

Coach Shaw talked to me about staying and phoned my mother the next day. She must have put on a tremendous front, as I look back on it now. "Everything is just fine here," she said. "Friends are taking me over every night to see your father and he's fine, doing very well. He doesn't want you to worry."

I phoned dad and he told me the same thing. I stayed in school and, again, my mother's strength had carried me through. I went home for Christmas and everything seemed all right, though I know now it wasn't. I went back and finished at NMMI.

I remember the San Angelo game that fall as one of the most exciting I've ever played in. It reminds me of the great Cowboy comeback against San Francisco in the 1972 playoffs.

We had beaten Air Force JV, 19–18, on a pass I threw to Dave Shafer (twelve yards with twenty seconds left) and a sportswriter in Roswell had started calling us the "cardiac kids." But the San Angelo game was even closer.

San Angelo was beating us all over the field. With 13:30 left they were ahead 28–14 and it could have been worse. Then with about three minutes left we were behind 34–28 and I *knew* we could win. I could just feel it.

I've still got films of that San Angelo game. It was amazing. Our winning drive covered sixty-four yards and Roger did everything. He scrambled all over the field like he became famous for at Navy. He also called a Statue of Liberty which gained about thirty yards.

But he got knocked woozy about their 20-yard line ... he was taking a good beating and naturally they were after him. They knew he was the key. Well, he came off the field for one play and then went right back in. He hit a pass to the 1-yard line with time running out.

—Bob Shaw

I'm not sure I knew what I was doing after I got hit in the head. Sometimes it's funny when things like that happen. You're there, but it's all like a dream. It's almost as if you're watching yourself. However, I had presence of mind enough to know time was running out and we had no time outs left. I called a quarterback sneak from the 1-yard line and scored. Bart Holaday kicked the extra point and we won, 35–34. San Angelo was no slouch either and they were also in the running for the Junior Rose Bowl.

Cameron clobbered us in the only game we lost, but afterward coach Shaw said if we beat Fort Lewis we'd still make the Rose Bowl. He said if we didn't his name wasn't Bob Shaw. We beat Fort Lewis. Tyler went to the Junior Rose Bowl. We all started calling coach Shaw, "Ol' What's-his-name."

—Bob Henry

Shaw also coached basketball and we disagreed on the style of play. He wanted to use a slow, disciplined offense. It took me a while to get in shape for basketball after football but I became a pretty high scorer, averaging about sixteen or seventeen points a game. I liked a faster game. Coach Shaw would get mad and yank me right out because he thought I was shooting too much. I think he just tried to control things too much for a basketball team. But he was the coach and we went all the way to the regional finals, which we lost.

Roger made one All-American JC team in football and was All-Conference in both basketball and baseball. I coached baseball and he was a tremendous centerfielder. He hit .385 and the pro scouts really liked him.

Babe Herman and some of the other scouts told me he was in the $60,000 bonus class if he wanted to sign a contract. They said he reminded them of Joe DiMaggio the way he glided around and got the jump on the ball in centerfield. There's no doubt in my mind he could have made it in pro baseball.

But he was a real cut-up and had a great sense of humor. I remember he had this girl friend in Cincinnati and he was loyal to her and the guys would kid him a lot about that. They'd call him, "Father Staubach." There were some real cute girls on some of those drill teams at Odessa and San Angelo Junior College and a lot of guys dated them. I'm sure some were after Roger. But he just didn't date much because of that girl in Cincinnati.

—*Bob Dennis*
baseball coach NMMI

I finally dated a lot down there. I must have had, oh, three or four dates at least. I did like this girl in Cincinnati, but during Christmas vacation I saw Marianne again. When I got back to Roswell I started corresponding with her.

Something was always happening to keep things lively.

We had this big fight with a fire extinguisher one night and got that foam all over the dorm. We stayed up all night cleaning the place up.

Rog was always sneaking out to go to the movies. He was always trying to get me to go.

—*Bob Henry*

Bob Henry was always sneaking out to the movies and trying to get me to go. You were allowed to leave the

40

grounds but we just decided it would be more exciting to sneak out without a pass. One night I took this guy Pete Geness and my roommate Jack Weldon with me. We got caught. A guard saw us and we should have run but we didn't. We got twenty demerits—twenty hours walking tours with the rifle.

I played centerfield and was a relief pitcher. I had this reputation for having a good, strong arm but something happened one day that just made me sick at myself. Around Roswell there are a lot of groundhogs. They were always running around the baseball field. One day one ran along the ridge, just off the field. He was about ninety feet away—just a small, little animal moving along like a top.

"Watch me hit that groundhog," I said, half joking.

"No, you can't do it," somebody said, egging me on.

I wasn't even thinking, obviously. I got a baseball and fired away. It was a once-in-a-lifetime deal. I hit that groundhog right in the head, killing him on the spot. I felt terrible. Then all these guys really got on me.

"Rog, look what you've done to that little animal," they said.

"You killed him. You killed somebody's daddy."

"You killed somebody's mother."

"Let me ask you ... just what did that poor little inno-cent animal ever do to you? Murderer! Fiend!"

They announced to the brigade that a groundhog was dead and everybody in school knew I'd killed it. They had a big burial ceremony near the baseball field. A bugler played taps and everybody stood at attention and saluted as they lowered the little box into the grave. I felt awful.

Our baseball team traveled around in Volkswagen buses. Riding around on those buses gave me a chance to see New Mexico and I became very impressed. I really fell in love with that state and still take my family there on vacations.

One time we drove those Volkswagens all the way to Trinidad, Colorado. You've heard of baseball games being rained out. Well, ours was snowed out. We were holed up there in a motel for three days.

NMMI always had prided itself on the behavior of its

41

athletic teams on the road. But these guys started drinking and we were all messing around. It was incredible! In one room the chandelier was knocked down, the bed was completely shattered, and a chair was broken. We knew we'd had it. So we got fifty rolls of athletic tape and taped everything back together. All you had to do was sit on something and it would have fallen apart. But it passed inspection.

I always checked the rooms before we left. I checked that room at the Trinidad motel and it looked fine.

—Bob Dennis

You could be expelled for stuff like that but we got home without anyone knowing what had happened. Then one day coach Dennis received a letter from the motel manager, with an itemized bill. Did he get mad! He called us together and started reading the letter in this gruff, serious voice. Then when he got to the part about the tape he broke up. The bill was approximately $600. We all chipped in and paid it. Fortunately, the motel people never did let the Commandant know. Had he found out, NMMI would have been without a baseball team.

We won our conference title and went to the regional finals to play the top Texas team, Paris Junior College, in Abilene. Paris was tremendous. Two of their pitchers, Luke Walker and Ernie McAnally, went on to the major leagues. You couldn't even see the ball when they threw. I had my best day at the plate. I think I went four-for-four and drove in three of our runs. The score was 4-4 going into the bottom of the tenth. I had pitched batting practice for an hour and coach Dennis hadn't planned on using me in relief. For some reason, he decided to bring me in that tenth inning. My arm felt terrible but I figured I'd just whiz it past them. I fired a pitch down the middle and this guy smashed the ball. I never saw it. They told me it cleared the centerfield fence and I imagine it's probably

42

still rolling out there somewhere in west Texas. We lost 5-4 and that ended my relief pitching career.

Coming back on the bus after that loss I sat between Rog and Tommy Jackson. Suddenly, Rog reached over and ripped the shoulder strap off Tommy's uniform. Tommy did the same thing to Rog. Pretty soon they were both in rags and down to their T-shirts. They looked at me and Rog said, "You look too good." So they started ripping up my uniform, too. Oh, well, school was almost out anyway.

—*Bob Henry*

I don't know how some of us, like Henry, ever got out but we made it. I knew long before the spring semester ended that I was going to the Naval Academy, although I received plenty of new scholarship offers from across the country after I became a junior college all-America quarterback.

I never talked to any of those schools, though. Coach Shaw told everyone who called that I had a moral commitment to the Naval Academy, but that didn't keep some schools from trying to make special deals for me. One offered a full scholarship plus a job which would pay me $100 for winding a clock—once a month. He never told me about these offers then, but they wouldn't have interested me. Everything had drawn me toward the Naval Academy since I first decided on going to NMMI.

I knew that once he settled down and began to blossom as a quarterback that he was going to remember how much we wanted him at the Naval Academy. There never was any doubt that he would be with us the next year. After he had that great season at NMMI, I told him, "When you go to the Naval academy you'll win the Heisman Trophy."

—*Rick Forzano*

43

I really fell in love with the state of New Mexico. I still take my family there on vacation. The state has everything and is as diversified in different regions as Texas. You can go from the red-tinted deserts to snow-covered mountains. There's Carlsbad Caverns. There's the old Mexican-style city of Santa Fe, with clay adobe construction that I suppose has been used since the settlers came. You have the dry, desolate areas and sandstorms which remind me of west Texas and then you have the cool, pine-covered mountains of Ruidoso. New Mexico is like going to a picture postcard rack in a drugstore ... all the colors, everything. You remember it and always want to go back. The population explosion hasn't hit New Mexico but I guess it will someday. Things change but I hate to see New Mexico change.

I will always remember New Mexico and my school year (1960–61) with a great deal of fondness. The professors there were excellent. Some of them came from MIT. They gave you a great academic background, which I found very valuable at the Naval Academy. Because of them I got off to a strong start in courses like chemistry, math, and Spanish my plebe year.

And there was Colonel Neil Murray, who served as coordinator for about a dozen of us who planned to enter the Naval Academy. He's still a great fan. I hear from him every week after a Cowboy game. He gives me a critique of my performance, and the whole team's. I can always count on it.

It was a big decision for me to go that far to school but it was the real beginning of my future. I learned something about the world, about discipline, and about playing quarterback. It was a springboard to the Naval Academy and the Cowboys.

5

Don't Give Up the Ship

I first met Roger when he arrived at the Naval Academy for Plebe Summer. Rick Forzano, the coach who recruited him, brought in a group of athletes, still wearing civilian clothes, to be sworn into the navy.

First thing Roger asked me was, "What time is daily Mass?" I said 5:30 A.M. and thought to myself, "Poor guy! He doesn't know how tough this place is going to be."

But he was there every morning of Plebe Summer. He never missed many during his four years.

—*Father Joseph Ryan*
Chaplain, United States Navy

Plebe Summer was my most difficult time at the Naval Academy. I believe most young guys find it that way. It lasted from early July until early September, when the rest of the brigade of midshipmen returned from cruises and leave. It's a time of constant indoctrination, orientation, and adjustment to a strange and demanding new life. You have so much on your mind all the time that you just go around in a haze.

My year at New Mexico Military Institute made the transition a lot easier for me but I still missed home. It was even tougher on guys coming right out of high school. Suddenly they were thrown into Plebe year. We started with a class of 1,200 and about 815 graduated so we lost nearly 400. Probably half of those left Plebe Summer.

Fourth classmen, the equivalent of freshmen at civilian

schools, were called Plebes for good reason. If you're plebeian, you are common and without status. That was us in the summer of '61. Some upperclassmen were there to supervise the Plebes and really kept us in constant confusion and anxiety. We were shuffled here and there, learning Naval Academy discipline, all the rules and regulations, marching to meals.

Generally, though, it was a good summer. The upperclassmen made it extra hard on you so you would be better prepared when the full brigade returned in September. I did what I was told and found that life there was quite interesting. There was enough variety to keep you from getting bored. We took some courses, learned how to take care of our uniforms—and how to spit-shine shoes again. We spent time on the rifle range and there were plenty of athletics and recreation. We got out on the water in knock-abouts and I learned how to sail. It was quite a change from the sand and tumbleweeds of Roswell, New Mexico.

The grounds of the Naval Academy and the surrounding area are beautiful. The brigade, over 4,000 midshipmen, lived in Bancroft Hall, a dormitory bigger than a battleship. It also contained the mess hall and all the headquarters for the six battalions which made up the brigade. There is a great campus atmosphere—tree-lined walks leading to the various academic buildings and a lovely chapel with the crypt of John Paul Jones in the basement. You're always passing statues and monuments to remind you of great men and great moments in the history of the United States Navy. Right in front of Bancroft Hall is Tecumseh, the old Indian warrior and the god of 2.5, the passing mark. On your way to exams it was traditional to fire a penny at Tecumseh for good luck. And he always wore war paint before the Army game, signifying the intensity of our rivalry.

There were athletic fields surrounding the grounds and you were right there on the Severn River, which flows into Chesapeake Bay. It really makes for an appealing, romantic sight. Then there's the old city of Annapolis, the capital of Maryland, right next to the Naval Academy grounds.

Annapolis also is steeped in tradition, with its narrow cobblestone streets and its old buildings, some of them dating back to colonial days in the 1700s. Once you settle amid all this and begin to absorb it, you realize you're living in a special place.

My first big mistake was not learning *Reef Points* during Plebe Summer. That's a book you are supposed to memorize. It contains all those sayings like "Don't give up the ship" plus the information you need to answer an upperclassman's questions. Like the one they asked at meals: "How's the cow?"

You should answer, "She walks, she talks, she's full of chalk, the lactical fluid, extracted from the female of the bovine species, is directly proportional to the number ..." And then you tell the number of gallons of milk you have on the table. It's just a disciplinary thing, a memorization tool, but I didn't latch on to it as I should have. That was the beginning of a very traumatic six months for me.

I suffered my first shoulder injury that summer during a baseball workout. I was in center field and when I went back for a fly ball, my cleats caught in the ground. I flipped and landed on my left shoulder. It popped and bent behind me. The pain knifed through the shoulder. After about fifteen seconds it suddenly popped back into place. I moved it around and I could use it again, but I knew something bad had happened.

I didn't go to the doctor and I didn't tell anyone. There were special squads for guys with an injury or illness, which allowed you to skip a lot of work and details, but I didn't want anyone thinking I might be faking it. The next morning when I woke up my shoulder was killing me. It had been dislocated, the first of seventeen dislocations to that shoulder while I was at the Naval Academy.

I just kept trying to use it that summer like it was normal and that was a mistake. I was a fairly decent boxer and I got to the physical education class finals with this guy who was going to be on the Plebe boxing team. We really got into it, the kind of fight that caused everyone to stand around the ring and watch us. I punched him in the nose and it started bleeding but he just kept coming. In the third round I swung with my left and completely missed him. The shoulder went out and I just hung there on the ropes for ten or fifteen seconds. Then it went back in. The instructor knew something was wrong, but I said it would be all right. He stopped the fight, though.

It was time for Plebe football workouts to start and I didn't know what I was going to do. I was scared to mention my shoulder at first, afraid they just might write me off. But then I asked them to make a harness to hold it in place. That helped. I began to relax and enjoy football, which was the real reason I had come to the Naval Academy.

It was obvious we had the makings of a really good Plebe team. The material was outstanding, the result of strong recruiting which Wayne Hardin, head coach, believed would restock the varsity. Navy had a fine team in '60, playing Missouri in the Orange Bowl. However, nearly all the players had graduated, including Joe Bellino, the halfback who won the Heisman Trophy. Bellino was back at the academy that fall, helping coach the Plebes. We had Pat Donnelly, a fullback and just a super athlete; a fine tackle named Jim Freeman, who had transferred from Southern Methodist; Fred Marlin, an older guy who had been in the fleet and would become a star guard; Doug McCarty, an outstanding tight end; Kip Paskewich, a fast halfback who was my roommate the fall semester; and a left handed quarterback named Skip Orr.

I first met Roger playing baseball during Plebe Summer. We started working out together in shorts, getting ready for football, and immediately I saw how good he was.

My going to the Naval Academy the same year Roger did was the best thing that ever happened to me. I don't think I could have made it as a big-time quarterback but I thought I could then.

Larry Kocisko, who had gone to New Mexico Military Institute with Roger, was in my company. He asked me what position I played. "Quarterback?" he laughed. "Forget it!" When football practice began, twenty-two guys came out for quarterback, but everybody knew Roger was the one. Most of us found something else to do. Me, I became a wide receiver, which worked out great. I got to catch Roger's passes.

—Skip Orr

Football players had an advantage over the other Plebes because we ate our meals at the training table. You ate by yourself and this removed you from Plebe life a little while. This meant a lot. The toughest part of being a Plebe was eating three meals a day at a table with upperclassmen. Having to sit at a brace and eat a square meal was really a pain in the neck. They made a guy sit on the edge of his chair and bring all food from his plate straight up and then at a 90-degree angle into his mouth. Then he had to bring his fork or spoon back to his plate the same way. The Plebe at the table always had to pour everyone's coffee, tea, or milk and make sure the upperclassmen got everything they asked for. Naturally, the Plebe was served last. Sometimes the food was almost gone when it reached him—there was never any dessert left. But I didn't have to go through this because I was eating at a training table—football, basketball, or baseball—the entire year. This really annoyed some upperclassmen in my company, the 16th, which was already notorious for harassing Plebes.

Kip Paskewich and I lived across the hall from a couple of first classmen who were just miserable. They came into our room all the time, particularly during study hall. Of course, any time they came in you had to jump to attention. One of them was a real little guy who enjoyed beating on my chest with a whiskbroom while he just sat there, talking about nothing. He must have gotten a special kick from it because I was so much bigger, 6-3 and 190 pounds. Finally a large red knot came up on my chest and I had a hard time getting my shoulder pads on. The only way I could wear them was with a piece of sponge covering the knot.

Kip was one of the hardest-headed guys I've ever known. He didn't like to wear a shirt when he studied but these guys told him to. He said, "I don't feel like wearing

49

a shirt." So they would come in with magic markers and draw all kinds of designs on his chest.

They also were very big on Plebe come-arounds. If they wanted you to, you had to get up early in the morning and run around to a first classman's room and tell him everything he wanted to know—Reef Points, all the news from the morning paper, the sports scores, the entire day's menu. And while you did this, you would be sitting on an imaginary bench with your legs rigid. Or doing pushups. It was just more harassment. And since I was weak on Reef Points I got into a lot of trouble.

Lights out for the Plebes was 10:00 or 10:30 P.M. I would have to sit in the john for about two hours some nights and study Reef Points. I also had my regular studies and I really had a difficult time. I kept getting demerits for not knowing Reef Points. The guys thought I had a bad attitude, plus they resented my eating on the training table, and they really piled the demerits on me. By Christmas leave I had 150 demerits and you were allowed a total of 300 for your entire Plebe year. If you went over that, you were out of the Naval Academy.

I was frustrated and sour about everything. My grades were good except in mechanical drawing, which I was on the verge of flunking. Every day after football practice I took extra instruction. I was having all that trouble back at Bancroft Hall and then this problem added to it just made everything seem that much worse.

Each Plebe is given a first classman who is supposed to look after you. Mine was Jerry Blesch, a fine guy. He and I became very good friends. I would tell him my problems and he did his best to help, but he had a difficult time doing anything about the disciplinary matters. It was getting so bad that Joe Bellino and Hal Spooner (another former football player who was helping coach the Plebes) asked the guys to lay off the harassment. Bellino and Spooner really had no authority to tell the first classmen what to do and they didn't like it. It just made matters worse.

My big break came when Navy beat Army, the third straight victory since Wayne Hardin became head coach. Whenever that happens Plebes are allowed to "carry on" from right after the game, in late November, until Christ-

50

mas leave. The entire Plebe system is off. You can walk down the hall naturally instead of holding your chin in, almost at a brace. There were no come-arounds, no square meals, nothing.

By this time I was really getting swept up in the Naval Academy football program. Despite all the trouble I was having elsewhere, I enjoyed Plebe football and was proud we had such a good team.

One of the big reasons the '61 Plebes were exceptional was Staubach. Hardin already was watching him closely. "When Roger was recruited," he said, "we knew he was going to be great. He gave no indication that fall that he was anything else."

Dick Duden, the head Plebe coach, knew he had a quarterback with an exceptional future.

"Roger had size, ability and a desire to excel. He did everything well—run, pass, and direct the team. He was our leader in every game. He had so many good games we came to expect them of him.

"He liked to scramble a lot but it was all right with me. He turned a lot of third downs into first downs that way. You know, it's difficult to lock up Roger. You can tell him what to do but when it's time to act he'll take matters into his own hands. It was all right with us as long as it turned out well—and it usually did.

"Roger's value had another dimension. There's usually so much anxiety among kids coming to the Naval Academy that you expect some good athletes to get discouraged and leave. But Roger was such an inspiring leader that probably 98 percent of the good ones stayed that year. He instilled confidence in everyone. We felt great about the future of our varsity football team."

The Plebes were an exciting, high-scoring team which finished with an 8–1 record, missing a perfect season by the narrowest of margins. The Maryland freshmen won, 29–27, on a twenty-three yard field goal with fifteen seconds left.

"We lost that game because of me," Duden said.

"They got possession of the ball and moved into position for that field goal because I sent in the wrong formation to Roger on third down. Say, that would be good for Tom Landry to know."

The Plebe team had a good nucleus of talent, players who obviously would contend for positions when they moved up to the varsity. There was a lot of excitement throughout the academy about our team. Our only loss was to the Maryland freshmen and it was unbelievable how that happened. We were on their 1-yard line and actually got the ball across twice, but they pushed our man back and the referee said we didn't score. Nevertheless, it was an unusual season and whetted our appetites for spring training.

I was just glad to see spring, period. Things eased off for me in my problem areas. I received only about twenty demerits that entire semester after getting 150 before Christmas, and I never had demerit troubles again. I guess I had only fifteen or twenty my remaining three years. I made both the basketball and baseball teams so I was able to play the three sports I wanted to play and still keep up with my studies.

I had only one real problem that second semester—a first classman whom I'll call Bad News.

This was exceptional, because as the year went on the upperclassmen started "spooning" you. That means they shake your hand, and you call them by their first names and there is no more harassment. But the entire year passed and Bad News never "spooned" me. This created a very bad feeling between us and I thought it was stupid.

Bad News had an immature attitude about harassing me because I was an athlete. It was an ego thing with him and he carried it too far. He seemed to resent me because he had little coordination and no athletic skills. He resented my eating on the training table all year and he didn't like my getting up early and going to Mass. He thought I was trying to miss come-around. So I had to hustle back from Mass and come around to his room. He carried the harassment too far and I became bitter toward him. But I soon got my revenge.

The last week of the semester is called June Week. It's the climax of the whole year—parades, ceremonies, social events, girl friends and parents visiting, graduation. Just before June Week you have your last laundry call of the year. You send all of your white uniforms to be cleaned because you'll be wearing them throughout June Week. My roommate, Tony John, also got a lot of flack from Bad News because he was my roommate. He and I took Bad News' laundry bag before it was picked up and crammed it into one of our cruise boxes.

When the laundry was returned, we hurried down the hall and tossed his bag of dirty laundry on the pile. A little later he opened it, expecting to see all those fresh whites. Wow! Did he ever blow up! I've never seen a man so mad in all my life. He burst into our room screaming and waving his arms. He knew we must have done it but he never asked us directly, which saved us from getting into a questionable area with the Honor Code if we had lied to him. We weren't going to admit it, of course, and now it was too late for him to do anything else to me. He was terribly frustrated. I loved it! I now felt like all those months of harassment and problems were worth it now.

June Week was fun for a lot of other reasons. You could relax and enjoy it, unless you were sweating out your exams. Fortunately, I had squeezed through in mechanical drawing. Marianne came for the week, which she did every year I was at the Naval Academy. She and some other girls stayed in a little house in Annapolis. There were parties and dances and we just generally had a good time. I felt I had come through Plebe year all right, although I wasn't pleased with my spring football practice.

I was well down the list of quarterbacks, fourth or fifth or sixth. Ron Klemick, who had been a nationally-ranked passer and done a fine job as a junior, was the starter and there were several upperclassmen behind him. I must have impressed coach Hardin as a wild Plebe quarterback, a guy with a good arm but one who ran a lot. That wasn't his kind. Klemick was a straight, drop-back passer, and he fitted perfectly into Hardin's offense.

I had thrown my shoulder out in boxing class again a week before spring football began, so I started wearing the harness again. That worried me and then when workouts began I was like cannon fodder out there. They had all of those older quarterbacks ahead of me so they started me out on defense. George Welsh, who's now head coach at Navy, was the quarterback coach and I was afraid I wasn't showing the coaches a great deal.

I couldn't do much on defense because I was afraid of hurting my left shoulder again. Finally they put me in some scrimmages with the fourth-team offense. It was mostly guys from the Plebe team going against the varsity defense. We were getting annihilated but I would break through for a long run occasionally. I was just scrambling and there was no consistency to my passing. I knew I would have to work a lot on my passing during the summer and try to show more when fall workouts began.

Father Ryan watched those spring workouts intently. "Roger's career on defense wasn't much," he chuckled. "Once he was so enthralled watching the offense run the play that he forgot to watch Ed Gill, an end coming downfield to block him. Gill knocked him three or four feet."

And Hardin was watching with more interest than Staubach realized.

"We knew what Roger could be to our team but we couldn't rush it," Hardin said. "We still had Klemick, who couldn't do anything but win. In '61 we were green and weren't supposed to win a game and he took us to a 7–3 season. He had to remain the starter until Roger proved to everyone he had earned the job.

"We tried to handle Roger's situation subtly and not focus all the attention on him. We were taking pictures one day and decided to take all the youngsters (upcoming Plebes) who might play the next fall. And we did have a lot of good ones.

"So we got them all together with Roger. He looked

over at me and grinned. 'Well, coach,' he said, 'you want a picture of next fall's starting lineup?' "

Hardin just laughed and said nothing. But in his heart he knew Roger was closer to being right than he realized.

6

Someone to Believe In

There was a new vitality, a mood of expectancy at the Navy team's fall training camp at Quonset Point, Rhode Island. The middies had some young talent which promised to make the Naval Academy a special name in college football.

A new superintendent had just taken charge at Annapolis. Rear Admiral Charles Kirkpatrick, a member of the class of '31, had a spirit in keeping with the times. An energetic, gregarious Texan, he had enjoyed a diversified Naval career and was delighted to return to the school he loved.

His brother graduated from the Naval Academy eighteen years before him and in the late 1930s, when Charles Kirkpatrick returned to Annapolis as a duty officer, his brother's son was a midshipman. Thus, Lt. (j.g.) Kirkpatrick soon acquired a nickname with the brigade—Uncle Charley. When he came back in '62, so did his nickname. He was no distant brass hat to the young men under him.

He loved sports and he believed a strong athletic program was invaluable in creating a vibrant spirit at the Naval Academy. So when the Commander in Chief came to visit the Navy team at Quonset Point it was only natural that Uncle Charley was at his side.

President Kennedy looked very young that day. He was tanned, spry and chipper. He had a bad back but you couldn't tell it the way he climbed out of the helicopter, his jacket flapping open and his hair flying in the breeze.

He was a navy veteran, of course, but also a great fan of Navy football. He obviously was happy he had an opportunity to visit us. I guess he was on his way to Hyannis Port, which wasn't far from the naval base where we were training. Everyone was excited when we learned he was coming. We were dressed in our whites and standing in formation as he landed. Suddenly here was the all-American family, the president, his beautiful wife, and their son and daughter. It was a very warm scene. He was so friendly—smiling and shaking hands with each of us as he came along the line. We became very close to him because of that meeting.

He said he would be following us that fall and hoped we would do well. It was a terrific feeling. Of course, I couldn't have felt more intensely about the season ahead than I already did. I was fighting for my life. I wanted to play my sophomore year. I didn't believe that I was ever going to sit on the bench and I was determined to be ready when we started training. I worked out every day that summer and had thrown the ball like crazy, even while on cruise.

I was assigned to the USS *Forrestal*, an aircraft carrier which cruised up and down the Atlantic coast. That was when Pat Donnelly, our fullback, and I first became close friends. We were among about a hundred midshipmen on the *Forrestal*. They treated us just like we were new seamen, the theory being that some day we would be officers and it was valuable for us first to have a feel for the life of an enlisted man on board ship.

Pat and I slept in the forward section of the ship, right under the catapults which launched the planes. You couldn't believe the noise when those jets took off in the middle of the night. I thought I'd never be able to sleep, but I got used to it.

Some of the men on the *Forrestal* weren't too crazy about having us on board. Particularly a boatswain's mate called Shorty. He would wake us up in the morning by screaming all the nasty language in the world. We got to where we would just yell back at him, then get up and go to work.

We were assigned to different divisions of the ship on a rotating schedule so we could learn about various operations. While we were in the engineering division we had to spend a couple of weeks in the boiler room. It was awful. It was hot and grubby and there wasn't much you could do except learn about the steam cycle of the ship. They didn't watch us too closely so I just got lost. I spent my time out in the sun, reading a book, *The Fountainhead* by Ayn Rand.

"Roger was pretty good at hiding out," said Donnelly. "It was easy to do on a ship as big as the *Forrestal*. He had a little place under the stairway in general quarters. He spent almost as much time there as his bunk.

"That time he was assigned to the boiler room was a real zero for him. At the end of the assignment, the commanding officer for the midshipmen's cruise asked how Midshipman Staubach had done. 'Midshipman Who?' was their reply.

"I was on cruise with him each summer after Plebe year and he took a football with him everywhere. That summer on the *Forrestal* it was always hot and humid, whether we were on board or putting into some port like New York or Norfolk, but Roger always stayed active. He had a way of getting people out to catch for him."

The carrier deck was long enough to throw a football around. In fact, it was as long as three football fields, but it was always greasy. Planes were parked here and there and guys were driving around on little tractors. It was rather hard to set up and throw but at least it was a place to loosen up my arm. There was also a little room on the ship where I lifted weights. I wanted to do whatever I could because I knew that was a very important summer.

We had a good training camp at Quonset Point before returning to Annapolis for the start of the fall semester. It was exciting but I really can't say I accomplished a lot. I found myself just a little ahead of my status in spring training. I was the number three quarterback. Ron Klemick, a senior, was the starter. Bruce Abel, a junior, was number two. As a sophomore, the prospects of starting that year weren't very bright.

Other sophomores were making big impressions. Pat Donnelly had won the starting fullback job in the spring and several more started moving in at Quonset Point. The best thing I did there was win the ping-pong championship. There wasn't much else to do except watch films.

I wasn't sure how I stood with Wayne Hardin but I was certain I liked his type of football. He had become Navy's head coach when he was only in his early 30s but no one doubted he had a fine grasp of the game and could run a major college team. He was a positive thinker and he instilled confidence in his players. With his red hair and freckles he had a pleasant look about him, yet his eyes were piercing and you soon realized he could be hardnosed. In reality, he was a fiery redhead, a tremendous competitor with a dominant personality. He really knew football. This was '62 and we ran a wide-open offense which was ahead of what most college teams used then.

He liked to keep the game exciting and interesting. Paul Dietzel, who coached Army then, talked about Coach Hardin's gimmicks but actually he was just a strong believer in motivational techniques. The previous year against Army he had all of the receivers wear fluorescent helmets so the quarterback could see them better. When we were going through our final workouts before our season opener with Penn State, I began wondering if I shouldn't try wearing one of those helmets. Maybe coach Hardin would see me better.

I remember a headline in the Annapolis paper: "To Have Better Team, Maybe Worse Record—Hardin." We were playing a very tough schedule that fall and the game at Penn State was typical of the problems we faced. They were good and they were ready to go. We had fine material but everything hadn't settled into place yet when we played Penn State. They won 41–7. I watched a lot that day, which is even worse than being on the field during a licking like that. Everything went wrong for us. The next week we barely beat William and Mary 20–14, and people began to wonder about this Navy team which had been looking for a really big year. It wasn't Ron Klemick's fault. He was a good quarterback. Then we went to Minnesota and really got worked over.

Minnesota had the number one defensive team in the country. Bobby Bell and Carl Eller, who would later become all-pros, were two of their stars. They beat us 21–0. I was in the game for only six or seven plays but I'll never forget one of them.

I ran out of the pocket, my first scramble for the Navy varsity. Bell caught me by my face mask, swung me around and slammed me on the ground like he was bull-dogging a calf. I was helpless. My feet came off the ground as I spun in a circle. It could have broken my neck. I got up and ran a few more plays, then went back to the bench for the rest of the game. I guess that was my welcome to big-time football.

"I went with Ron Klemick in the early games out of loyalty," Hardin said. "He was a senior and had done a fine job for us the year before. I felt Roger had to beat him out fairly and squarely. I was anxious to see how he would perform against someone as tough as Minnesota but it was a short look. For a second it looked like it might be a short game. When Bell slung Roger down and the official nearest the play didn't throw his flag I raced onto the field. I was ready to take the team off. It was an unfair, unjust, obvious penalty. No one in the stands believed that official hadn't seen it. But another official came rushing in from about fifty yards away and threw a flag.

"Roger didn't have much to show for that game except being the victim of a vicious foul. His talent was obvious, though, and I decided he would play a lot against Cornell the next week. He had earned it."

The day before the Cornell game Roger had written his parents, "Boy, did I feel bad about not knowing it was your anniversary. I'll win this game tomorrow for you both."

Navy was struggling against an underdog Cornell team when Hardin replaced Klemick with Staubach in the first quarter. Roger directed six touchdown drives and Navy won, 41–0. He hit nine of eleven passes for ninety-nine yards and ran eight times for eighty-nine more.

"He was super-fantastic," Hardin said. "From here on he began to develop."

When I went in everything just started to go right. I'll never forget a play in the first series of downs. It had to be one of the biggest plays in my Naval Academy career. It was third-and-seven and I threw a short down-and-out pass to Jimmy Stewart. It was a low pass on the sideline but he caught it for a first down. If we hadn't made it coach Hardin might well have given me just that one series and then put Bruce Abel in. I had a good game but I know most people weren't impressed because it was against Cornell, which didn't have a good record that fall.

We had another tough test coming up at Boston College the next week. Boston College had a very good team, with Jack Concannon at quarterback. They were favored. I started shakily but then everyone settled down and we won 26–6. It was a very unusual game. We brought our Navy blue jerseys but Boston College wore maroon instead of a light color. It was a sunny day and when you looked on the field you could scarcely tell who played for which team. Concannon threw some interceptions and put one right in our linebacker's hands. It looked like he just couldn't see who was who.

It was one of those days when the whole team was clicking. We felt a new excitement when we got back to the Naval Academy.

Staubach threw for two touchdowns against Boston College while completing fourteen of twenty for 165 yards. His flair for leading the team convinced Hardin he'd never look back at his decision to put a sophomore in charge. "Roger had that charisma," Hardin said. "The quality that made things turn out right."

Skip Orr noticed the atmosphere change around the team when it realized Staubach was the starter. "Once he got to play, the whole spirit turned around," Orr recalled. "They saw he was such a rare one. They knew he would go down in history."

Admiral Kirkpatrick was thrilled by the prospect of what a player with Staubach's style could do for the entire Naval Academy. "Roger caught the imagination of that football squad," the superintendent said. "He was a winner and a leader. I don't think he necessarily set out to be a leader. The ability was just there.

"When he called plays in the huddle he had confidence. Boy, I could encourage that! Because of Roger, the team had confidence. The whole damn brigade had confidence!"

Next we had another tough one, Pittsburgh, in the Oyster Bowl at Norfolk, but we felt we were well prepared. Our offense was clicking now and we also had a trick play which coach Hardin felt sure would be good for a touchdown. It was, but it also created a big controversy.

The officials were told about the sleeper play before the game so they would understand what we were doing when we pulled it. After Pitt kicked off to us, one of our tackles faked a block near the sideline and rolled off the field, leaving us with ten players. Then while we huddled, one of our receivers, Jimmy Stewart, went limping toward our bench and Dick Ernst ran on the field. Of course, what the Pitt players thought they saw was one guy limp off and another replace him. But Ernst lined up at tackle and Stewart stopped on the edge of the playing field. He stayed close enough to the huddle to be legal, though, and we had the standard eleven players on the field.

The Pitt defense paid no attention to Stewart. I took the snap, dropped back and watched Stewart sprint down the sideline. The Pitt safety just stood there staring at me. He couldn't believe that I was throwing the ball. It was the weirdest thing in the world. Stewart was all alone and he caught the pass for sixty-six yards and a touchdown. That got us off to a good day and we went on to win 32–9.

Pitt thought the play was unethical and Hardin caught a lot of criticism after the game. In the locker room reporters kept asking about it and we just said it was a special play and that Pitt missed its coverage. Of course, everybody knew it was a gimmick play but at the time I felt it was a heck of a play. I just thought it was football and that was the way coach Hardin was. He was always giving us tricky plays to work on in practice. They weren't a major part of our offense but they seemed to be good for our morale, although I didn't think we needed it. Looking back on it now, I guess we were taking advantage of Pitt, especially with Stewart acting like he was limping off the field.

Whatever the play was, it helped Staubach have a perfect day passing. He completed eight of eight for 192 yards. Suddenly the entire country was aware of Navy and its young quarterback for a couple of reasons.

Lawrence Robinson of the *New York World-Telegram and Sun* wrote, "He threw passes with defenders hanging on his neck and blasted at tacklers like a fullback. It was his real test under fire, confirming the promise shown in the Cornell and Boston College games. He now is an authentic ace, probably the most talented quarterback in Navy history."

The public's awareness of Staubach improved as the weeks passed but Navy's record didn't. The middies lost to the Notre Dame 20–12 in the rain and then Syracuse whipped them 34–7. This hardly seemed the tonic to bolster them for their toughest trip of the season. They had to play Southern California, the eventual national champion, in Los Angeles Coliseum and they found they still were being needled for the trick play against Pitt.

Jim Murray, the *Los Angeles Times*' syndicated

columnist, wrote, "This is a team that patterns itself not after Frank Merriwell but Mata Hari and Willie the Actor Sutton. They might all show up wearing trick mustaches and using trick footballs that the air comes out of when *you* throw them. Anchors Aweigh has been changed to 'Steal, Navy, down the field.' "

But the middies simply stuck with Staubach that day and almost pulled the upset of the year. Southern Cal squeezed out a 13–6 victory but Roger was remarkable. He passed and ran for 219 yards, including an eighteen-yard scramble for a touchdown, and was so impressive he was voted Pacific Coast Back of the Week.

That probably was one of the finest days I ever had as a quarterback. Southern Cal had a great team, one which went on to beat Wisconsin in the Rose Bowl, but we had them beaten. Late in the game they had that seven-point lead but we had been moving the ball on them all day. We had a first down on their 4-yard line and I handed the ball to Pat Donnelly. I don't believe Pat had fumbled all year, but he lost the ball right on the goal line. Pete Beathard, their quarterback and safety, hit Pat just right and punched the ball out of his hands. They recovered in the end zone and got the ball on the twenty.

If we had scored there and made a two-point conversion we would have had the lead with time running out. It was a disappointment to come that close against a great team and miss, but that game did wonders for our morale. Our record was only 4–5 but we went back to the Naval Academy feeling we could hold our own against anybody.

"The whole team already knew Roger was a great player," Donnelly said, "but he proved against Southern Cal what a terrific competitor he is. They were rough on him, trying to make him hesitant to do some things he did best. But they didn't change his style at all."

S.C. coach John McKay had plenty of other reasons to remember Staubach. "What hurt us was not their plays they had worked on, but the ones when they were trapped," he said. "Staubach looked like Red Grange running when he couldn't pass. They couldn't have practiced that play too much."

By then Hardin knew that Staubach often was most valuable simply doing what came naturally. "If you can just reach the happy medium of giving him his freedom but stay within the rules," Hardin said. "That's all he wants."

And all Hardin wanted now was another victory over Army—his fourth straight. Although this team had won only four of nine games while all of the young players settled into the line-up, he felt very confident.

We fired up to our highest pitch for the Army game. It was a classic, a national institution, and there was a deep feeling about it throughout both branches of the service. Plenty of admirals and generals would be either delighted or disgusted for the year that followed. It always drew more than 100,000 fans to Philadelphia Stadium. It was more than a game. It was a state of mind.

Both teams always had an open date before the game, giving us two weeks to get in the mood for our showdown. You never had a moment when you weren't thinking about Army. There were pep rallies and bonfires nearly every night. Banners hung from windows all over Bancroft Hall. A lot of them began "Uncle Charley Says ..." because our superintendent had had such a positive and stimulating effect on the brigade. That fall Admiral Kirkpatrick had told us, "You can do anything you believe you can do." That really stayed with us.

There were the usual pranks being played by both sides, middies stealing the Army mule and cadets kidnapping the Navy goat. One middie must have made a couple of thousand dollars selling panties with "Beat Army" on them. The last day or two before the game the atmosphere around the academy was electric. You knew you had the entire brigade depending on you, as well as the entire

65

navy. I remember a newspaper photo of a submarine in the Atlantic with "Beat Army" painted on it.

Army had a better record that season and was favored. Paul Dietzel was in his first year as head coach after all his success at Louisiana State and he had his special unit called the Chinese Bandits. We were thinking we would just lay low and then go to Philadelphia and give it our best shot. But we had a big pep rally two nights before the game and coach Hardin announced that we were going to run up the score on Army. None of this "I think we have a chance to win" stuff. Naturally, it was in banner headlines in the Philadelphia papers when we arrived the next day. It was unbelievable strategy. Coach Hardin always was strong for pregame statements and that one really worked. It was amazing how sharp we were against Army.

Navy players wore a skull-and-crossbones insignia on their helmets when they lined up against Army. The Jolly Roger. Many thought it was in honor of their swashbuckling quarterback, but Hardin said it had a different meaning. "In Naval lore there was a story of a phantom ship flying a flag with the skull and crossbones on it. It came from nowhere and never lost a battle."

The middies won every battle that day, routing Army 34–14, behind a spectacular Staubach. Roger hit ten of twelve passes for 204 yards, including touchdowns to Neil Henderson (twelve yards) and Nick Markoff (sixty-five yards). He scored two touchdowns himself on runs of twenty and two yards and was named National Back of the Week. Once, scrambling to throw under pressure, he caught his own deflected pass, threw the ball and completed it. All he got for his trouble, however, was a five-yard penalty. That was about the only thing that went wrong for him all afternoon.

President Kennedy was there. He sat on the Navy side with Admiral Kirkpatrick during the first half. "He was supposed to be unbiased," said Admiral Kirkpatrick, "but it was perfectly clear to me he was highly pleased with how the game was going. At half-time we went to midfield and met General William Westmoreland, the Army superintendent, who would escort him to the Army side. General Westmoreland said, "Mister President, I hope you can bring us as much luck this half as you did for Navy." President Kennedy told him, "I don't know, General. The Admiral is quite a rooter."

And Hardin recalled, "When he visited us at Quonset Point before the season he asked about the Army game. I told him we'd play a game fit for a president. I believe we did.

It was wonderful to see that Army game turn out as it did. I had been a nervous wreck the night before. I only slept about two hours. I'm normally not that way. I even slept the night before the Super Bowl game in New Orleans. But I was so keenly aware that I was only a sophomore and I had the pressure of being the starting quarterback. I was glad to have the responsibility, but I couldn't get it off my mind.

When the game started, however, I was ready to go. I remember the first play. Coach Hardin had told me just to roll out to my right. I did and gained nine yards. He did that simply to get me involved in the action immediately. I lost my nervousness and on the next series we drove for a touchdown.

Paul Dietzel tried some gimmicks with Army, too. The Chinese Bandits came on the field in white shoes. They looked like ballet dancers. That was a good Army team but we just did everything right against them.

"I really learned to appreciate Roger's running ability in that game," Donnelly said. "He had a wonderful feel for it. He wasn't particularly fast but he knew when to start and stop—or duck. It was like he had eyes in the back of his head. Several times he stopped and an Army guy would go by in front and another in back. Then he'd start again."

Beating Army meant we broke even for the year—five and five. You would have thought from the crazy scene in the locker room we had won the national championship. We had a big party at our hotel that night, with champagne and steak. Mom and Dad came to the game, as they did all the Army-Navy games. It was a wonderful weekend, one I'll always remember. Winning that game was like winning the whole season. It was amazing what it did for the spirit of the entire school. And the Plebes loved it because it meant they could carry on until Christmas.

There was quite a flap about something I said in the locker room. I was asked if I would be interested in playing pro football and I answered, "It depends on how much I like the navy. I'll make up my mind in the next two years. I would like to play pro, though. At least I'd like to try it." Some people interpreted that as meaning I might try to leave the Naval Academy before graduation and turn pro. But I never meant I wouldn't graduate and honor my four-year service commitment. I just meant that I would like to consider trying pro football some time in the distant future.

Finally all the excitement of the Army game died down and I started concentrating on school again. I didn't go out for basketball, but later in the winter the coach, Ben Carnevale, asked me to come out along with two other football players, Jim Campbell and Doug McCarty. Jim played defensive end and Doug played offensive end and both were pretty physical under the backboard. Coach Carnevale thought the team needed more of that.

Gradually I got to where I could help the team, too. We came to the end of the season and Army was coming to Annapolis. Coach Carnevale started me. I played guard and my main job was defensing Army's top scorer. He was a great shot and I had to play him man-for-man while the rest of the team played a zone. I played maybe twelve or fourteen minutes in the first half and he didn't score a point. I didn't either. I was so nervous on my first shot that the ball banged off the backboard and bounced all the way to the stands. However, I did play enough to letter that year.

"General Westmoreland came down from West Point to see the game and sat with me," Admiral Kirkpatrick recalled. "He saw Staubach coming on the floor and asked, 'Why is the coach putting him in?' I said, 'Westie, the coach knows he's a winner. Your players know he's a winner, too.' Sure enough, our whole team came alive with Roger on the floor."

Spring was real busy but it was fun. I was the starting center fielder on the baseball team and I had my best year, hitting .421. It just seemed everything I hit went to the right spot. And spring football practice was altogether different from the year before. Coach Hardin thought I had really improved after getting that experience my sophomore season. We felt we would have a good team but we didn't know just how good.

Hardin wanted to be sure he set the stage properly for Staubach's junior season. "He is the only player I've ever had who made me change my offense," Hardin said. "I prefer to use the drop-back pass, but Roger is a roll-out, scrambling type of quarterback, so we've adjusted to *him*."

No one knew better than Hardin that Navy possessed a rare talent in Staubach. "He has a sixth sense," he said. "He's not fast but he's quick. He somehow gets where he is supposed to be. He's exciting and one of the easiest to coach I've sever seen."

The nation was aware of Staubach now, but no one could know how long this would last.

7

Undefeated in 49 States

Among the dinner guests at the White House one summer evening in 1963 was Admiral Charles Kirkpatrick. During the reception beforehand, President Kennedy was recalling the fun they had sitting together for the first half of the previous Army-Navy game.

"Say, Admiral," he asked, cocking his right arm as if to throw a football, "do you still have that man?"

"Yes, sir," the Naval Academy superintendent assured him, "we sure do!"

Many people were already aware that Roger Staubach was prepared to lead Navy in pursuit of a truly special season. As a sophomore he had closed with a brilliant game against Army and now he was surrounded by some of the finest talent in the middies' history.

President Kennedy may have been wondering what to expect, but back in Annapolis Wayne Hardin's butcher already had predicted that this would be *the* year for Navy. "One day before spring practice I was in his shop," Hardin recalled, "and he said, 'Hey, coach, I have it all figured out. Your team is going to be No. 1 in the country next fall!' 'You gotta be kiddin',' I said. But he started explaining how he figured that with Staubach and our other material we could get off to a strong start and gain the momentum to carry us through our schedule and into a bowl game. In his mind this Navy team could be so spectacular that they'd have to rank us No. 1."

The more Hardin thought about it the more he

liked the idea. He called a meeting and told his team that they realistically could be playing for the national championship the next season. When the middies reported for fall practice they felt a quiet confidence that they could achieve something unusual if they played up to their potential. Hardin gave them a motto, "Drive For Five"—a fifth straight victory over Army. That would delight all the old Navy men but Hardin kept thinking how nice it would be to give them even more.

It felt good to get fall practice underway. For the first time in a number of years the team reported directly to Annapolis instead of going to Quonset Point, Rhode Island, for a couple of weeks. We practiced twice a day until classes started and we felt the difference in the heat, which had been one reason for going to Quonset Point. But being at the academy was more convenient and I guess less expensive. And being right there probably added to our enthusiasm for the season.

The quality of service academy football has suffered in recent years because so many good players prefer to attend civilian schools where they can move immediately into pro football after their college careers. But that was not yet a problem. Our '63 team had the talent to be highly competitive against tough major college teams.

We had six juniors including myself in the starting lineup, a good indication of the quality of our '61 Plebe team. Pat Donnelly, of course, already had played a full season as the regular fullback. Skip Orr, who originally had been a left-handed quarterback, really came on at flanker back in early workouts and moved up from fourth to first team. Freddie Marlin played guard and was also our kicker. Jim Freeman and Pat Philbin won the starting jobs at tackle.

The other starters were seniors. We used two tight ends, Jim Campbell and Dave Sjuggerud, and Johnny Sai gave us great speed at halfback. Al Krekich was the other guard. Then there was our captain, Tommy Lynch. He played center and linebacker and was a big key to our success. He really held us together with his leadership.

71

In those days everybody on the offensive team also played defense with the exception of me. The rules allowed you to substitute for one player after each series of downs and coach Hardin preferred to have his quarterback beside him on the sideline than out there playing in the secondary. We had plenty of other fine players, both offensive and defensive specialists. They gave us the depth we needed to play a major schedule. By today's standards, comparing those players with men in professional football now, we had a first-class team.

It was a pleasure to be playing football again because my summer flight training at Pensacola Naval Air Station had been a pretty sad experience. They kept sending us up in the back seat of those trainers and I got sick nearly every time. The first time was terrible. The pilot started doing loops and rolls and I couldn't stand it. I grabbed a barf bag in the cockpit, used it, and then rolled it up. I was sick as a dog when we landed but I didn't want the other guys to know what happened up there, so I stuck the bag in my helmet and tried to walk past them nonchalantly. Everything might have gone all right but the lousy bag broke. I spent two hours cleaning out my helmet. I never did get that smell out, and every time I put it on it reminded me of the whole mess.

Flying got so bad for me that I finally promised my instructor two tickets to the Army-Navy game if he would just get me down as fast as he could. We became good friends and he started cutting my hops short. Eventually I overcame my problem. I'm okay when I fly now, but that was an awfully sick summer.

I spent a month's leave at home after that and worked out every day. I was in good condition when fall practice opened and so was everyone else. We had a closeness, a sense of dedication, and we were eager for the opening game against West Virginia.

This had looked like a rugged one for us. West Virginia had a fine team the year before and was expecting great things with nearly everyone returning. They had a lot of big men and although we were excited about our prospects we really weren't sure what we had until we played them.

Well, we played a great game and beat the heck out of West Virginia, 51–7. Our passing really clicked with Skip Orr in his first big game at flanker. The running game was sharp and the quickness in our line, both offensively and defensively, was impressive. We knew then that we would have a good year.

"That was the first test for the roll-out offense we had put in to capitalize on Roger's ability," Hardin noted. "We found we had the perfect offense by accident against a good team. West Virginia was big but slow and just couldn't stop what we were doing— Staubach to Orr, Donnelly up the middle, and Sai around end. We knew we had something."

We also beat William and Mary the next week. [Roger set a Navy total offense record of 297 yards while playing three quarters in a 28–0 victory.] Then came the game which was the turning point of our season. We went to Ann Arbor to play Michigan and we knew it would be a tough, physical game. But we took control, playing a great game and beating them 26–13.

I remember that one well for several reasons. Robert Kennedy, who was then the United States Attorney General, came to the game with his family. So did Paul Fay, the Under Secretary of the Navy. Fay was an old friend of President Kennedy, dating back to their navy days during World War II and he was also a great fan of ours. He was very athletic and used to come over to the academy often to play tennis. He and all the Kennedys played touch football on the lawn outside our hotel that weekend. The Michigan game was one of my best, right up there with the ones against Southern Cal and Army my sophomore year.

Everyone in the country was aware of Staubach by now. He completed fourteen of sixteen passes against Michigan for 237 yards and two touchdowns. He ran eighteen times for seventy yards, scoring once from five yards out. His 307 yards total offense broke his

73

week-old Navy record and his statistics for three games were spectacular: 614 yards passing with a completion percentage of 78.1 and 175 rushing, a total of 789. "The greatest quarterback I've ever seen," said Michigan coach Bump Elliott.

Roger could do no wrong that day. Once he scrambled and retreated under a heavy pass rush until he was twenty yards behind the line of scrimmage. Finally with tacklers pulling him down he saw Donnelly up field and threw the ball to him for a one-yard gain. "That," announced Navy publicist Budd Thalman, "was our Hail Mary pass."

Time magazine was working on a cover story, "The Year of the Quarterback." There were a lot of outstanding ones around the country that fall—George Mira at Miami; my old Cincinnati rival Steve Tensi at Florida State; Don Trull at Baylor; Gary Wood at Cornell; Pete Beathard at USC; Pete Liske at Penn State; Jack Concannon at Boston College; Dick Shiner at Maryland; Jimmy Sidle at Auburn; and of course, Joe Namath at Alabama. But I was enjoying such a good year right then that they decided to put my picture on the cover and feature me in the story. The magazine came out the week after we played SMU in Dallas so it naturally told a lot about that game. Wouldn't you know it! That would be the one we lost!

We played in the Cotton Bowl on a Friday night during the state fair, the night before the traditional Texas-Oklahoma game which is always sold out. Navy and SMU only drew about 30,000 so the stadium wasn't even half full. It's funny, but since I've lived in Dallas I've talked to at least 150,000 people who claim they saw the game. They usually say, "Hey, one game I'll never forget watching was the one when SMU beat you. Boy, what an upset!" It was that, all right. We should have won but our defense couldn't stop John Roderick, a sprinter who had come out for football and just ran wild. We kept swapping the lead but SMU scored to go ahead 32–28 near the end. We still thought we could win and with one second left we were on the SMU 7-yard line. I threw a pass to Skip Orr in the end zone and he almost caught it but it was knocked down by Tommy Caughran.

Our losing to SMU must have made a great impression around the country. In December one of the wire services conducted a poll and that game was voted the Upset of the Year. I guess it was, but it also was something else. My left shoulder was dislocated twice and there were some nasty feelings on both sides. It turned into a really knock-down, dragout affair.

"It was the dirtiest, stinkingest game I have seen in my twenty-five years of football," Hardin said more than ten years after the loss to SMU. "The only time I ever saw Rog lose his temper was in that game. He was hurt the first time after he had handed off the ball. One of the SMU players (defensive end Johnny Maag) hit him in the small of the back and knocked him a somersault when the play was almost over. The film shows an official standing right there, reaching into his pocket for the flag. But then he left it and there was no penalty.

"Rog went to our locker room for some treatment and Bruce Abel went in at quarterback. When Rog returned we had the ball inside the SMU 5-yard line. He went back in and scored on a quarterback sneak. There was a pile-up and while he was on the ground they pulled his helmet off and scratched and clawed his face. He was enraged when he came back to the sideline. 'They deserve anything they get, coach!' he told me. 'They've really got it coming!' "

SMU, meanwhile, reacted bitterly to the play of Nick Markoff, a reserve fullback and linebacker who seemed to pursue Roderick like a headhunter. But Roderick, like Staubach, was having a fine night regardless of his treatment. He rushed for 146 yards and scored two touchdowns. Markoff was also involved in an incident with one of SMU's male cheerleaders. Once after he was bounced out of bounds, Markoff appeared to come up swinging at the cheerleader. Markoff said the cheerleader had kicked him and that he was only trying to defend himself.

Regardless of what went into the game, SMU achieved its greatest distinction of '63 that night. The Mustangs earlier had lost to Michigan 27–16 and were rated a two-touchdown underdog against Navy. They won only three other games that year.

No one had a very good taste in his mouth after that game. The press coverage was pretty bad. We stayed over and went to the state fair the next day and watched Texas beat the heck out of Oklahoma, 28–7, and knock Oklahoma out of its No. 1 national ranking. I felt horrible. When I woke up that morning my shoulder was as sore as could be. The team doctor didn't think I could play any more that season and said I needed an operation. But they built a harness for me the next week and I played against VMI. We won 21–12, but I didn't have a very good game. I just protected the shoulder. If it had popped out again I would have been finished for the year. But I made it through okay and was ready to play against Pittsburgh.

We had a chance to put ourselves back in the running for a good record and a bowl invitation if we beat Pitt, which was undefeated and ranked third in the nation. We played in the Navy-Marine Corps Stadium at Annapolis. Temporary seats were set up and a record crowd (30,231) watched the game. Pitt was a good solid team but we won 24–12. We were sharp that day, ready to play. Our defense was super, making four interceptions. I had a good game passing (sixteen of twenty-one for 167 yards with no interceptions) but the Pitt defense didn't let me have anything running.

Roger wound up with a net loss of thirty-three yards against Pitt but whether he realized it or not, he was gaining ground in a far more prestigious race, the one for the Heisman Trophy. The Downtown Athletic Club of New York awards it at the close of each season to "the outstanding player in college football" as determined by vote of more than 1,000 sportswriters and sportscasters across the nation.

The trophy has a massive base. On it is a figure of a ball-carrier, vintage 1930, in the classic Red Grange pose—stiff-arm out and one leg stretched behind him as he pivots away from some would-be tackler. Heisman critics figure it's fitting the player is carrying the football. No interior lineman has ever won it. Perennially, it has gone to backs, most often quarterbacks, and it has never been voted to anyone at the smaller schools which often turn out great pro players. Still, it is the best-known and most-publicized award in football, college or professional. At the Naval Academy, where halfback Joe Bellino had won the Heisman in 1960, there was great excitement over the prospect of another middie winning it just three years later.

Navy went to South Bend, Indiana, to play Notre Dame on November 2, prime time for making the case for a candidate. The game was important to Staubach for other reasons. He wanted to keep the middies moving upward and he always had a special feeling for playing against Notre Dame, the school which waited too long to offer him a scholarship.

The teams were tied 7–7 at halftime and Admiral Kirkpatrick enjoyed telling what happened in the Navy locker room. "Tommy Lynch, our captain, got Roger out of the room and then he talked real straight with the rest of the players. He told them Roger had a real good shot at the Heisman Trophy but it wouldn't be helped if they lost to Notre Dame. They settled down and really played the second half and we won 35–14."

Staubach finished the game with 1,420 yards total offense in seven games, breaking the Naval Academy's single-season record with three games yet to play. Hardin told the press, "If he doesn't win the Heisman Trophy this year the game is crooked."

By now I was receiving a great deal of publicity but I wasn't crazy about it at all. I would have been on the phone every night if I had tried to return calls to everyone who wanted an interview. Any free time during the day would have been spent with the press, too. So the Naval Academy adopted a strict policy where I was concerned. Except for a couple of times when special press days were arranged, I wasn't available for interviews during the week. After games there was a little time but not much. Sometimes I would just be carted right off on the team bus.

The Naval Academy's official position was that I was there to concentrate on my studies and to play football—if I were constantly available for interviews everything else would suffer. Budd Thalman, the athletic department's public relations director, took a lot of flack because of this, but it had been done at the insistence of Wayne Hardin. He didn't have a lot of good press anyway and that hurt him even more. But it was fine with me because I didn't particularly like being harassed all the time. Now I look back at how little time we gave the press after a game and I realize those guys were just trying to do their jobs by wanting to interview me.

However, the Heisman Trophy thing slipped up on me. I honestly didn't understand its significance. I don't think the Naval Academy staged a big publicity campaign in my behalf. Budd Thalman, an outstanding publicity man, did send out some pamphlets, "Meet Roger Staubach," but it was no big deal. Navy people kept recalling how Bellino had won the Heisman three years before, so I became more aware of it, but we had played most of our schedule before it hit me that it was a very big award.

Throughout the fall Roger had been absorbed in a public relations project of a different nature. "Roger would stop at our office almost every other day for some pictures. We couldn't figure out why," Thalman said. "Then his roommate told us Roger was trying to answer all of his own fan mail, and paying for the postage. We practically had to force him to bring the mail to our office. When he did, there were several

78

boxes full of letters he had been tackling in his spare time."

His roommate was Dick Smith, a second classman like Staubach but a non-athlete. "Oh, we talked about communism, segregation, girls, and classes," said Smith, who roomed with Roger for two years. "But the only time we talked about Navy football was when I asked him."

Dick was a great guy. Each time I left for a game he'd tell me, "Bring home the eggs." I guess he was tired of hearing people say bacon.

By the time we played Maryland in our eighth game we had moved up to No. 4 in the national ranking. We had come back strong after losing to SMU and the spirit of the brigade was fantastic. Our team was already closely-knit, but the great atmosphere around the academy gave us even greater drive.

Admiral Kirkpatrick was a big key to that season. We had a pep rally before every game and he always spoke. The rallies were held at night with all 4,100 midshipmen standing under floodlights in front of Bancroft Hall. They always screamed, "We want Uncle Charley!"

Usually you heard from the superintendent at the first of the year but rarely thereafter. But Admiral Kirkpatrick was so outgoing they always wanted to hear from him. He was very positive and kept telling the brigade, "You can do anything you believe you can do." It finally got so that when he went to the microphone all 4,100 members of the brigade would say in unison, "You can do anything you believe you can do!" It was a great scene.

Admiral Kirkpatrick recalled meeting one of the player's mothers. "She told me, 'Admiral, you keep telling them that and they'll keep doing it!' "

He had an electricity about him that I think helped to get the brigade behind the football team better than it ever had. His philosophy really helped me later, both in the service and in professional football.

79

Maryland was a big game for us since College Park is close to Annapolis. It was a strong natural rivalry, sometimes a fairly bitter one. Well, we stomped Maryland 42–7, but I strained my knee and left the game in the third quarter. I wondered if I would play against Duke the next week but I wore a knee brace and played. It was a tremendous game, at least in the first half. Both sides scored a lot and then it quieted down. We scored one more touchdown in the second half and won 38–25.

Now, we had an 8–1 record and were ranked No. 2 nationally. Texas, which had a perfect record for nine games, was ranked first and there was lots of talk of a Navy–Texas game in the Cotton Bowl on New Year's Day—if we beat Army. We had the usual two weeks to prepare for that game and the tempo of the season was building up daily.

With a break in the schedule, Hardin attended a New York football writers meeting to talk about the Army game—and his quarterback. "Roger reminds me of Wyatt Earp," Hardin said. "He's going to be a legend in his own time." He also said Staubach was the greatest quarterback he'd seen, including pro greats Johnny Unitas and Y. A. Tittle.

When he returned to Annapolis, Hardin told Roger he thought he would win the Heisman Trophy. Results of the balloting would be announced on November 26, four days before the Army game.

All the anticipation, all the excitement suddenly disappeared on Friday, November 22.

Everyone remembers that date and can recall what he was doing when he first heard that President Kennedy had been assassinated. I was between classes and had gone back to my room. I was stretched out on my bed, half asleep and half awake, just resting a few minutes before I went to thermodynamics class. I heard some commotion in the hall, which was unusual in the middle of the day when it normally is quiet, so I got up and walked out.

The hall was filled with a strange emotional electricity.

Guys were running back and forth yelling. I said, "Hey, what's going on?"

Someone yelled, "The president has been shot!" I couldn't believe what I was hearing. I asked again. "The president has been shot!"

I started asking how badly he was wounded. One guy said it was critical but another guy said he thought he was going to be okay. At that moment no one knew. The only thing anyone knew was the news which had been flashed across the country, that President Kennedy had been shot in Dallas and was being rushed to a hospital.

I was in a state of shock. I walked down a couple of flights of stairs, left Bancroft Hall and started to class. Everybody was yelling back and forth about President Kennedy but no one knew anything definite about his condition.

Everyone in thermodynamics class just sat and stared. The professor wasn't there. He was somewhere listening to a radio. Finally he came in and announced the president was dead. I got a terrible sick feeling in my stomach. I remembered how I had seen him at Quonset Point, so happy and full of life. I just couldn't believe it had happened.

The professor said we could stay for class or leave. Everyone sat there, their minds far away, while he went through the motions at the blackboard. Then we started drifting outside.

I went to the practice field. Everyone was just standing there. Our team felt we were closer to the president than most people. He had visited us at Quonset Point and then tossed the coin at the last Army-Navy game. Coach Hardin looked like he had been crying. He told us he didn't know what would happen to the Army game but that the afternoon practice was canceled. We knelt and said some prayers. Then we left.

There was a memorial service that night. The entire academy had been plunged into mourning. All the banners for the Army game had been torn down, the war paint removed from Tecumseh. A lot of college games scheduled for the next day were being postponed and canceled. We heard the Army game tentatively had been called off but no one knew for sure. Maybe our season was ended. Maybe it wasn't.

The next Tuesday we received the word from the Pentagon. The game would be delayed one week and would be played in President Kennedy's memory at the request of his family. The same day I got some other news. I had won the Heisman Trophy.

The team had a celebration in the locker room. There was a big cake and they threw me in the shower. But the spirit around the academy was very subdued. There was some talk of the Army game in the mess hall, but there was no real excitement, no new banners. We had a pep rally the night before we left for Philadelphia and that was it.

I was proud of the Heisman Trophy but I felt no joy. There was so much riding on the Army game but you had to wonder if we would be emotionally ready for it. As game time neared I wasn't nervous but I did realize the pressure was much greater than last year. Now I was the Heisman Trophy winner.

Philadelphia Stadium, the big old place where Army and Navy have played for years (now called JFK Stadium) was filled with the usual crowd of 100,000 and millions of people were watching on national television. But everything else was different from the year before.

The presidential boxes on each side of the field where President Kennedy had planned to watch this game, were empty and draped with black rosettes. There were none of the pregame pranks. Instead of parades by the corps and brigade, the cadets and midshipmen for the first time in history marched on the field together. There was a memorial service and then everyone settled back and waited for the kickoff. It was a crisp, beautiful day—perfect football weather. At last it was time to play.

It turned out to be a memorable game, probably one of the best Army–Navy games ever played. There was a lot of offense and a lot of big plays. I threw the ball well and ran a few times but Pat Donnelly was the hero. He scored our three touchdowns. We only had the ball five times during the entire game. Army's offense did just as well and our defense couldn't control them. They had the ball most of the time, it seemed.

It looked like we had the game, though, when we went ahead 21–7 in the fourth quarter. With about six minutes left, Army scored and then went for two and made it. The score was 21–15 but the way our offense was moving we felt we could control the ball the rest of the game. We had had it only twice in the second half and scored both times. But Army pulled a perfect onside kickoff. Rollie Stichweh, their quarterback, recovered the ball on the 49-yard line. With that much time left it looked like they had a great chance to score again. I stood beside coach Hardin and watched Army move toward our goal line. We started talking about the plays we wanted to use when we got the ball back after they scored. With a minute and thirty-seven seconds left they had a first down on our 7-yard line. Then they really let the time get away from them.

We stopped their third down play on the 2-yard line with twenty-nine seconds left. Army had no more timeouts but asked the referee to stop the clock because the crowd noise was so great when they tried to line up. They went back into a huddle but pretty soon the referee started the clock again. Finally they tried to line up with a couple of seconds left. The gun went off. Tommy Lynch grabbed the ball and started running off the field with it. It was a weird ending. I must have said about a hundred Hail Marys the last couple of minutes.

"Army predicated its whole game plan on stalling," Hardin said. "Twenty seconds in the huddle and four seconds to snap the ball. They were trying to prevent us from getting the ball so Roger couldn't do his thing.

"They were wasting the clock on that last drive. Then they got near our goal line and realized time was almost gone. They really didn't understand why the referee would stop the clock a few seconds and then start it again."

Rollie Stichweh told me later that they were just physically exhausted when they were down there on our goal line. They just weren't thinking straight. They tried to use the crowd as an excuse to stop the clock but mainly it was because they were just tired. They tried to blame the foul-up on the referee, which was ridiculous. They could have gotten off a play all right, although fourth down from the two was far from a cinch touchdown for them. I'm just glad they didn't get the chance.

If Army had won, it would have received the invitation to play Texas in the Cotton Bowl. The Cotton Bowl officials looked very happy when they came to the locker room to invite us. Their game became a much bigger attraction with the nation's No. 1 and No. 2 teams playing.

We were screaming and hollering, "We're No. 1! We're No. 1!" Field Scovell was one of the Cotton Bowl representatives there. He said our enthusiasm was fantastic. We were supposed to vote on it and receive official sanction from the Naval Academy, but everyone knew we were going to play Texas.

We couldn't have arranged a better game from Navy's standpoint but there was a funny feeling about going to Dallas. I felt very leery of the city. In fact, I didn't like Dallas. We had lost to SMU in a distasteful game and had received bad press coverage. Then there was President Kennedy's death. Stories in the national press made Dallas seem like a pretty bad place. Later we learned they were in bad taste and inaccurate, but I read stories in the Washington papers that kids cheered in their classrooms when they were told the president had been shot. We just went crazy at the Naval Academy when we read that. Later we learned the children were cheering because school was dismissed the rest of the day. They weren't old enough to understand what had happened. It was propaganda but it really hurt Dallas in the eyes of the world.

Since I've made my home in Dallas I've learned it has an altogether different atmosphere, but in December of 1963 I was no lover of Dallas. We wanted to go back and knock the heck out of Texas. We were anxious to make amends.

Before Navy began its Cotton Bowl preparations, Roger spent a whirlwind week in New York. As the

Heisman Trophy winner and everybody's all-America quarterback, his schedule was crammed with dinners, lunches, brunches. There were countless interviews and TV appearances. The *Time* magazine all-America team, picking players based on their professional potential, picked Roger No. 1 and quoted Pittsburgh Steeler coach Buddy Parker: "For his position, the best college player I've ever seen."

Jim Murray of the *Los Angeles Times* wrote, "Staubach has gotten every award but the Good Housekeeping seal this season. He can run, pass, catch, kick, cook, and sew, to hear the Naval Academy tell it. He plays basketball, baseball, football, and would be a threat in any contest up to and including the Pillsbury bake-off. If you could bottle him, you'd get rich."

The pace was pretty wild when you're used to the disciplined, organized life at the Naval Academy, but I had some great experiences. The Downtown Athletic Club did a beautiful job with the Heisman Trophy presentation. They invited my parents and Marianne to New York, put a limousine at their disposal and really treated them royally.

I had just been drafted as a future in both pro leagues. The Dallas Cowboys of the NFL picked me in the tenth round, the Kansas City Chiefs of the AFL in the fifteenth. Naturally, I was asked how I felt about a pro career at a press conference before the Heisman Trophy dinner.

"I can't say for sure I'll never play pro football," I said. "I have a year and a half to go at Annapolis and after that four years of navy service. Right now I'm thinking along the lines of the navy rather than pro ball."

The dinner was beautifully arranged, probably the nicest affair I've ever attended. Dad was asked to say a few words. He said, "Well, we've only got one child and God couldn't have given us a better one." That really made me feel great!

I was in town a few more nights and our captain, Tommy Lynch, came up for one of the dinners. We had some free time one night and Budd Thalman said, "Hey, you guys should go out and live it up." We wanted to but I didn't have any civilian clothes with me. Budd took off his pants, sports jacket and necktie and I put them on. In a minute Tommy and I were in a cab heading for the Playboy Club. A girl in a low-cut dress was a big thing then and those Playboy bunnies were like something you couldn't believe. We were pretty excited when we got there but never got in. It's a private club and we didn't have a key.

We asked one couple if we could go in with them. They looked at us like we were crazy. We got so embarrassed that we grabbed a cab and went back to our hotel. We had a cheeseburger and a milk shake in the coffee shop, then went upstairs. Budd Thalman couldn't believe what happened to us.

I had my first real TV experience on the "Ed Sullivan Show." Being behind the scenes was a rude awakening. There were dancers on the show that night and all the girls were changing their clothes in an elevator. There I was standing back there in my football uniform wearing my gym shoes and my old crewcut. That was big-time show business! It was just a lousy backstage atmosphere.

Ed Sullivan was very nice. I sat in his office about ten minutes and then I went on. I was really unpolished, just a young gangling kid. Some of the guys had dared me to wave to them on TV. We had this little inconspicuous way of waving your hand under your chin. While Ed Sullivan was interviewing me I gave that little wave. The guys back at the academy laughed so hard they fell out of their chairs. Ed Sullivan asked what I was doing and I said, "Just waving to the guys." He got a kick out of it, that I would have the nerve to do that.

We had a week of practice for the Cotton Bowl game at the academy then everyone went on leave for about a week. Each player received a plane ticket from his home to Dallas, where we would assemble on Christmas night. Back in Cincinnati I learned that my old pals hadn't changed a bit.

Vince Eysoldt and I went to a gym to work out. We

were throwing a football and Vince noticed a man nearby exercising. Vince yelled, "Hey, here's Roger Staubach the Heisman Trophy winner!" Then this guy started yelling at me to throw him a pass. I tried to get out of it as casually as possible. I lobbed the ball to him and he gave me a disgusted look. He kept throwing it back and insisting I throw harder. Finally he said, "Hey, is that as hard as the Heisman Trophy winner can throw?" I cut loose. The ball hit his arm and broke his watch to pieces. He just picked up the pieces of his watch and left.

Vince and Jim Higgins went with me when I went to a department store to buy Marianne's Chirstmas present. I should have known better than to let them do that. Both were big guys and I guess Vince must have weighed 260. Well, we got on an elevator and there stood a little old lady. Vince looked her in the eye and told her this was a hold-up. It scared her silly. I tried to look away but didn't know what to do.

The elevator stopped and she got off. "Hey, lady," Vince yelled, "just tell everybody Roger Staubach tried to rob you!"

Later we were on an escalator. Jim and Vince got off first and then wouldn't let me off the last step. People started jamming up. A woman right behind me started screaming at me and hitting me with her purse. Just then my buddies hurried off into the crowd. There I was alone in the middle of the store with some wild woman beating me with her purse.

When the team met again in Dallas it was in a different mood. All season we had been closely-knit, hungry, and dedicated. Now we had the opportunity to play for the national championship and some of the guys were complaining about not getting enough Christmas leave. Of course we would have almost another week of leave after the Cotton Bowl game on New Year's day but these guys were griping about leaving home on Christmas Day. They were awfully shortsighted as far as I was concerned. Christmas at home is a big time of year, an important time, but these guys couldn't look one week ahead and see what we might gain in Dallas.

A lot of the complainers were guys who weren't playing much but this friction affected the entire team. Tommy Lynch was having trouble keeping everyone's minds on our goal. The night before the game we had a meeting and everybody said, "Come on, let's get back on the track. Tomorrow is for the national championship." We shouldn't have even found that meeting necessary. But I still thought we were going to win. I felt we were capable of beating Texas.

We had been treated very well in Dallas that week. They had a big reception for us when we checked in at Holiday Inn Central, with good-looking girls giving us cowboy hats. Everyone was friendly and helpful. We practiced at the Dallas Cowboys' field, which then was located on North Central next to where the club's office building is now. It was very convenient, just a five-minute bus ride from the hotel. I saw my first rodeo one night when they took the team to the State Fair Coliseum across the street from the Cotton Bowl. They brought in new movies for us to watch at the hotel. There were a lot of Navy supporters in Dallas plus many more coming in from bases in that part of the country. The atmosphere was good, no problems at all.

The assassination had happened there a month before and it was still on everyone's mind when we arrived, but I soon realized the people of Dallas were just as concerned as the rest of the United States. Our minds were put at ease and the game with Texas became the main order of business.

The game was far from what we had hoped it would be. Everything was off from the Navy standpoint, even the pregame introductions.

The weather was ideal for the game, sunny and crisp. The stadium was jammed with 76,000 people and they could hear the introductions and remarks which were going on national TV because the microphones were tied into the loud speakers. Of course, the players and coaches could, too.

Coach Hardin was introducing our line-up and when Pat Philbin, one of the tackles, stepped up he forgot his name. He had to ask Pat to tell the national TV audience his name. It was embarrassing, and rather amazing that coach Hardin forgot Pat's name. I'm sure he felt badly about it. That got us started and we never really got straightened out.

A few moments later the announcer asked Coach Hardin to describe his feelings for the game. Hardin came on strong, saying that we were there to challenge Texas for its ranking and if we won Navy was the national champion. A little later the announcer asked Darrell Royal how he felt about this. Coach Royal just said, "We're ready." Unfortunately we weren't.

The biggest reason for our unreadiness was legitimate, however. Pat Donnelly pulled a hamstring in practice four days before the game and was nowhere near the tremendous fullback and linebacker he normally was. He started the game but probably shouldn't have even played. He was ineffective and it killed us. He just couldn't run.

Texas never had shown much of a passing attack with its starting quarterback, Duke Carlisle. He was a fine field general, however, and a big reason they were number one. But the game wasn't very old when he already had thrown two touchdown passes to his wingback, Phil Harris.

Harris was behind Pat both times, but neither pass should have been for a touchdown. The first ball just floated up there and Pat couldn't recover and get back to it. The second pass was thrown so badly that Pat did get back to it and jumped to intercept it. But the ball bounced off his hands and right to Harris, who ran it in for a touchdown. So there we were, down by fourteen points already, and Texas became a different team. If the game had been tight we could have come at them with a more wide-open attack. But with Pat hurt we couldn't establish a running game. We were so far behind so quickly there was nothing to do but pass. Texas was gambling, which they didn't normally do, and taking chances. And they had the finest defense I ever played against in college football. They were all over the field.

I remember the first time I scrambled. I was running

around in the backfield and I ran into the referee. I bounced off of him and into a Texas man standing right there. They were penetrating and just waiting for me to scramble. It became an awfully long afternoon.

Besides everything else that was against us, the Texas coaches knew our defensive signals and picked them off as our coaches gave them from the sideline before each play. That had to play a great role in their offensive success but, of course, they had a tremendous defense going for them too. Tommy Nobis was a sophomore then and a regular linebacker. I thought he was their best defensive player although Scott Appleton, a senior, was an all-American tackle and a fine one. They had Jim Hudson at safety and he later starred on the New York Jets' Super Bowl champions. But one guy I especially remembered that day was George Brucks. He played a terrific game at defensive tackle. Overall, Texas was fantastic and deserved its rating.

Texas won 28–6 after leading 21–0 at halftime. Roger, despite the terrific rush, completed twenty-one passes, a Naval Academy and Cotton Bowl record. But there was never any real hope of catching up.

"Texas had a fine team," Donnelly said. "It seemed they had about fifteen men on the field, all coming at you."

"I never apologized for my pregame remark and I'm not apologizing now," Hardin said in 1974. "I just said when No. 1 and No. 2 are playing in this game the winner should be No. 1. Texas won the game and God bless 'em.

"Naturally, injuries did affect us. We had five among the first eleven players, including Donnelly's. I don't think our team got beat, though. I just got out-coached. Darrell Royal did a beautiful job."

The game was a weird ending to a very exciting and emotional season—one in which we achieved a lot for Navy football. I had another season to go and we had some other top players returning, so we hoped to pick up where we left off. After all, we were undefeated in forty-nine states. The Cotton Bowl game certainly didn't satisfy us but we proved something there. We proved who was No. 1.

8

A Year of Turmoil

The mood of the Naval Academy changed dramatically in January 1964. Some of it was caused by the letdown after the loss to Texas in the Cotton Bowl, but there were other factors.

Shortly after classes resumed there was to be a Change of Command ceremony, complete with a full-dress parade by the brigade. Rear Admiral Charles Kirkpatrick, after a rousing year and a half as superintendent, was being promoted to vice admiral and reassigned to Washington as Chief of Naval Personnel. His successor, Captain Charles Minter, Jr., another great football fan, had served as commandant of the brigade under Admiral Kirkpatrick and was being promoted to rear admiral.

There was no ceremony. The night before it was to be held Admiral Kirkpatrick suffered a heart attack. He recovered, but within several months retired from active duty. Now he lives in Virginia Beach, Virginia, and still avidly follows the adventures of his favorite quarterback.

Meanwhile, Roger Staubach was adjusting again to the less glamorous side of academy life. As the Heisman Trophy winner he felt he should attend a few key banquets but feeling pressure to keep his grades up, he soon shut them off and tried to concentrate on academic life. He made an exception, of course, when he was invited to dinner at the home of Under Secretary of the Navy Paul Fay in Washington.

Since he was a big Navy football fan, I guess Under

Secretary Fay wanted to include some of us at his dinner honoring General David Shoup, the retiring commandant of the United States Marine Corps. Coach Wayne Hardin and Mrs. Hardin, our captain Tommy Lynch and I were invited to represent the team. It was snowing when we left Annapolis for what we thought would be a very large party. When we finally made it we discovered that it was a small group of about thirty people, strictly the Kennedy clan. General Shoup evidently was part of that close group around the Kennedy family and Under Secretary Fay, of course, had been a close friend of John Kennedy since their navy days in World War II.

Jacqueline Kennedy was not there but Robert and Ted Kennedy attended with their wives. The party was seated at three tables and I found myself next to Ethel Kennedy. She was very bitter toward Dallas, which was understandable at the time, but then she became irate with me because we had lost to Texas there. "You went down there to play in the Cotton Bowl and you were representing the Navy and the country," she said, as if Texas wasn't part of the country then. I didn't feel that way about the game. There wasn't anything to hold against Texas or Texans. But the more she got on me about that game I began to feel, well, maybe we had let everybody down.

She reminded me how John Kennedy had loved the Naval Academy and said the Army–Navy games were his games. She kept emphasizing how important it was that we beat Texas, but this was a month after the game. It was still a very emotional time for the Kennedys. I believe the shock of the assassination had just begun to wear off and they were going through a very difficult time.

The anti-Johnson attitude among the Kennedys permeated the atmosphere at the dinner. Some stories were thrown around about President Johnson and I felt uncomfortable. I was a Naval Academy man, he was my Commander in Chief and I respected him. I had felt a loyalty to President Kennedy because he was a great man and the head of our country but I didn't feel the intense family loyalty these people did. We were the only outsiders there and it was an interesting experience—but a difficult one.

Despite the tensions, the night gave me an insight into the Kennedy family which has stuck with me to this day. The idea of losing that game has bothered me a lot because I knew how they felt about it. The incident with Ethel also brought home the importance so many people place on football—the significance of certain games, whom you represent, and how you represent them. It is almost scary.

When spring football practice arrived there was fresh excitement. Hardin had a number of his top players returning but he was enthused about '64 chiefly because of Staubach. He felt his quarterback could become the first player to win a second Heisman Trophy.

"An additional season's experience will make Roger an improved passer, a wiser play caller, a smooth ball handler and a smarter runner," said Hardin. He appeared to be bouncing back strongly from the Cotton Bowl defeat. Since becoming Navy's head coach, Hardin's teams had beaten Army five straight years, leaving the cadets with only a one-game edge in the all-time series. Hardin gave the middies a new motto: EVEN THE SCORE IN '64.

I was feeling pretty good about our prospects for my senior season, but then I began to worry if there would be a senior season. I was struggling like mad to pass metallurgy.

The course dealt with hydrocarbons, graphites, all kinds of metals and rocks. Unlike most of my studies, metallurgy was the type that you build on. It was necessary to learn certain facts before going on to others. I began skipping parts because I missed time on baseball trips; consequently, I was in deep trouble when time for the final exam rolled around.

Before a final I usually stayed up most of the night and crammed, going over everything in the course. It worked in my other subjects but I was too far behind in metallurgy to do any good. The night before the exam I found myself sitting there feeling bored. So I got a lacrosse stick, tied a water balloon on the end of it and lowered the thing to the window of Pat Donnelly and Fred Marlin, who lived below me. I shook it and the balloon burst right in the middle of their desk. When they came rushing into my room with more water balloons, I was sitting at my desk in rain gear. That started a big water balloon fight. I didn't study one more minute.

Next day I took the metallurgy final and made the lowest mark in the entire class—over 800 guys. I flunked, and became ineligible to play in the next baseball game, one of two scheduled after finals.

I had one more chance, however. I was able to take a re-exam. But I had to pass that one or I was in real trouble—like out of the academy.

If that had happened I would have been eligible immediately to sign a pro football contract because it had been four years since I graduated from high school. But I didn't want that. I desperately wanted to pass that re-exam. I was really scared, so I got a tutor and studied almost around the clock for three days. But I did take time out to see the baseball game strictly as a spectator. It was the only time in my athletic career that I was ineligible because of academics. It was weird, just sitting there watching.

I don't know how hard they graded that re-exam but by the time I covered the half mile from the exam room to the baseball practice field, the phone was ringing in the locker room. I passed.

That summer was the most interesting I spent as a midshipman, for several reasons. Pat Donnelly and I were assigned to a guided missile destroyer, the *William D. Pratt*, in the Mediterranean. This was the summer when midshipmen, before their first class year at the academy, became junior officers on board ship. You were given responsibilities and learned what regular officers must do during a cruise.

It was very difficult to get serious on board ship after studying hard in school for nine months. You wanted to have a good time but they expected you to work. We put into some great ports in France, Greece, Italy, and Malta. We even managed to find time for sightseeing.

When the cruise ended, we took eleven days leave, toured Europe, then went to Frankfurt, Germany, for a military flight back to the United States. Pat and I met Skip Orr, who had been on another ship, put on our civilian clothes and took off. Our money was limited so we stayed in the cheapest hotels and ate the cheapest food we could while visiting the nicest places. We had a tremendous time.

We had a football and one day went to a soccer field in Nice to work out. Suddenly we had a crowd of about a hundred people watching us. They were amazed how far I could throw the ball and how well Pat and Skip caught it. Of course, they thought at first I was throwing a rugby ball, which is much bigger than a U.S. football.

That evening we decided to go up to Monaco about twenty miles from Nice. We had rented motorbikes but Skip's broke down so he took turns riding with Pat and me. It was a beautiful setting as we rode up the mountainside to Monaco. Naturally we went to the casino and placed our dollar bets. We also went to an art exhibit and Princess Grace was there, which was funny because we had been joking about how we were going to call on her. Then there she was, really good looking too.

About ten o'clock we headed back down the mountainside. Skip was riding with Pat and I was following them. As we came around a bend Pat was close to the center line and suddenly there was a truck coming at them too close to the center. Pat's great reflexes probably saved both their lives. He swerved his bike so quickly they didn't hit head-on, but they sideswiped the truck and Skip went flying across the street and landed against a fence. It was amazing, but Pat held on to the motorbike, like a guy riding a rodeo steer. He held on to the handlebars while the bike was sliding across the street on its side. He let go when it hit the curb and he rammed into the fence, too.

All of this happened in a split-second and I watched it like a nightmare scene in the movies, when you want to get up and walk out of the theater. When I got to them I thought surely they were all broken up but miraculously they weren't. Their clothes were ripped and they were skinned and cut all over their hands, legs, and faces. Skip hurt his ankle and foot, which was the only lingering problem. It still bothered him when we reported to fall football training a month and a half later.

That ended our workouts during that leave but not our experiences. We went to Rome for about two and a half days and I spent two of them at St. Peter's Basilica. I had a general audience with the Pope, being among thousands of other people seeing him while he gave a talk. I met a Catholic priest, Father Higgins, and he took me into the sacristy and showed me a lot of things you couldn't hope to see if you just walked in with the other tourists. I went to Mass right under Pope John's tomb in a small chapel in the basement. I was intrigued with everything, the architecture, the statues, the history. As a Catholic I found it to be an incredible experience, but I believe a non-Catholic would feel much the same.

We also spent some time in Switzerland, which by the way has a Staubach Falls. Our last stop before Frankfurt was Munich, where I learned more about strong German beer than I ever cared to know.

We met a couple of other Navy players, Neil Henderson and John Mickelson, and with some girls from San Jose State, went to the Hofbrauhaus. It's like a big auditorium with pillars and long wooden picnic-style tables. I had drunk a little beer before, but just with my father when we went to a fish fry. But now I was twenty-one years old and in Germany on my own. We were having a great time and I didn't realize how that beer could affect you.

We played a game called Thumper. You would start pounding on the table and then someone would give a sign. If it was your sign and you didn't quickly give another sign you had to take a big gulp of beer. It became a riot! No one could do anything wrong, it seemed. I had control of myself but I was more than high. I had the feeling that can come with getting too much alcohol in your system. I have experienced it twice—that night in Munich and once in Vietnam at a going-away party.

I was a big loser and when we got up to leave the Hofbrauhaus I felt terrible. Everyone was going on somewhere else but I wanted to go back to our hotel. I found a cab but I couldn't speak German and didn't know the name of our hotel or the address. I just knew it was near the train station. Finally I got a pad of paper from the driver and drew some railroad tracks and a little station. He recognized it and said, "ya, ya!" But I kept drawing. I drew a little train on the tracks and some smoke coming out of the train. He started laughing. I don't believe he'd had many fares like me. He took me to the train station and after walking around a few minutes I found my hotel—just in time. The next day I had a terrible headache. But that's part of the pains of youth—learning to control yourself.

Coach Hardin also had an unpleasant experience that summer, but the effects of his lingered throughout the year. While lecturing at the Texas High School Coaches Association Clinic in Fort Worth, he made a statement at a press conference that received national attention. I remember picking up the Cincinnati paper and reading the headline: "Navy Is Nothing Without Staubach." I was embarrassed to read the story. The pressure of the upcoming season was bad enough without something like that.

Whether he said it as strongly as it appeared in print or not, Captain Bill Busik, our athletic director, took the statement as a slap at the entire Navy team. Captain Busik was a former Navy football player and took great pride in the athletic program. He immediately recalled coach Hardin from the clinic and they really went at it. The incident led to real turmoil which lasted through the season. There had been a strained relationship there prior to this, however, as both were forceful, independent men.

The situation was made worse by the talk that coach Hardin hoped eventually to move into the assistant athletic director's job held by Rip Miller, an institution at the Naval Academy. Rip is an old-timer who probably has done more for Navy athletics than any other man in history. The regular Navy officers who served as AD's came and went but he was always there coordinating important programs like the Navy bird-dogs, the men around the country who spotted promising athletes and tried to interest them in the Naval Academy—just as Dick Kleinfeldt did with me. He had talked about retirement, though, and I believe coach Hardin, who had a contract to serve as assistant to Rip as well as head coach, may have had aspirations to become assistant AD. Rip didn't like that and this caused more friction. Rip, by the way, was still there ten years later.

While coach Hardin's situation was shaky, we were optimistic when we opened fall training. We had finished last season as the No. 2 team in the country and had a very experienced team. We had lost some key players like Tommy Lynch, our center and captain, but we had seniors coming up to replace them. Fred Marlin, who had been a regular guard the year before, was the captain of the '64 team. We were looking forward to a fine year but things soon started going wrong.

We went to Penn State for our opener and won 21–8. Penn State went on to have a great year, later beating Ohio State at Columbus by something like four touchdowns. It was a goofy game—rainy and overcast and I didn't throw many passes but we moved the ball and got some breaks. In the second quarter, though, I was scrambling and stopped to dump the ball out to Doug McCarty. Just as I was about to release the ball I was hit by two big linemen, one of theirs and one of ours. Bruce Kenton, our center, was blocking on their middle guard, Glenn Ressler. They both fell over on my ankle and I felt something snap.

It hurt like crazy so I went off the field and our trainer taped it a lot tighter. I couldn't put much pressure on it the rest of the game and the next morning I could hardly walk. But the doctor figured it wasn't sprained because it wasn't swollen. That week I had all the treatments—heat, ice, whirlpool—but it wasn't any better. They put me in the infirmary one night to see if complete rest would make it better. It didn't improve.

I wasn't going to play against William and Mary since we felt a week's rest would help my ankle. Bruce Bickel, the backup quarterback, was doing fairly well, but the game was a real problem for us. With six or seven minutes to play we led 14–6, but William and Mary was threatening to turn the game around. So coach Hardin put me in for a few plays. First thing I did was hand off to Kip Paskewich and he ran seventy-six yards for a touchdown. The crowd went crazy. Kip came back and said, "That's the loudest cheering I ever heard for a guy who just handed off the football." Next we recovered a fumble and I threw three passes. John Mickelson caught the last one for a touchdown. That ended my day. Four plays and we scored two touchdowns and went on to win 35–6. After the game I was the hero, which was ridiculous.

My ankle wasn't any better and I was worried about the big Michigan game coming up. They built a special leather ankle brace and tried all methods of taping but I still felt pain. Every time I put pressure on it I just couldn't move. Doctor Steele, the head orthopedist at the Naval Academy, examined me and said the ligaments were badly sprained and the achilles tendon was strained. A couple of days before the Michigan game they shot it with a combination of Novocaine and cortisone to numb it. For the first time I was able to run. I couldn't believe it. Of course, there were mixed emotions at the Naval Academy about giving a player Novocaine, but I guess the doctor felt it wouldn't make it any worse. So I got another injection just before the game.

Michigan had a great team but we came out strong and almost scored on the first play. It was pretty tricky, with a couple of fakes off one of our basic running plays and my throwing a long pass to Skip Orr. Skip ran right past Rick Volk, the safety, but my pass was just an inch over his fingers. Next I ran for thirty or forty yards. I didn't feel a thing but everybody said I was limping. We spent the afternoon moving the ball up and down the field but we didn't score. We fumbled away three chances inside the 10-yard line. Michigan won 21–0 and to make it worse I hurt my ankle again.

They had given me another shot at halftime because the first one was wearing off, but when Bill Yearby, Michigan's all-America tackle, fell on my ankle in the third quarter I felt the pain in spite of the Novocaine. When we returned to Annapolis I was in worse shape than ever.

Nothing was working on the ankle so they put my leg in a cast and put me in the hospital. The doctor said I should be completely immobilized for ten days to two weeks. I definitely was out of the Georgia Tech game at Jacksonville, Florida.

We lost 17–0 and I watched a closed-circuit TV back at the academy, dying every minute. I couldn't believe it. Four games into the season and I hadn't done anything.

The next Thursday, just before the team was to leave to play California at Berkeley, I left the hospital. They took the cast off my leg and I could run. I felt stiffness and some pain but not the same type as before. It was better so they said I could at least make the trip to help team morale but not to play. They built some special high top shoes for me and I still was hoping there would be a way I could play.

We worked out at Kezar Stadium in San Francisco the day before the game and I had a good workout. I was running pretty well and my arm was still okay. Every day in the hospital I had gone out in the yard, stood on my cast and thrown the ball. I was encouraged.

Cal had a fine offensive team led by Craig Morton. He and John Huarte of Notre Dame were in the same position I had been in the year before, receiving heavy publicity as the top quarterbacks in the country. Craig was 6–4, strong, and could really throw the long pass. Still, our defense played tough early and managed to trap him a couple of times. We blocked a punt for a safety and Cal couldn't do anything. Later we drove inside the 10-yard line and Hardin sent me in on third down. All I had to do was fake to the fullback off tackle and come back and throw across the field to the tight end, Bill Stutt. There wasn't a soul within ten yards of him in the end zone but he dropped the ball. We wound up kicking a field goal.

If we had scored a touchdown it could have been an entirely different game but after that it got close. Coach Hardin kept sending me in some. I was in for twelve plays, completed six passes and had four interceptions. Cal

101

finished strong, with Craig throwing a couple of long touchdown passes, and we were dead at the end, especially me. To make it worse Pat Donnelly hurt his knee and it was doubtful he could play any more that season.

After the game I saw Craig standing outside the locker room with a crowd of friends and fans around him. Everyone was happy and I remembered how I had been in that situation the year before. He saw me and came over and said he was sorry I had been hurt. He was really a nice guy.

Captain Busik was enraged when coach Hardin let me play so soon after leaving the hospital. Evidently he had told Captain Busik I wouldn't be playing. It was mostly my fault because I had begged him to let me play. Then I didn't do well and that caused more problems. Coach Hardin was really depressed on the plane. He came over and sat by me and said that this team really lacked discipline and pride, which was true. Some of the guys didn't care that we had lost. They just wanted to get their Cokes and sandwiches back in the locker room.

The lowest point of my college career was during the days after the Cal game. I still didn't know if my ankle was okay and we had a tough game with Pittsburgh coming up. But then we found new life and scored a moral victory, a 14–14 tie.

I played the entire game and although I wasn't in top form I occasionally showed some spark, especially in the first half. Then I got tired. I had missed so much football that it was like going to summer camp again. Still, it was encouraging the way we came back after Pitt took an early 14–0 lead. We scored two touchdowns in the second quarter to tie it and had other opportunities later but missed a couple of field goals. We also lost Skip Orr with a knee injury. Now we were without our flanker back plus our fullback, Pat Donnelly, and our fine end Neil Henderson, who had pulled a hamstring early in the season. Notre Dame was next!

This was Ara Parseghian's first season as Notre Dame's coach and they were going great. They had a perfect record and we were really struggling along. We played in Philadelphia and in the locker room before the kickoff coach Hardin tried to motivate us. He said he really wanted us to play well so we were going to share some blood. All the players lined up and the trainers pricked our fingers and we let some blood drip into a bowl. We sat down and he talked some more, then as we went on the field each player touched the blood to make us one. When the game started guys were rubbing blood on their shirts, their fingers still bleeding. We lost to Notre Dame 40–0. After the game some of our guys were pretty sarcastic, saying we lost because we were too weak to play.

It was all so frustrating. I was embarrassed even to look at anybody. That night I went to a movie by myself. I took a seat in the top of the balcony and just stared at the screen. I sat there all night. I was humiliated to say that I was even on the Naval Academy football team.

Suddenly the middies came together as a team again. In a bristling game with bitter rival Maryland they followed Staubach's lead in a wild offensive display. Roger completed twenty-five of thirty-nine passes for 217 yards and three touchdowns. Calvin Huey, a sophomore subbing for Orr at flanker and the first black to play on the Navy varsity, caught the last two late in the fourth quarter as Navy rallied for a 22–21 lead. But the brigade's cheers were silenced by Ken Ambrusko's 101-yard kickoff return for a touchdown. Maryland won 27–22.

While finding more thrilling ways to lose, Navy still was stuck with a 2–5–1 record and hadn't won since the second game of the season. The middies finally recaptured the winning touch in Roger's last game in Navy–Marine Corps Stadium at Annapolis. They beat Duke as he broke his Naval Academy single-game total offense record with 308 yards, completing twenty-one of thirty passes for 217 and running seventeen times for ninety-one more. Only the Army game remained but Navy looked like it was regaining its old flair.

The brigade was all fired up for Army but we didn't give them much to cheer about at first. We got off to a terrible start. Army drove right through us for a touchdown, then I was trapped in the end zone for a safety and they led 8–0.

But coach Hardin put Pat Donnelly in the game for the first time since he was hurt against Cal and he really made a difference for our offense. We made a long march for a touchdown, then we decided to go for two points on the conversion. I probably have never been involved in a more unbelievable play. I was trying to pass but was chased all over the field. A guy grabbed both my legs and another reached for my passing arm so I moved the ball over to my left hand. Then as I was going down I moved the ball back to my right and threw it about fifteen yards into the end zone. Phil Norton jumped up and caught it for two points and it was 8–8 at halftime.

We displayed some tremendous defense but finally Army started moving with Rollie Stichweh throwing to his big tight end Sam Champe. By then it was gloomy and dark and the lights were on in JFK Stadium. Our defense tightened but Army kicked a field goal to make it 11–8.

We started moving on passes late in the game. Donnelly had reinjured his knee on our touchdown drive and couldn't play any more but we were still moving. We had a first down on the Army 25-yard line, but then their defense gambled and came after me with an all-out blitz, like nine men. They trapped me for a couple of big losses and we were back on our 40-yard line when the game ended. It was tough to lose to Army like that but even more so for me. I thought that might be my last football game and I had wanted to go out the right way.

I was very depressed when we returned to the Naval Academy but I had lots of company. This was our first loss to Army in six years and the Plebes were mad because they wouldn't get to carry on until Christmas leave. I was just taking over as company commander and I had a tough time getting myself in the right frame of mind to handle the responsibility. A year before everything had been exciting. Now it was blah. But at times like that you learn to appreciate your best friends even more.

Chief Donald Pelletier worked in the academy's medical department and we had been friends since I was a Plebe. When that season ended he gave me a beautiful silver platter engraved with my career records. (Among them a total offense of 4,253 yards.) I am happy that he has remained a special friend through the years. Today we keep that platter in a place of honor in our home.

But there were more disappointments. One day coach Hardin called me to his office and told me he had been fired. This seemed incredible. I didn't see how they could justify firing a coach with his talent and abilities. His overall record was outstanding—five wins over Army, the '63 team ranked No. 2 in the nation and the '60 team ranked No. 5. I guess it went back to that athletic director conflict and his not conforming to the Naval Academy's ways of doing things. They fired a successful coach and a great recruiter, that was the beginning of the downhill slide for Naval Academy football. It didn't recover for years.

Coach Hardin and I had one more game together, though. He was coaching in the North-South Shrine game at Miami on Christmas Day and I was the only player who played in that one and then went on to the East-West Shrine game in San Francisco.

Our South squad included a lot of famous players, including Bob Hayes and Jerry Rhome. Hayes had won those Olympic gold medals and then finished the football season at Florida A&M, signing with the Cowboys. He was the world's fastest human but he also was a genuine football player, a great threat as a pass receiver. He was incredible on reverses in that game and wound up the most valuable player although we lost 37–30. Rhome and I were alternating at quarterback. He had just broken all those NCAA passing records at Tulsa and also was signing with the Cowboys. He had a real aloof attitude but I think he was just tired. He came in late from the Bluebonnet Bowl where he had been the hero, and I guess he also had had those pro contracts on his mind. I was a little disappointed

105

in the strength of his arm but it was obvious he was smart and competitive and could throw the short pass.

We gave everyone a good show in Miami. The North led 30–6 going into the fourth quarter but then we got hot. I started running, hit some passes, and Hayes was flying on those reverses. They had a rule that the team which was behind could keep receiving the kickoff after it scored. We kept receiving and scoring. Finally it was 30–30. Then the North got the ball and Huarte hit Snow for a touchdown with five seconds left.

The game in San Francisco wasn't nearly as exciting but it was more surprising. I received the MVP trophy, which I didn't deserve. We played the game in a heavy rain and I guess the press was impressed because I threw a thirty-seven-yard pass to Dick Gordon to set up the East's only touchdown in the third quarter. They had to turn in their ballots before the game ended, which was unfortunate because Craig Morton threw a touchdown pass to Jack Schraub, his tight end from California, with a minute left and the West won 11–7. Craig had had a fine day passing and he certainly deserved the award, not me.

The final months at the Naval Academy moved swiftly. Roger enjoyed another big moment in baseball, hitting the home run which beat Brown 5–4. "I just can't say enough about the guy," coach Joe Duff said. "He can look pretty poor for the first two strikes but always looks awfully good for the last one. He is at his best in pressure situations."

Soon it was June Week and Marianne came to visit again. While other top quarterbacks leaving college thought about their first pro training camp Roger was preparing for active duty in the navy as an ensign. But just before graduation he experienced his last grand moment in Naval Academy athletics.

My biggest thrill in college was when they retired my jersey, number 12. We were having the annual athletic awards program in the field house and I had no idea they would do it. The midshipmen had petitioned the Naval Academy Athletic Association to retire my jersey. This had happened only once before, to Joe Bellino, who won the Heisman Trophy in 1960.

The ceremony already had been special for me. I had received the Thompson Trophy which is awarded to the overall athlete of the year and I was the only athlete to receive it three years in a row. Also, they presented me with the sword which goes to the outstanding senior athlete. Then when they called me back to the stage and presented me with my jersey I just broke down.

Roger received three standing ovations that day. Admiral Minter, the superintendent, said, "Such a young man comes along only once in a great while in the life of an institution. A superb athlete and a complete gentleman, his performance, both on and off the field, reflects great credit on the institution he represents and on college athletics in general."

Roger's jersey was placed on display in the Naval Academy field house, a lasting reminder of a rare era. "His kind," noted Baltimore columnist John Steadman, "will not come this way soon again."

9

Time for Decisions

During 1965 the AFL and NFL war over collegiate talent was, perhaps, at its highest pitch. The AFL had gained a surprisingly strong foothold in professional football and some believed the leagues eventually would find merger inevitable. But the infighting continued.

Two of the most competitive teams were the Dallas Cowboys and the Kansas City Chiefs. Lamar Hunt's team had originally been the Dallas Texans but had abandoned the city of its birth when it became obvious Dallas would not support two teams. The move to Kansas City, however, far from ended the rivalry.

Dallas had drafted Roger Staubach in the tenth round for 1964 and Kansas City had chosen him in the fifteenth round.

When the College All-Stars played the Cleveland Browns in August of 1965 I thought it would be my final game. I had never considered anything but fulfilling my four-year commitment to the navy. Four years seemed like a lifetime then, though it now seems like a short period of my life. I only faintly considered going into professional football some day. So I wanted to make this game count and it was very important for me to get the starting assignment.

Otto Graham coached the All-Stars that year and the atmosphere was serious. We worked hard at Northwestern University, practicing twice a day for three weeks. Graham told us the starting quarterback job was up for grabs. I was competing against Craig Morton of California, the

Cowboys' No. 1 draft choice that year, John Huarte of Notre Dame, and Bob Timberlake of Michigan. We had a vast array of talent in that All-Star camp. Great defensive players like Dick Butkus, and some fine receivers in Lance Rentzel, Fred Biletnikoff, Bob Hayes, Jack Snow, and Roy Jefferson. We had running backs such as Pat Donnelly (my friend from Navy), and Gale Sayers, Junior Coffey, Tucker Frederickson, and Ken Willard. There were also a couple of guys in the line named Malcolm Walker and Ralph Neely, who were later to be my teammates with the Cowboys.

Pro scouts visited our workouts and I think that's when they first realized I could play pro football. They were impressed by the strength of my passing arm. They knew I was a scrambler and had good statistics. However, a lot of guys come out of college with good records and statistics but just can't make the transition due to some intangible factors which just aren't apparent.

Competition at the quarterback slot was close, but I finally got the edge in a scrimmage against the Chicago Bears and became the starter. Huarte was very disappointed. He was coming off a great year, the Heisman Trophy winner for 1964, and Notre Dame stars are always popular, especially in Chicago. He had just signed a big bonus contract and the day he found out he wasn't starting he didn't show up for practice. This caused some tension for a few days.

After minutes we could have taken a vote and elected Staubach captain. I don't know why—it's just something about that guy that exudes leadership. He's got it.

—*Ralph Neely*
At College All-Star Game

Although I got the starting job, coach Graham didn't particularly care for my tendency to jump when I threw short screens and flare passes. I had dislocated my left shoulder a number of times in college and he warned me,

"Hey, you keep jumping like that and somebody's gonna cream you underneath that arm."

I took Graham's advice about everything except the jumping. I just shrugged it off. It's something I'd always done.

Jimmy Brown, Cleveland's all-time running back, was playing his final year and the Browns also had Paul Warfield at wide receiver. Oddly enough, I once played against Warfield in a high school all-star game when he was Ohio's top halfback. Paul suffered a broken collarbone during the College All-Star game and was out the entire season. I didn't fare much better.

We were doing fairly well in the first half, trailing 7–3. A deep pass was called with a swing pass to a running back as a safety valve. I faded to throw and saw an outside linebacker, Galen Fiss, blitzing. I jumped up just as he got to me and dropped the ball off to a back in the flat. Fiss let me have it! His helmet caught me right under the left arm and finished off my shoulder. It had been dislocated seventeen times during college and it always slipped back in a matter of seconds. Not this time.

They carried me into the locker room. The ambulance had just taken Warfield to the hospital so there was no way to move me from the stadium. The doctor tried to get my shoulder back into place, putting his foot under it and pulling, but it wouldn't go back in. I was in that locker room about an hour and fifteen minutes before the ambulance came back. My friend, Marianne Hoobler, had come to the game and I don't think she enjoyed it very much. She ended up riding to the hospital with me in the ambulance. They hung weights on my shoulder and it finally popped back into place after a couple of hours.

I was upset about getting hurt in what I thought was my final game, and the next day I did something very stupid. I had my car in Chicago. Mother worked for General Motors and through her I had bought a new 1965 Chevrolet Super Sport, a blue convertible with white top and wire wheel covers. I got behind the wheel and drove all the way to Annapolis alone.

My shoulder was bandaged and I still felt the effects of

110

medication. I could have lost control of the car or gotten drowsy and gone off the road. I was lucky. I got back to Annapolis with nothing worse than a bad mood.

Cleveland had won the All-Star game 24–16 and that just added to my disappointment. Several weeks later coach Graham sent letters thanking us for playing in the game. But mine had a little message scribbled at the end.

I told you not to jump, Roger.

That fall a doctor at the academy, Captain Steele, operated on my shoulder and did a great job. I've never had any problems with it since. So the All-Star injury actually turned out for the good. It caused me to finally get my shoulder repaired properly. If I hadn't, it could have bothered me for years.

The College All-Star game was the most important and the most serious of the post-season games, but I played in another one earlier that summer—the Coaches All-American game at Buffalo.

I thought I got less than I deserved in that one. I was the starting quarterback and co-captain in every all-star game but this one. Ara Parseghian of Notre Dame was the coach and he named his own quarterback, John Huarte, as the starter. Rollie Stichweh, the Army quarterback, was also there and Parseghian wanted both of us to play defense. We'd been working out three days when Parseghian came over to me. I guess he wanted to show how friendly he was when he said, "How's it going, Rollie?" So I played on defense and the specialty teams in that game, getting in at quarterback only about a quarter.

That trip to Buffalo was a blessing, though, because it inspired me to make one of the great plays of my life.

Marianne and I had dated for years. She came to the Naval Academy for June Week every year, but we had never gone steady. She dated other guys back in Cincinnati and I dated other girls around Annapolis and Washington. Yet we always had a special feeling for each other. I knew she had all the qualities I wanted in a wife but I never mentioned marriage to her while I was in the academy.

111

Of course, it was against regulations for me to marry while I was in school, so that made me more inclined to let things ride. After graduation I realized it was time to think about a different life. I had no reason to expect Marianne to wait around for me indefinitely.

All during the week of the Coaches All-America game, however, I dated Miss Buffalo. She was official queen of the game and met each player when he arrived and had her picture taken with him. She invited me to a party the first night and the next evening I went to her house for dinner. She was pretty and had a nice personality, but by the time the game ended that Friday night, I knew what I wanted to do. As soon as I got home I was going to propose to Marianne.

It was Saturday night when I got to Cincinnati. Marianne was working late at the hospital. I picked her up when she got off work and we went to her house. As soon as we got in the living room, I proposed. She said yes and I gave her an engagement ring. After all those years, it was settled just like that.

Roger and I had known each other since the fourth grade. I first remember him as the smart-aleck kid who cut up in class a lot.

We both had some other romantic interests through the years but we always wound up together again. I felt it was getting serious when he invited me to Annapolis, for June Week and graduation. I really thought he would propose. A lot of our friends were getting married or engaged and kept asking us, "When are you getting married?" Roger would just say, "Oh, we don't know each other well enough."

When I went home to Cincinnati after June Week and he hadn't proposed, I was crushed. In August I would have worked two years in intensive care at Good Samaritan Hospital and I made up my mind to move to another city. I just wasn't going to be there every time he came home for a visit.

That Saturday he was coming home from Buffalo I

made certain I had to work late. His plane came in at 4:00 p.m. and I didn't want to meet him at the airport. I figured he could wait a few hours and pick me up when I got off at 11:30.

—Marianne

In late June I had to report back to Annapolis to start six months as an assistant physical education instructor and assistant Plebe football coach. Then I had to report to the College All–Stars, so we planned our wedding for September 4. We wanted to be married in St. John's Evangelist, in the parish where we had always lived, but our priest, Father Guntzelman, had moved to a big cathedral downtown, St. Peter in Chains, so we were married there.

It was a combined civilian-military wedding. Some of my best friends from Cincinnati days were attendants, and so were some of my best friends from the academy. Marianne was attended by girls who had been close to her for years. After we were married we left the church under crossed swords, just like the ceremonies at the Naval Academy.

The Hoobler family was large. Marianne was the oldest of five children and her family, like mine, didn't have much money. She helped pay for the wedding by selling her car—a Corvair.

Roger didn't attend the rehearsal the night before the wedding. In fact, few of his attendants were there. They were coaching the Plebes at the Naval Academy and the head coach wouldn't let them off early enough. They flew in later that night.

We were married on Saturday morning and then went to Washington for the weekend. It wasn't that short a honeymoon, though. It was Labor Day weekend and Roger had Monday off. But on Tuesday we were at Annapolis and he was coaching again.

—Marianne

When we returned to Annapolis, we lived right outside the academy grounds on Cornhill Street in a little carriage house behind a bigger home. There is still a colonial atmosphere in Annapolis and there are cobblestone streets around the area. It was a nice, neat section and we enjoyed living there. Skip Orr, the flanker at Navy, was there as an assistant too. We had served as best man in each other's weddings. The four of us had a lot of good times together—inexpensive good times.

One day I received a phone call from a man with a very unassuming voice who said his name was Lamar Hunt. It took me awhile to figure out that this man was *the* Lamar Hunt. This was actually the second time I had been contacted by a pro team. Gil Brandt of the Cowboys had visited my parents' home while I was a midshipman. He told them of the advantages I'd have if, for some reason, I decided to leave the academy. This really upset my mother and she just about threw him out of the house. But Gil was only doing his job.

We went ahead and drafted Roger because he was just such a super prospect and also because there was some question whether his being color blind would keep him from active duty. Whether this happened or not I still, personally, felt he would play again. He was just so competitive and football was in his blood. And if he did play, we wanted him in Dallas. I would say he turned out to be a helluva tenth-round draft choice.

—*Gil Brandt*
Dallas Cowboys
vice president in charge of
player personnel

Anyway, Lamar Hunt came to our house and we had dinner together. You would never have known that he was a man of such stature—a millionaire no telling how many times over, a founder of the American Football League, owner of the Kansas City Chiefs—and yet a man of great

114

humility. I couldn't figure out why he came in person to see me, why he just hadn't sent a scout or some other club official. But I understand that's the way Lamar is sometimes. Dallas and Kansas City still had their big rivalry going, and Lamar had a plan where he could at least sign me to a future commitment if I ever did decide to play football again.

His plan called for the Chiefs to pay me a bonus immediately—I believe it was $5,000—and then give me $250 to $300 a month the remainder of the time I was on active duty. I would sign a future contract for three years at some $25,000 a year and receive a $50,000 bonus, if upon leaving service, I did decide to play again. But under the terms of his contract, I was under no obligation whatsoever if I wanted to stay in the navy. I could keep the money and the future contract would be void.

Captain Paul Borden, a legal officer at the academy, looked over the contract and everything was in order. It was agreeable to the navy. I couldn't believe anybody would pay me for doing nothing, but I wasn't going to argue about that. Of course, I realized the key fact was that I was also drafted by the Cowboys. Kansas City wanted to know on a long-shot basis that I would play for the Chiefs, not Dallas. Had there been only one club involved, they would have just waited until I'd served my four years and then tried to sign me.

Coach Petersen, an assistant basketball coach at the academy who knew Gil Brandt called him and told him I was working out and looking very good, and that Kansas City had definitely been talking to me. I believe the Cowboys had already heard about this anyway. They contacted us and Captain Borden told them the basics of the Chief's offer but did not mention any money figures. He said that he felt it was the kind of contract I could sign, a good way to do things. He told them we would consider only one offer from each side.

When the Cowboys played in Philadelphia that December Captain Borden went up there and talked to Clint Murchinson, the Cowboys' owner; Tex Schramm, the general manager; and Gil. The Cowboys said they would pay

115

me $10,000 to sign and $500 a month while I was in service. I would sign a future contract with them and, if I decided to play, I would receive a bonus of $25,000 a year on three separate one-year contracts. If I took the bonus in a lump sum it would be $55,000 to $60,000 but it would come to $100,000 on a deferred basis—$10,000 a year over a ten-year period. Captain Borden called me from Philadelphia and I agreed immediately.

I felt bad about Lamar because he was such a tremendous man and had thought of the plan in the first place. But the Cowboys had offered me more money, had drafted me higher and the NFL just had more charisma at that time. I phoned him and broke the news.

"I don't want to haggle over this and for each side to keep making counteroffers," I told Lamar. "I'm sorry but I just took what I felt was the best offer for me."

"I wish you hadn't agreed to their offer," he said. "I'd like to have made a counteroffer but I guess it's settled now."

I signed and the Cowboys paid me the bonus and money every month the remaining three and a half years. I was in the service. I gave most of the bonus to my parents and Marianne's because they needed it. I also paid Captain Borden a fee, although he didn't want to take it. We kept a couple of thousand for ourselves, which was a real windfall for us. We had that couple of thousand in the bank and were getting $500 each month to add to the $400 I was making as an Ensign. Eventually we banked most of those monthly checks, too. We called it our Cowboy Account.

The navy made an announcement that I had signed the option, a future-type contract, in case I *did* decide to play again after my four-year obligation. But then Steve Perkins of the *Dallas Times-Herald* wrote that I was getting out of the navy because my shoulder was a problem and that I was joining the Cowboys. This was unbelievable. Steve had called me and I had explained the contract in detail. He apparently decided to do the story no matter what I told him. Captain Borden contacted the Cowboys and asked them how something like this could happen and be so misunderstood. Perkins wrote a corrected version, though it came out as only a small story across the country. You can image what people, especially the navy people, were thinking of me.

I enjoyed coaching the Plebes that year. Dick Duden was the head coach and I was backfield coach and helped to put in the plays. I remember being more nervous on the sidelines as a coach than I'd ever been as a player. However, it was a satisfying experience. A couple of days before we played the Maryland frosh I was watching films and decided to put in a play where the split end ran a corner route and the tight end ran a post. The back came out of the backfield, splitting them over the middle. Boy, he was wide open and we scored. That was as much of a thrill as throwing a touchdown pass.

When my final six months in Annapolis ended we moved to Athens, Georgia, where I entered supply school. We got settled in an apartment and were excited about the future. Marianne was pregnant and our baby was due in June.

We made new friends and I began playing on the basketball team. Once we were playing in a tournament at Gainsville, Georgia. I'll always remember it. Someone stole the wire wheel covers off my convertible while it was parked outside the high school gym. It burned me up and I called the sheriff immediately.

He asked me, "Son, where you from?"

"Ohio," I told him.

"What kind of license plates you have on that car?"

"Ohio."

"Well, Son, you lucky they didn't take the whole car."

The reason I ended up in the Supply Corps instead of navy line (which is sea duty, or flying) is that I'm slightly color blind. As far as the navy is concerned, that's like being a little bit pregnant. It took a very odd twist of fate for me to even get into the academy. I should never have been accepted, but the academy didn't find out I was partially color blind until it was too late to do anything about it. I've always had trouble with color tests. I can see basic colors but only to a degree. When I take tests where there are colored dots which contain a pattern for a number, I just can't make the number out.

I took my final physical for the academy at Fitzimmons Army Hospital in Denver. My eyes were strong, about 20/15 or 20/10, for the regular eye test. Then they sent a group of us over for the color test. A seaman was sitting there with his feet on his desk, just a very loose guy. We walked in and he looks up, shrugs and says, "Okay, another bunch."

I stood back across the room and read the red and yellow over green dot test. I had no idea I missed any of them but the seaman said, "Hey, you missed a couple, but that's not bad." He passed me. That's the first and only time I've ever passed a color test.

Strange. I later found out the test for color blindness is supposed to be one of the most stringent parts of the academy's entrance examination. The first physical I took at the academy, they said, "Hey, man, you're color blind." But once you're in the academy they can't do anything about it. So I stayed. And the academy took what I felt was some unfair criticism when it all came out years later, after I was on active duty.

Even today if the house is a little dark I'll put on my socks and Marianne will say, "You've got on one blue sock and one brown one." It still amazes her.

I nearly chose to go into the marines while I was at the academy, which could have certainly changed my future. The marines had tried to recruit me for Quantico, saying I could play football there. (We had a choice of going into the navy or marines upon graduation.) I finally decided I just didn't seem to have the marine instincts. Guys at the academy who were set on the marines wore their combat boots while they studied and you'd see them in their fatigue hats walking down the halls. That was their thing. I just wasn't that gung ho so I felt it was better to go into the navy.

I volunteered for Vietnam after my schooling at Athens. I wanted to go because I believed that we, the United States, were doing the right thing—trying to stop the threat of communism in Southeast Asia. Later the war became controversial and I saw things I disagreed with and questioned. But at the time I went, I strongly felt I had my duty to do. So I choose shore duty in Vietnam for a year. That may have been the longest year of my life.

10

Vietnam: Another World

Vietcong forces, supported by communist North Vietnam, began raiding farm villages in South Vietnam in 1957. Soon United States military personnel were helping the South Vietnam Army (ARVN) in an advisory capacity.

On July 30, 1964, two U.S. destroyers were patrolling near the Gulf of Tonkin. They were attacked by North Vietnamese PT boats, which apparently had been in pursuit of South Vietnamese vessels. After these attacks, U.S. planes bombed North Vietnam PT bases—the first U.S. attack on North Vietnamese territory.

Citing the attack and the aggression from the North against South Vietnam, President Johnson asked Congress for power "to take all necessary measures to repel any armed attack against forces of the United States and to prevent further aggression."

The United States was in the Vietnam War.

It was a small black box, hardly big enough to hold a large television set. They locked me in this box for four or five hours. I had to stay in a half-squatting position, with my back bent forward. A guard would walk back and forth in order to make sure I didn't try to sit down. I thought I would go crazy. The walls were close, squeezing me in. My back, neck, and legs ached—a dull, throbbing kind of pain. I wanted to straighten up but I couldn't. There wasn't room.

Finally I was taken out of the box over to the compound where I went through indoctrination—a continual flow of propaganda which would not stop. Then they put me in an even smaller box where I could not move at all. I couldn't stand it. I almost cracked up. I pushed with all my strength and just about broke the lock and burst out. I was going crazy and they only kept me in the smaller box for about five minutes.

This took place in a mock prisoner of war camp, which we went through before going to Vietnam. It was unbelievably realistic and I guess I'll never forget those small, black boxes. It tears my up inside when I think how some of the prisoners of the Vietcong and North Vietnamese were put in those boxes for five, six, or seven months. You wonder just how much a man can stand. I know the group I was training with only went through the ordeal for about twenty-four hours and some of the guys broke and told everything they knew.

They wanted to get us ready for all possibilities in Vietnam. About forty of us were sent to survival training school in Coronado Beach, California. At first we were taught Vietnamese customs because there had been a great deal of trouble with Americans going over and, through ignorance or otherwise, disregarding Asian customs. For instance, if you're sitting in a chair and cross your leg, it's very rude to show the heel of your shoe to someone. We also learned about communist strategy and how it was being used in the small villages.

Then we had weapons training, which I found a little ironic. My parents had never let me have so much as a BB gun when I was growing up and there I was shooting everything from a .45 to a machine gun. As a supply officer I didn't particularly need this training, but they sent us all through it just in case.

The mock prisoner of war camp was on Whitney Island, just outside of Seattle. When we got there they immediately put us out in the woods, with absolutely nothing. We finally did get a rabbit and tried to make a stew, using it with wild peas. But it made me sick. About the only thing I ate for five days were wild berries and I lost about fifteen pounds. They captured us out in the woods and put us into the POW compound. The entire setup was based

121

on information given by returning POW's from Korea and what little knowledge we had about Vietcong camps. Even the guards were dressed in communist uniforms and I had to keep reminding myself this wasn't for real.

They never hurt us physically but it was tough, just from the strain of the boxes and the constant propaganda. They did everything to get us to reveal information, but all I ever gave was my name, rank, and serial number as specified in the Geneva Convention.

They would barrage us with propaganda about President Johnson and other officials. They'd continually tell us the American people were against the war. They told us President Johnson had justified the war by saying more men were killed on the highways each year than in Vietnam. Everything was done well. It was a big act, but I think it gave me more than the average guy's appreciation of what our prisoners went through.

One night they took us to a hut for indoctrination and questioning. They put bags over our heads so we wouldn't see as they marched us along and then took them off as we got inside the hut. I was carrying my jacket and as I entered, I slipped my hand up and moved the bag from my eyes. Just slightly. But it was long enough for me to see how far the barbed-wire fence was.

The guard nearest the fence was a pretty good distance away and there was another guard on the other side of the hut. I thought I could make the fence if everything went well. As I came out of the hut, the bag still over my head, I took off running to where I thought the fence was. I tore the bag from my head and just as I got it off, there was the fence. I threw my jacket on the fence and tried to dive as high as I could and then roll over. The jacket saved me from getting all torn up. I cut my arms and my clothes were torn to rags but the jacket saved my face from the barbed wire.

One guard apparently didn't see me in time to point his gun and the other one was taken by surprise. By the time he got his gun I was over the fence and running into the darkness of the woods. I didn't know where I was running but I didn't stop. I had escaped. Finally, the guards called me in, telling me I'd made a good escape.

When you made what they term a good escape you got an hour's rest. So I went back and had coffee and cookies with the guards. who were just regular guys then. But the socializing ended pretty abruptly. When the hour was up, this guy came over to me.

"Well, have you enjoyed yourself?"

"Yes sir," I said.

Then he drew back and slapped me across the face. "Now you're back in the problem again," he said. They threw me out of the room and back with the other guys. That night they stuck us in cold water.

Soon after this ordeal I got some time off before I went to Vietnam. Jennifer had been born by then and I was able to spend time with the family in California. In August 1966 I was flown to Vietnam.

When you fly along the countryside near Da Nang the view is beautiful. Trees carpet the region, covering the mountains and hills giving it a soft, restful appearance. Some of the most beautiful beaches in the world are there. The French had planned to turn the area into a vacation resort and many of the buildings in Da Nang had been built for this purpose. Of course, the beautiful appearance was the antithesis of what was actually happening.

Da Nang is in the northern part of South Vietnam on the South China Sea. It's a tropical area, sometimes warm and sticky. Then the monsoon season comes with rain and wind, making it cold. The land is good and rich for agriculture. South Vietnam is divided into four corps technical zones. Da Nang was the uppermost zone, Zone 1.

I was a supply officer in a support capacity. I had a necessary job but it wasn't like being out in the rice paddies with the army and marines. When I first landed I had no idea what my assignment would be. The next morning we were to get our orders and everybody was talking about the fight that had taken place with the Vietcong at the navy's petroleum, oil, and lubricant facility (the POL), which was about six miles south of Da Nang.

Lieutenant JG Andy Havola was the supply officer and ran the facility. Marines were on duty near there and also helped guard the POL and there were about twenty navy men from the supply corps on hand. When the gunfire began he started running around, telling his men to get into the bunkers. There had been a lot of trouble there and everybody was a little trigger happy. One of the men accidentally shot Havola, blowing off his right arm.

My assignment came. "Ensign Staubach, you'll take over the POL site just to the south of Da Nang."

Oh well, I thought. Anyway, they gave me a truck and I'd drive the six miles from Da Nang two or three times a week to the POL site, passing through a few villages along the way. I carried a .45 automatic but never had to use it. Looking back now, I know guys had been ambushed and killed in some of those villages and I feel very fortunate that nothing happened to me.

I was also in charge of shipping and receiving of all personal effects, which was really depressing. We had to ship back possessions of guys who had been killed. I also felt I just wasn't contributing enough, that I didn't have a very responsible job. I asked to be transferred to something more important and they decided to send me to Chu Lai, a military base some sixty miles south of Da Nang. I liked that idea, I would be in charge of the freight terminal division there with 120 men under me and we would off-load and load all ships that came into Chu Lai.

I had spent about four months in Da Nang and just before I left an old friend of mine from the academy, Tommy Holden, tried to contact me and another friend, Freddie Marlin. Tommy was on R&R (Rest and Relaxation) and had come through Da Nang but missed us. He was some guy. He was a guard on offense but played linebacker on defense at the academy. He was one of those real hard-nosed guys, all guts—the kind of guy you find on the specialty teams in pro football. Boy, he was tough, not afraid of anything. Tommy had gone into the marines and I can remember how proud he was, how happy he was to be a Marine. I was sorry I missed him because we've had a lot of good times together.

I was just sitting there behind my desk one day and a guy told me that Tommy had gone back out into the field and been killed. Just like that. The war really hit me personally then. I'd felt badly about all the people who had been killed but I knew Tommy, he was a friend. He was a platoon leader and had been directing his men in a fire fight against the Vietcong. Just as he charged over a hill he was shot right in the chest.

I couldn't believe it. He was such an active guy and loved life so much. I felt this sickness inside. I remember the football games we had played together and how happy he had been. I thought of June Week at the academy and how he was smiling and having such a good time. Then I got mad. I looked around me. I wanted to get a gun and charge out there myself. I wanted to get even for what had happened to Tommy. But I couldn't do anything or change anything. Tommy Holden was dead.

Americans split over the Vietnamese War. Some felt if communist aggression was not stopped, Southeast Asia would eventually fall, that the free world must stand up and fight or the smaller countries would fall like dominoes.

Others felt Vietnam was in a civil war which was no business of the United States, that democracy in South Vietnam was only a sham for dictatorship anyway. And they feared endangering relations with Russia and the threat of Red China.

Americans remained divided throughout the war, though there was a swing toward moderateness. They are still divided.

And the men who served in the armed forces in Vietnam? Well, they fought, suffered, died.

A mortar makes a whomp-like sound. It's an eerie, whistling kind of sound which gets louder the nearer it comes to you. You hear the whistling and WHOOOOMPPP. I heard the sound very close at 2:00 A.M. one morning near this small hut I lived in at Chu

Lai. I jumped out of bed and headed for the door, all the time yelling at my roommate.

I hit the screen door, knocking it right off its hinges. I never stopped. I bet I was in the bunker ten seconds before anybody else. The mortar attack, some of which hit within 100 yards of our hut, killed four people and injured others. Odds against a direct hit are very low but when your life is in danger, you don't worry too much about the odds.

Death was always there. Close. There would be twenty or thirty ambulances lined up near the helicopter pad, waiting to put the dead in bags to be shipped back to the United States. We volunteered to help. It just tore our guts out. These had been human beings and now they had become just bodies, or pieces of bodies, wrapped in cloth for shipment.

A friend of mine, Mike Grammer, was in the marines. Mike and I had been Plebes together at the academy and I hadn't seen Mike since we left. I was down on a beachhead one day and we were loading ships. I got to talking to some of the marines and one of them knew Mike.

He said, "You mean you haven't heard? Mike and this sergeant were found dead in a South Vietnamese church. They .. their hands were tied behind their backs and they had been shot through the head."

I suddenly got a sick feeling in my gut. I had heard a lot of the marines talking about the atrocities the Vietcong and North Vietnamese committed on prisoners, but Mike had been captured and couldn't do anything and ... they just shot him. You feel you can't just sit back and take things like that. But what do you do? Do you, in turn, use the same methods against the enemy? Do you get revenge for the Mike Grammers by doing the same thing to the communists? That's something that will be debated as long as there are wars.

When I found out about Mike I could, in a way, sympathize with marines going into the villages where they were supposed to help the South Vietnamese. You didn't know where the Vietcong were in the South. You knew some South Vietnamese had been forced to kill Americans because relatives they had in the North had been threatened by the communists. There were Kamikazes with grenades stuck up their butts; a villager comes up, drops a grenade and kills a buddy; a friend goes into a hut and it's mined. So sometimes you fire too quickly at the wrong person. It's terrible, but I can see how it could happen.

Don't get me wrong, I disagree with things that happened, like at My Lai. Lieutenant William Calley was convicted of being responsible for the killing of at least twenty-two captured civilians in 1968.

If he was guilty of murdering all those people, there was no doubt in my mind he needed to be punished. People also seemed to forget that the men who judged him were Vietnam veterans. Vietnamese are human beings too. War turns many people into a lot of things but there still has to be a degree of humanity.

American servicemen had other problems in Vietnam but I don't see why everybody thought it was so shocking. Drugs were easy to get, especially marijuana. The poppy seed was growing right in the villages, like shrubbery. Smoking marijuana was much more serious in 1966 than it is now so when they caught some guys with it, they instituted a complete search of all the barracks. Later, when guys came back from Vietnam and took bloodtests they were found to have a serious drug habit. But the hard stuff was usually gotten in the Far East when guys would go on R&R to Hong Kong and other places. I am certainly against the use of drugs in any form but I think it's also important that we try to understand the guys who came back from Vietnam and what they went through.

We were also surrounded by poverty areas and naturally there was a serious problem with VD. Many of the women sold themselves to buy food for their families or to support babies, but the only way you could really judge them was in the context of their country, their society and what was happening—certainly not from the perspective of our country.

I also think it's very important that we try to help Vietnam veterans—whether they returned healthy, with a drug problem, handicapped, or from a POW camp. The Viet-

127

nam War became very unpopular with much of our country and there were many protests. The Calley thing came out and also cast a bad reflection. But these veterans were sent over there to perform what they felt was their duty, risking their lives every day.

Feelings in this country about the Vietnam War changed somewhat when we saw the POW's returning. I cried like everybody else when I watched them on television. They were so proud, and as American as can be. Some had been stuffed into those boxes, isolated, gone through God-knows-what, and yet they came back and stood there saluting the flag.

The Vietnamese War was a screwed-up mess. Some of our allies, such as France, were sending supplies to our enemy. People in our own country were protesting the war and we weren't fighting the war as a war. It was like playing for a tie. We'd be allowed to fight a certain point and then stop, whereas the enemy went all out.

Most of the six months I spent in Chu Lai I believed strongly in our job in Vietnam. We were trying to stop the communists from shoving their doctrine down the throats of the Vietnamese people. We were fighting so they could choose the type government they wanted and by doing this we were curtailing the spread of communism throughout Southeast Asia.

Some marines from the Republic of Korea were near us in Chu Lai and they certainly influenced the way I felt. I'd help them get supplies and I got to know one South Korean captain pretty well. He told me some of the terrible things the communists had done when they tried to take over South Korea. He said the communists were hated and how, once they were stopped, South Korea had been able to build a good, strong republic. I felt Korea was analogous to Vietnam—the North had come to the South and tried to force the communist way of life.

But I began to see some mistakes we made, though we were there to help, and certainly, unlike the communists, we were not imperialistic. Still, I think, we tried to force-feed democracy to the South Vietnamese.

Most of the country is quite primitive. The people exist from day to day, trying to get enough food, enough of the necessities of life to stay alive. You'd find a family of six living in an eight-by-eight foot hut that had only a single table in the middle with a candle on it. And then you had the small minority, the upperclass. They have most of the country's money and drive around in big cars.

We stepped in and tried to bring Americanization to all the people, with all the wonders of soft drinks, television, and things such as that. I don't know. They were under a kind of dictatorship with Diem. We tried to install free elections and Thieu made a farce of those.

But on the other hand, the communists were there to take over. Inflicting the Marxist philosophy on countries such as Vietnam isn't the answer either. Still, if you tell a peasant living in squalor that you know a way where everybody will become equal, he'll jump at it—without knowing he'll lose his freedom. I'm not sure what the answer is and I suppose this has been debated for centuries. I just know in my mind and heart that there is no freedom under communism.

I also became extremely disenchanted with the way the war was being run. With some of our limited war policies it was like sending a quarterback into a game with one arm tied behind his back. I know, with hindsight, it is easier to say that we should have escalated our war effort and gone all out to win. The tragedy, though, was in sending our troops over there to fight and then limiting what they could do. If you ask a man to put his life on the line, you should let him have full maneuverability and give him all available weapons to defend himself.

If you sat back in Washington and pushed buttons maybe you forgot you were dealing with men's lives. Each man's life is important. We dragged out the war with belated escalation policies and this just cost more American and Vietnamese lives. When we finally did go after the strategic sites, railroads and fuel dumps, it didn't seem to create any more interest as far as Red China was concerned. But we waited, and while we did, the North Viet

Vietnamese figured out every angle, started using Cambodia, better arming themselves.

I blame the Defense Department when it was under Secretary Robert McNamara for many of the problems. McNamara apparently had a tremedous influence on President Johnson. I was in Washington a few years ago for a banquet and talked to Admiral Moore. Admiral Moore told me he thought President Johnson had the gut feeling what we should do but listened to advisors too much.

The Department of Defense was behind one of the more ridiculous things I saw during the war. A decision was made to build a wall, like the Berlin Wall. It would stretch across the DMZ (demilitarized zone) and prevent troops and supplies from coming to South Vietnam from the North. They actually sent Seabees and the engineering corps to start construction. Can you imagine? All the North Vietnamese had to do was just come along the Cambodian border or the Ho Chi Minh Trail and enter South Vietnam. They wouldn't have had to cross over the wall. This finally occurred to somebody and the wall was never finished.

I can understand why people began to protest in the United States. We weren't making any progress, and we were losing a lot of lives. The negative thing about the protests was that this added fuel to the enemy. My own personal philosophy about our policy changed because I kept seeing men die and no progress being made. Some who protested, I'm sure, were thoughtful but then you had other idiots, who were so naive about the entire situation it was unbelievable.

I just hope with all my heart that lives lost in Vietnam weren't lost in vain. There is certainly hope for South Vietnam—hope that the country will get back on its feet and become a free, productive society if only the people can have honest leadership.

This is the dark side of the war. There just aren't many bright sides. Despite everything though, I didn't forget football completely the year I was in Vietnam and had taken some equipment with me to Da Nang. I worked out there almost every day at a soccer field with Steve Roesinger, who had played football at the Naval Academy.

The Chu Lai area was chewed up and rough; I had a difficult time finding a spot big enough to work out on. Luckily, I had a friend who was the the public works officer and I got him to send out some tractors and level a spot. Some of my friends put up this sign with a picture of Snoopy on it and the name, Staubach Stadium.

But the ground was still rough and it just tore up the football. So I sent a letter to Gil Brandt, just after the Cowboys had lost the NFL title game to Green Bay in 1966.

Dear Gil,

I'm just a small part of the Dallas Cowboy organization but I want to congratulate the team on a great season. All the guys over here have been following the Cowboys.

By the way, if you get a chance I'd appreciate it if you'd send me another football. The rough terrain has worn mine out.

Regards,
Roger Staubach

Gil sent me another football. I worked out whenever I could and made a concentrated effort to stay in shape. I knew if I could stay in shape in Vietnam, I could certainly do so during my next two years on active duty back in the states. Different guys worked out with me. There wasn't much else to do in our spare time, except go to the movies. I ran sprints and threw passes to anybody who'd catch them.

I left Vietnam in August 1967 and reported to Pensacola. I counted the days as my time to leave drew near. I hadn't seen much of Jennifer. Marianne met me in Hawaii on a brief R&R period after my first six months in Vietnam. When I had to leave her it was as if the whole world had ended, knowing I had six more months away.

131

But when my year in Vietnam ended and I left for good, it was just ecstasy.

Probably the happiest feeling I've ever had was just knowing I was going home to Marianne and Jennifer.

11

The Road Back

We didn't win many games but we never lost a party.

—*Pensacola Goshawks motto*

I had known the shiny, glittering side of football at the Naval Academy. There was so much fanfare: the Heisman Trophy, all-America honors, and more banquet invitations than I could possibly accept. After I returned from Vietnam and settled in Florida at Pensacola Naval Air Station I found that fame is a fleeting thing and past accomplishments just yellow and die on some old sports page. For instance, I was invited to Anniston, Alabama, to speak at a quarterback club meeting. The guy who met me at the airport said they had a very big surprise for me when we got to the motel.

I was surprised all right. On the big marquee outside the Holiday Inn in block letters was, WELCOME TO ANNISTON, ROGER STEINBECK. Oh, well, I'll always be with the Anniston Quarterback Club, win or tie.

During this time I was very determined to get back in shape and make a place for myself in football. I had two more years in the service and then perhaps I would get my chance as a pro. I wanted to be ready. Pensacola, along with Quantico, had the only remaining service football teams and I knew I could get a taste of the game again.

My memories of Pensacola are good. It's a neat, trim, sprawling place near untouched beaches. Of course, anything would have looked good to me after that year in

Vietnam. I was with my family—Marianne and my daughter Jennifer—and my life was coming together again, taking a normal shape.

The main purpose of the Naval Air Station is to train pilots. It is often called, "The Annapolis of the Air." Me? I was in charge of shipping and receiving at the base. Most of those who worked under me were civilians and I was constantly barraged with complaints—a chair was either lost or broken, and someone always needed something in a hurry. I kept busy.

And after work there was football. Our team consisted mostly of pilots. Many of them would still be flying when we'd work out about 4:30 in the afternoon but we did the best we could with whoever was there. Pilots had to be average-sized guys so we had no big linesmen, which was not especially conducive to keeping the quarterback off the seat of his pants. They called the team the Goshawks, which I understand is a bird of prey, almost extinct.

I reported for football about two weeks late and found out, for the first time, how much you could lose being away from the game for a couple of years. I could throw the ball and had fairly good movement but just didn't feel comfortable. It was difficult getting used to wearing the equipment again, to setting up to throw, and working against defenses. It was like . . . well, starting all over again. We had a tough schedule, playing small four-year colleges such as Middle Tennessee State, McNeese, Southwest, Northeast Louisiana, and Louisiana Tech but we hung in there.

Roger came in late. We already had three good quarterbacks, including Bill Zloch, who had quarterbacked Notre Dame between John Huarte and Terry Hanratty. I had played at Gettysburg when Jim Ward was the quarterback so I had been around a top-flight passer before. I knew right away Roger had it as a passer, though he would be brilliant at times and not so good at others. He played a lot with a bad ankle, but wouldn't come out of the lineup.

134

We hit it off right away. We'd go out and have a beer and talk. One thing I noticed about him is that he didn't want to be the center of attention. He'd avoid that.

—*Tom McCracken*
wide receiver
Pensacola Goshawks

Toward the end of that first season my ankle was bothering me but I could feel it all coming back. My legs weren't as heavy and my recognition was improving. The equipment was feeling natural again, like a second skin. We had a 5–4 record, I believe, but ended the season on a high note, beating the Quantico Marines which Pensacola had never done before.

Service football isn't exactly do or die for ol' alma mater. We were flown to games in an old C-47. We'd hit town, get a boxlunch, stay at a motel for a couple of hours, go play and then take off again in that C-47. We were like a band playing one night stands.

One game two of our players didn't show for pregame warmup. The one was a starting halfback and the other a receiver. They were pretty flashy guys. Hollywood types. It seems they'd met two girls at the motel and just decided to stay with them. They finally showed up about halftime.

Things like that were always happening and we lost a lot of players by transfer. We won our first seven games my second year, in 1968, and then lost the final two when about fourteen players were transferred. Things got to the point near the end of the season that you'd have to introduce yourself in the huddle.

I got my old scrambling instincts back fast. I had to. Word got around that I was the guy who had won the Heisman Trophy and been all-America: I was like a target in a shooting gallery. I'd get all these cat-calls during a game and some of the guys on the small college teams would really get after me. So I was on the run a lot. We had some really fine players, like Tom McCracken and Steve Dundas, the ends, but there wasn't time to pick up blitzes and backs missed blocking assignments so I was on the move a lot.

I remember one game we beat Youngstown something like 56–32. Service football records were skimpy in those days but Roger must have passed for over 400 yards. We had no running game and I believe we ended up with minus yards rushing, which gives you some idea.

One time we were playing Northeast Louisiana and they had us down about eight or nine late in the game. They were kicking off but our kickoff return man was hurt. I was looking around for Roger so we could talk about what we would do when we got on the field. I couldn't find him anywhere. So just before the kickoff I looked out on the field and there he was ... back there to return the kickoff. Fortunately, they kicked short and he didn't have to return it. But you know how he thinks ... He was going to run that kickoff back and then pass us to a touchdown and win the game someway, if he had to do it by himself.

—*Tom McCracken*

We had our own version of a bowl game after that first season in Pensacola and, appropriately I suppose, it was about the weirdest game I've ever played in. We went to Mexico City for five days to play the Mexican All-Stars. I really enjoyed the people in Mexico City and I have since learned they are great Cowboy fans. Now, they haven't played much football in Mexico and it was about like playing a junior college team. For instance, they had no conception of pass defense. We could score at will. Had it been soccer, I'm sure the tables would have been turned.

They did have us a little scared before the game started, though. We had heard all these stories about Latin fans—how they'd come out of the stands and attack soccer players and that some had even been killed. If they needed military protection to keep the fans off the players, you can imagine how we felt. The game was played on a soccer field and it was difficult to tell where out of bounds was, and those fans were jumping up and down and yelling so much we didn't know what to do.

I remember óne of my teammates came up with a good suggestion, "Let's just let them win and get the hell outa here."

The Mexican All-Stars showed up and had the same color jerseys we did. It was very confusing. They also must have had eight officials for the game and each one had probably memorized a couple of rules each. (I think they got one official out of a tortilla factory.) The first three times we got the ball we went right down and scored. But each time this one official dropped his flag and said we had lined up offsides. Bill Zloch got tired of this, so one time when that official dropped the flag Zloch sneaked over and stole it. He hid it in his pants. Later when we were looking at the films, you could see the lonely official over to the side looking for his flag, like somebody searching for Easter eggs.

We were way ahead and Bob Moss, our coach who was from West Virginia, told us he didn't want any more scoring. But ol' Zloch said he hadn't played quaterback in a long time so he wanted in there for a while. Zloch immediately started throwing bombs. I moved over to end, which he had been playing. I dropped one bomb and then caught another for a 60-yard touchdown. Suddenly the fans started coming out of the stands and crowding around the scrimmage line. They would just stroll up to the huddle to see what you were doing or want to shake hands. Nothing happened to us though, and we later became good friends with some of the Mexican players.

We won 35–18, something like that. Later, looking at the films we noticed we only had ten men on the field for extra points. We found out later the eleventh man had gotten drunk and just didn't show. We laughed about it and then got to wondering why they didn't block all our extra points. Then we discovered why. The Mexican team only had nine men on the field.

Before my second season at Pensacola I took a two-week leave and went to the Dallas Cowboy training camp in Thousand Oaks, California. I went through the rookie sessions just before the veterans reported. I ran, lifted weights, and did everything I knew to make a good impression.

I've never seen anybody work harder. He'd get me to go out with him almost every day. I'd run so many patterns that I'd finally just fall exhausted on the ground. I'd literally be on the ground and ol' Roger would just keep on throwing the ball at me.

—*Tom McCracken*

Marianne thought I was crazy. I probably was and still am. We'd be watching television and I'd jump out of my chair and rush outside to run some more. I became fanatical.

I had submitted my resignation and my four-year obligation would be up the following July. Stories were going around that nobody would ever be able to lose four years in the service and still make it in professional football. This kept burning inside of me. I kept telling myself, you've got to do it, you've got to do it. I just had to. Naturally, I was worried about those two weeks I'd spend with the Cowboys. If I didn't do well it could have a bad psychological effect on me, something that might stay with me my final year at Pensacola. I might get to thinking that I couldn't do it.

All in all things went pretty well. About ninety percent of the guys at camp were rookies, though there was a smattering of veterans who reported early for one reason or another.

Only July 18, 1968, the Dallas Cowboy rookies, with a few veterans such as center Malcolm Walker, had a scrimmage game with the Los Angeles Ram rookies, plus veteran linemen Diron Talbert and Dave Cahill. Roger Staubach completed ten of fourteen

138

passes for 161 yards and two touchdowns, which came on 51- and 48-yard bombs. Two of his passes were dropped and he also scrambled four times for twenty-eight yards.

"This guy can play in our league. He throws well, long and is an exceptional runner. He reminds me of Fran Tarkenton, except he has a stronger arm," said LA coach George Allen.

"There's no doubt he can be a pro," Tom Landry declared.

"Listen, we've got to do something about Staubach," said Don Meredith, Dallas' No. 1 quarterback. "He's gonna have to learn what an NFL quarterback is like. He needs to grow his hair long, start smoking, drinking, and things like that to keep up the image."

On my way back from Vietnam I had stopped over at Thousand Oaks for a couple of days in 1967. I was out there throwing one day and coach Landry told me some things to work on. When I came to the two-week rookie camp he saw that I had worked on what he had suggested. My setup was better and I think he saw I had the potential. I believe coach Landry and the other coaches were surprised I ran as well as I did, even though it was against the Ram rookies. They also saw I had a strong arm. They knew that, physically, I was able to play again. All I had to do was learn.

Before I went back to Pensacola coach Landry gave me a playbook. I don't think he had planned to give it to me but some of his assistants talked him into it. During my second year at Pensacola I was also the backfield coach. Therefore, I was able to put some of the Cowboy offense into our attack. I made sure the Cowboy terminology and numbering system—odd to your right, even to the left— was used by the Goshawks and we also used some of the Dallas formations. I also continued to work like a maniac after our season ended.

Roger would skip lunch and run sprints. He was always working. The closer the time came for him to get out and join the Cowboys, the harder he worked. He always thought he could make the transition to professional football. Some of the guys at Pensacola didn't, but maybe they didn't know Roger well enough. There was never a time we talked or watched a Cowboy game on television that Roger didn't think he could become the Dallas quarterback.

———*Tom McCracken*

I wanted to think that mother and dad would eventually be coming to see some of my games with the Cowboys, like they used to when I was at the Naval Academy. But that Christmas I realized there was little chance dad would make it.

When we got back to Cincinnati on leave we found him in bad shape and getting progressively worse. He was still at home but couldn't do anything for himself. This made it harder than ever on mother. He insisted on driving his car although he was in no condition to, and I knew that as long as he was home he was going to drive that car. He could have hurt himself and somebody else too. I knew he needed to be in the hospital.

I talked to his doctor about it but he was slow to respond. I got mad because this was such a difficult—and dangerous—situation. So I went over this doctor's head and talked to his superior, saying, "Hey, you'd better get him into a hospital before I go back to Pensacola or there is going to be a lot of trouble."

When this doctor saw dad's condition he got him to the hospital immediately. Dad's heart was strong but his kidneys grew weaker all the time and hardening of the arteries was setting in. Later they moved him to a nearby nursing home and for months mother went to see him almost every night.

Dad's situation was on my mind a lot while at Pensacola, but I knew it was being handled in the best way possible. I also knew I had a lot to be thankful for in my life. I was about to have the opportunity in pro football I had wanted so long, and I had had some great experiences during my navy career.

I liked the navy. Marianne and I enjoyed the people we met and made a lot of close friends. By the fourth year we had become accustomed to this way of life. I had become a lieutenant, making about $700 a month with all of medical and dental expenses taken care of. But, nevertheless, I *did* get a raise when I joined the Cowboys.

When I left the service Jennifer was three; our second daughter, Michelle, was one; and our third, Stephanie, had just been born. I'm sure that as they grew older, navy life would have been tougher for them, having to move them from one school to another. But there's an excellent chance I would have stayed in had it not been for football. Football was just so deeply embedded in me that it was impossible to get rid of the feeling that I had to play again. It was like a disease. I wanted, and planned, to prove I could play again.

People will continue to speculate and say how much better off I'd be in pro football if I hadn't lost those four years fulfilling my obligation to the navy. But if I had it all to do over again, I'd do the same thing. I say this even considering the bidding war I missed between the NFL and AFL plus all the experience I could have gained.

The Naval Academy is a tremendous school. That four-year obligation after graduation is used by many schools to recuit against the Naval Academy. But many college coaches are recruiting only to have better teams. That's what they want good players for and they miss a big point, the education and preparation for the future. It should be instilled in a young man that college is the climax of his educational process, the catapult which will shoot him into life. The academics and experiences he has in college are the platform for his entire life.

The Naval Academy points you in the right direction. No matter whether you're going to stay in the navy or get out and go in some other directions, it's still a sound basis. Navy life creates a positive effect on your life. You mature greatly in the process and learn responsiblity. The business world is looking for young men with their feet on the ground who have fulfilled their service obligation. Sure, you might be twenty-six when you get out but by that time you really have a direction in life. The pay isn't that bad either, and it's getting better.

Football was still my first love and the closer I came to picking up my career again, the more excited I got. A few weeks before my discharge I was able to take another leave and attend Tom Landry's ten-day quarterback school in Dallas. We studied and worked on techniques—it was a big help. It had become clear that Jerry Rhome would be traded, but I was able to meet a couple of guys named Don Meredith and Craig Morton.

Both are extremely nice guys. One of the first things I noticed was how close they were. I believe you need to be friendly and compatible on the field, but I'm not sure its the best thing to do when you run around together and socialize off the field. You can become lethargic about competing for the same job. I think you can lose some of your competitive edge. Craig and Don were very close and still are. I think it might have been a factor as far as their competing against each other. But it *was* beginning to get to Craig a little during the quarterback school and he told me one day, "This will probably be my last year with the Cowboys if they don't give me a chance to start. I've waited for four years to play and they've never really given me a chance to start. Even with Don here, it's time I get the chance or just forget it in Dallas."

So the competitive edge was getting to him, though I doubt it was as strong as it might have been had they not been so close.

Observations of Roger Staubach during quarterback school:

Roger could make the transition to playing quicker than an ordinary rookie. After he's exposed to the NFL this coming season he could be able to play and do something very positive on the field—if he's what we expect him to be.

—*Tom Landry*

142

Something has to be done, Roger. You can't go around with that crewcut. At least, grow long sideburns or muttonchops. Well, then again, I guess that would look funny with a crewcut.

—*Curt Mosher*
Cowboy publicity director

I got a big break the day I was discharged. I left the navy on July 5, 1969 and that was the same day Meredith announced his retirement. He felt he didn't have enough desire to play again. I was getting calls from sportswriters, so I felt I might have a shot at it. Although I was still a little afraid Landry would trade me for a back-up quarterback with experience. I held my breath. I believe those two weeks in rookie camp saved me. I think coach Landry saw enough and gained enough confidence in me to count on me as one of his quarterbacks. I had my chance, which is all I ever wanted. I did a lot of thinking on that flight to Thousand Oaks. I had to prove to everybody that I could become a fulltime player with the Cowboys. I just had to.

12

No. 2—And Trying Hard

I coached in Canada for a while after I left New Mexico Military Institue. Then I joined Tom Fears as an assistant coach when the NFL put a franchise in New Orleans in 1967. I told Tom he ought to give Dallas a call and offer a No. 1 draft choice for Roger Staubach. I told him if the Cowboys wouldn't take that to offer them two No. 1 choices and, if that wasn't enough, offer them three No. 1's.

I knew Roger could play. No matter if he did miss those four years I knew he was such a great athlete and competitor that he could play.

—*Bob Shaw*
Staubach's junior college coach, 1960

Staubach couldn't win the job this year. Let me put it this way: If late in the season Staubach is our number one quarterback, it'll mean this was a lost season. He just has no experience. It will just take him a while to know our system, which is very difficult, and be able to read and key defenses.

Now I'm not saying he isn't an outstanding player. He is. He has a good arm, great determination and the guy's a fine runner. Fran Tarkenton has the ability to sense trouble out of the corner of his eye but Roger is a better runner. And, of course, he has a stronger arm.

—*Tom Landry*
1969

Marianne, professional football isn't as tough as I thought. I moved up to second string quarterback and I haven't done a thing.

—*Roger Staubach*
July 1969

I'm afraid I didn't exactly distinguish myself that first year with the Dallas Cowboys, though I can claim one unofficial record. In one preseason game I scrambled for thirty-one seconds on a single play, breaking Fran Tarkenton's Cotton Bowl record of twenty-three seconds. Tom Landry wasn't too impressed.

I worried about a lot of things when I reported to my first full training camp in July of 1969. I had an unbelievably positive attitude but I knew people were saying I couldn't make it back after four years. Also, I couldn't help but think that Coach Landry might just decide he needed to trade for a back-up quarterback with experience, since Don Meredith had retired and Craig Morton became the starter. Maybe they'd just put me on the taxi squad. When you're a twenty-seven-year-old rookie you can't spend a year being taxied. I had to make every year count for something. And the time to prove myself began in earnest that summer in Thousand Oaks, California.

I settled my bonus situation, choosing to receive $100,000 over a ten-year period in payments of $10,000 each, instead of taking a lump sum of $55,000–$60,000. The ten-year deal was better for tax purposes. Then I turned my complete attention to camp.

Thousand Oaks is a relatively quiet, peaceful city, though things pick up somewhat, I'm told, when the neon lights come on. It's about forty miles down the Ventura Freeway from Los Angeles in what they call the Conejo Valley. The first summer I was there Thousand Oaks must have had about 40,000 people. though I'm sure it has doubled by now. Temperatures stay around 75 to 85 degrees, though occasionally it gets cool enough for a sweater at night. Club officials and writers who follow the Cowboys especially appreciate the place because it's only a forty-minute drive to the ocean and Malibu and Zuma beaches.

We live and train at California Lutheran College, which is situated just at the foot of a mountain. We have two good practice fields and excellent facilities. Officials, coaches, writers, and visitors live in one two-story dorm, which is connected to the players' dorm by a long hallway and foyer. I hate to be away from my family but I like training in Thousand Oaks.

Did I honestly think I could get the starting assignment that year? I don't know. To be truthful, probably way down deep I *did* think I'd be No. 1 quarterback when I went to that first camp. I always think I'm going to be No. 1 somehow, some way. You have to have a positive attitude to succeed, though some people think mine is too positive. It hit me like a thunderbolt when I really knew I wouldn't be No. 1. When just the rookies were in camp, we used basic formations, but then the veterans came and the coaches threw the entire playbook at us. There were some twenty to twenty-five formations, not to mention all the plays off each different set. Quarterbacks were also expected to call the blocking at the point of attack. I just couldn't grasp it all. I knew Craig Morton was the man.

Craig was in his fifth year and had all the confidence in the world when he called plays. He ran the first team like a precision machine. The guys on my second team were also veterans and they were really watching me. I was the No. 2 quarterback and the players and coaches expected me to call the play and get out of the huddle. I'd get mixed up. The coaches would get mad. Ermal Allen, an extremely intelligent man, was the backfield coach then and Jim Myers coached the line. They'd both jump me. "Come on Staubach, get your head up!" Ermal would yell. I wasn't used to taking criticism and it made me press even harder, which wasn't good.

There was no doubt that Craig was the master in the huddle. I still wanted to beat him in something. Anything. So we ran the 40–yard dash and I beat him, just barely, and that made me feel a little better. But mentally there was no way I could compete.

PHOTO: Dick Darcy, *The Washington Post*

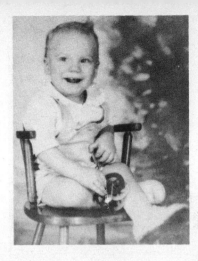

Even at ten months Roger looked like he was in the mood to scramble.

Naval Academy just ahead and New Mexico Military Institute behind, Roger enjoyed reunion with Marianne during visit home in June of 1961.

Roger discovered new pressures, and several chins, during rigorous Plebe year.

An exciting start to varsity career: President John F. Kennedy visited Middies during fall practice in 1962. Coach Wayne Hardin accompanied him as he met the players.

Roger, in front of lucky old Tecumseh, hoped for a great day in his first Army game. He got his wish.

Ready for his Heisman Trophy season in 1963, Roger had two fine offensive teammates and two great friends in Pat Donnelly and Skip Orr.

PHOTO: J. E. Bailey

Roger flashed style all his own in big game against Michigan, which furnished frustrated witnesses to birth of the Hail Mary Pass. Chased twenty yards behind his line of scrimmage, and seemingly trapped, he saw Pat Donnelly upfield and completed pass for one-yard gain.

Happy and riding high in November '63, Roger and Pat Donnelly are congratulated by their superintendent, Admiral Charles Kirkpatrick, after victory over Notre Dame.

PHOTO: Jack Beers, *Dallas Morning News*

Pursued by top-ranked Texas and watched by millions, Roger set Cotton Bowl Classic record for pass completions, but Middies couldn't muster much to go with it in disappointing battle for national supremacy.

Middie career ended in June of '65 when Roger received the school's most coveted athletic awards, Thompson Trophy and Naval Academy Athletic Association Sword.

PHOTO: Tom C. Dillard, *Dallas Morning News*

During the game between Navy and Texas Roger sees too much of relentless Longhorn defenders to suit him—or any Navy rooter for that matter.

Once more, with feeling. Marianne helped Roger hold up his Navy jersey after it was retired.

Proud moment for Staubach family: Roger, Dad, and Mother share the thrill of graduation day.

Marianne and Roger step beneath crossed swords and into life together after their marriage in September of 1965.

Playing for Dallas someday was a distant dream during the year in Vietnam, but Roger stayed in condition with daily workouts on makeshift field named for its star.

Football at Pensacola in 1967–68 was a patchwork affair, as were Roger's pants.

At his first Cowboy quarterback school in May of 1969, Roger seemed intent, Craig Morton confident, and Don Meredith disinterested. Meredith retired two months later.

PHOTO: Richard Pruitt, *Dallas Morning News*

Roger earned starting job for '71 opener at Buffalo but forfeited it due to injury, so he settled for seeing Niagara Falls with Mel Renfro, Rayfield Wright, Jethro Pugh and Dave Manders.

This became a familiar trio through the years: Cowboy coach Tom Landry, Craig Morton, and Roger Staubach.

Happy moment in locker room after winning NFC title: Roger receives congratulations from former President Lyndon B. Johnson.

PHOTO: Gary Barnett, *Dallas Morning News*

The Cowboys moved past Miami with impressive skill and strength in Super Bowl VI. Roger was voted Most Valuable Player.

Aglow with Super Bowl success, Roger strolled through New Orleans' French Quarter with Mom and Marianne on day after game.

PHOTO: Richard Pruitt

Straining to rebuild shoulder and regain strength in passing arm, Roger worked long and hard to play again in final weeks of '72.

PHOTO: Baylor University Medical Center

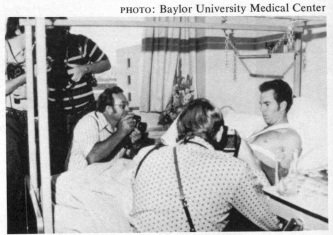

Feeling low after shoulder surgery in August of 1972, Roger found everyone wanting one more picture. Then for a long time no one wanted any at all. . . .

No. 1 again in '73, Roger directed a diversified attack featuring 1,000-yard rusher Calvin Hill.

A winning combination: Bob Hayes and Roger Staubach.

Through the years the Heisman Trophy has proved to be a popular attraction in the Staubach household. Michelle shows her daddy why.

PHOTO: Russ Russell

PHOTO: Jim Work

Mile-high Denver proved perfect place for Roger and Cowboys to get up for their rush into 1973 playoffs.

PHOTO: Jim Work

Back in his own backyard, Roger finds his happiness lies with Michelle, Marianne, Stephanie, Jennifer, and, of course, Bridget, their Lhasa Apso.

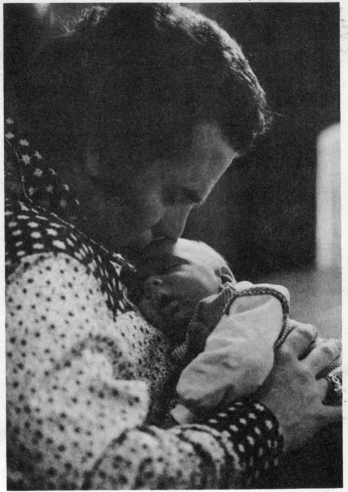

Roger enjoys a special moment with the new quarterback in the house, Jeffrey Roger Staubach.

Things got worse before they got better. They scheduled a big rookie game in Oakland. The Raiders used a number of veterans and built up the game to the public and it drew about 30,000 fans. I had some navy friends in the area who came to see the return of Roger Staubach. Banners were even up. "Go Staubach!" I ran well in the game but I hit only one of thirteen passes and really got clobbered. So did we all, 33-0.

We moved the ball well but things kept happening and we couldn't score. I was off on some passes and my roommate, Richmond Flowers, dropped some. But I'll never forget getting blindsided. Calvin Hill missed a blitz and this guy really hit me, right in the back. I went down as if I'd been shot. The blow cracked some bones in my back and badly bruised a kidney. I was really hurting mentally and physically when we got back to Thousand Oaks. Veterans were kidding us about getting beaten so badly and I went to bed thinking coach Landry would certainly get another quarterback now.

We had two workouts the following day and I could hardly move. But I didn't tell anybody I was hurt and just made myself go out. I knew I couldn't afford to miss a practice. Still, I couldn't straighten up and went around limping for two days. Finally, the trainers figured something was wrong and took me in for X-rays, which showed the cracked bones. They also found blood in my urine.

"I don't believe it," Dr. Marvin Knight, a team physician, told me. "There's no way you could practice like this."

"I couldn't afford to miss," I told him. He just shook his head. He didn't understand.

They wouldn't let me work out for three or four days. I just stood around watching my whole world cave in. I started working back in a little the next week before our first preseason game with Los Angeles in the Coliseum. Word was that coach Landry wasn't going to let me play but I kept insisting my back was fine. There was a big crowd in the Coliseum. This was my first real game as a pro and for the first time in my life I didn't play. It was as if I wasn't even really there, just watching things happen

147

and not being a part of it. I didn't know what to do, how to handle it. I kept grabbing the phone and calling Ray Renfro, an assistant coach, in the press box. "Hey, Ray, I'm all right. Tell coach Landry I'm all right. Tell him!"

"Okay, okay," Ray finally said. "I'll tell him."

It didn't do any good. Craig needed the playing time even if it was only the first exhibition game. Coach Landry was going to let him go all the way. He was oblivious to me. His opinion of me was that I would catch on a little faster than most, but it would still take a few years. That didn't matter to me, I wanted to play! I wanted to be a Dallas Cowboy quarterback. I was just stunned, though not too stunned to see that Craig Morton was an excellent quarterback.

Los Angeles won 24–17 and we went back to Thousand Oaks for our final week of training camp. My back was better. Something else happened to lift my spirits. I was in charge of the annual rookie show and came up with an innovation. California Lutheran was having a play nearby which featured this really good-looking girl. I went over there and talked her into being in the show. When showtime came, all these guys were out in the audience expecting to see nothing but a bunch of men dressed up weird and doing crazy things. Then, all of a sudden, here comes this great-looking female walking across the stage carrying envelopes announcing contest winners—ugliest coach, biggest nose, biggest loafer, etc. The guys went crazy, cheering and pounding on the chairs.

After that the veterans started talking to me. "Hey, nice rookie show," they'd say. I felt a part of the team. Things were looking up and I was more relaxed. I threw touchdown passes to Obert Logan and Lance Rentzel in a scrimmage and felt even better. Bob Lilly came over to me after the scrimmage and said, "Why don't you go out with the veterans tonight?"

We went to Los Robles, a plush restaurant and night club overlooking a golf course. I was the only rookie there. Willie Townes started giving me a rough time. "Hey, rook, what are you doing here?" he said. "Hey, guys, get this rook out of here!" Morton and Lilly invited

148

me out on the town with them and we stopped at one place and then ended up at Orlando's, a favorite spot for the players. Walt Garrison, Danny Reeves and Ralph Neely were there, too. I got a little nervous around midnight. Rookie curfew was 12:30 and I couldn't afford to miss it.

"Don't worry," Neely told me. "You're out with the veterans tonight and on the veteran's curfew."

"Listen, I better get on back," I said.

"Don't worry," Walt Garrison told me. "Just relaxxxx."

"Listen you get into trouble and we'll all chip in and pay your fine," said Reeves.

I got back to my room late. There was a note from coach Landry. He leaves notes if you're not in for curfew and if you don't go to see him when you come in, you get counted absent the entire night. I left the player's wing of the dorm, went through the foyer into the coach's wing and down the hall for what seemed a mile to coach Landry's room. "Oh geeze," I kept saying to myself. "Oh geeze." I knocked. He finally opened the door; standing there all sleepy in his pajamas.

"Where have you been?"

"Uh, hi, coach. I've been out with the veterans."

"You're supposed to be on rookie curfew. That'll cost you $100."

"Uh, thank you, coach. Goodnight."

The veterans asked me the next day what happened. "Okay," I said. "Who's going to help me with my fine?" They told me not to sweat it. Reeves even went to talk to coach Landry. But the fine stood. Remember all those guys saying they were going to chip in? I haven't seen a penny yet. I paid the whole thing.

There were some other new faces in training camp besides rookies that year. Mike Ditka, the former all-pro tight end, and Joey Heatherton, for instance. Lance Rentzel had just married Joey and she would come to practices with her entourage. Every time she'd come around we'd just stand there like a bunch of kids, gawking at her.

One of the best friends I made was Calvin Hill. He was Dallas' No. 1 draft choice that year and some people thought it was odd to pick a player so high from an Ivy League school like Yale. Now, of course he has become one of the NFL's premier runners, and made national headlines before the '74 season when he signed a terrific contract to play in the new World Football League in '75. Calvin and I went to a lot of movies. That was about our only entertainment. I was the expert. I would see every movie in town a couple of times. When anybody was going to the movies, they'd call me. I'd tell them the time it started and what it was about.

Veterans never did harass me very much. Guess I was just too old. I only had to get up at a meal one time and sing, "Anchors Aweigh." (They never asked me again but I think that had something to do with my voice.) They were really getting on the other rookies, though, especially my roommate, Richmond Flowers. They'd make rookies bring ice to the veterans' rooms and always send them on errands. Richmond was very forward, an outspoken guy. A newspaperman asked him how it was going one day and Richmond really let it all out, telling him that veterans treated all the rookies alike—like dogs. The story was printed and when word got back to camp the veterans really came down on him.

Well, the night before we broke camp to play the 49ers in San Francisco before returning to Dallas, Richmond and I were asleep about 2:00 A.M. when suddenly our door flew open. It scared me to death. I thought it was the end of the world. I really did. I had just opened my eyes and got them in focus when I saw Cornell Green standing over Richmond with a trash can full of water. He dumped the whole thing on him. Richmond screamed and jumped out of bed, going after Cornell. But he slipped in the water and crashed against the door. I thought he had broken every bone in his body. That only started things. Somebody went downstairs and dumped water on Willie Townes. There were big plastic coolers full of lemonade in the dorm, and they started throwing these on people. We had a big fight in my room and some of the lemonade leaked through to the room below and we had to pay for it.

150

I guess things remained pretty serene in the coachs' wing, although a newspaperman poured a fifth of vodka in their cooler of lemonade one night. They sure must have felt loose the next day.

I got to play a quarter and threw my first professional pass against the 49ers. Ditka was open over the middle. I saw him and drew back and fired. The ball hit him right in the chest . . . on the first bounce. But at least I had offically begun my career.

Sideline conversations during training camp:
"Look at Staubach, he's still out there working," said the writer. "Man I'd hate to have him after my job."
"You'd begin to hear footsteps after a while," said trainer Don Cochren.
"Yeah," added the writer. "He'd be working while you were playing or sleeping."

I tell you how to block for Staubach. You throw your block and just lie there on the ground. He'll be back sooner or later.

—*Walt Garrison*
Cowboy fullback

When the team returned to Dallas after training camp I had no idea where I stood. I've always been the type of guy who thinks its better for an athlete if he has some idea how he stands. Coach Landry is thinking about what you're doing but he just never says anything. Until you understand that's the way he is, it makes you feel like a wall. You're just there, unnoticed. Maybe he had all sorts of ideas about me but he just didn't tell me anything. He never said a word, was never personal.

I did create something of a furor which got a vocal reaction out of him. A rookie isn't supposed to bring his family to Dallas until he's made the team, but I had been away from my wife and three kids all that time and just decided I was going to bring them to Dallas. It was different for me. I had four years in the navy, I was older, and had a family. So I just rented an apartment and moved them in. Coach Landry was upset but finally told the team, "Well, I didn't specifically tell Roger that rookies couldn't bring their families, like I normally do. So Roger has brought his to Dallas and I just want you to be aware of it. They're here and I'm not going to ask him to send them away."

The whole team knew about it then and I felt awful. I was afraid everybody was thinking I was trying to be a prima donna.

I also lost my dog, a collie named Cola, after Pensacola. They wouldn't let me keep the dog at our apartment but Walt Garrison's father-in-law, B. F. Phillips, said I could keep her at his ranch. One night somebody broke the lock on the pen where they were keeping her and stole the dog. B. F. felt terrible and put ads in the papers and looked everywhere but we never did find poor Cola.

"Got good news and bad news," Dennis Homan told me. "Good news is that they found your dog. Bad news—she's dead."

Garrison looked at me during the meal one day and said, "This sure tastes like dog meat to me."

Some jokers, those guys.

I got my first real chance in our fifth exhibition game with the New York Jets in the Cotton Bowl. The situation was looking bad for the offense. Bobby Hayes suffered a dislocated shoulder in pregame warm-ups and Craig injured a finger. We were trailing 9–3 in the first period and he was passing. He let the ball go and his hand came down on John Niland's helmet. It dislocated his right index finger. "Staubach," said Landry, "Go in."

Everything happened too fast for me to be scared. I didn't know how badly Craig was hurt or if he'd be coming back into the game but I just got in there and . . . well ran.

Roger Staubach guided Dallas to a 25–9 victory. When he first entered the game Staubach took the

Cowboys 76 yards in nine plays for a touchdown, which he scored.

His touchdown was described in the *Dallas Morning News:* "On first and ten at the Jets' seventeen— with the clock making a serious attempt to end the first half—Staubach faded, apparently could not find a receiver and went into his dance. He looked ... paused and raced out of the pocket as Landry, on the sidelines bit his tongue, lip and mouth. Roger faked past John Elliott and then Ralph Baker and, when challenged at the goal line, catapulted, upside down, into the end zone with four seconds left in the half. Dallas was ahead and never trailed again."

Staubach hit ten of sixteen for 160 yards and one touchdown. He also ran three times for twenty-one yards, scoring the Cowboys' other touchdown.

Craig wasn't ready the next week when we finished the preseason against Baltimore. That was coach Landry's most memorable game. His quarterback—me—ran for 118 yards (12 carries). But I also threw four interceptions and we lost 23–7. Baltimore knowing I had no experience, blitzed me all over the field. As during the first part of my career, I wasn't reading my keys. I'd drop back and just see flashes, people running around. I basically knew who I was going to throw to, and maybe I'd read the safety, but I didn't look at the linebackers and couldn't feel the blitz coming. The Colts trapped me six times.

I did run like a jackrabbit and lost fifteen pounds that game. That's when one of my runs lasted thirty-one seconds and approximately eighty yards, though I gained only fourteen yards forward. Poor coach Landry. Everybody was excited about my running. They didn't realize I was missing all those keys and that my passing was awful. Landry looked at it realistically. I can just see him thinking ... Oh, me, I lose Morton and I get this wild man running all over the field.

Staubach ran us into the ground out there. He's quicker than Tarkenton. Shoot! I hate him. I never ran so much in my life chasing anybody. I don't ever want to play against that cat again.

—*Bubba Smith*
Baltimore defensive end

Roger will be fine. He was just missing keys. But he learned something out there.

—*Tom Landry*

Coach Landry didn't criticize me at all before the team when we looked at films of the Baltimore game. "He'll learn," he kept saying. The players were laughing at some of the runs I made. At least they thought I was a good runner. Coach Landry failed to see the humor. He had other problems. Morton's finger was out of the brace but he still hadn't thrown the ball and the doctors made the decision to keep him out another week. Coach Landry was going into the regular season against St. Louis with a rookie quarterback.

I felt like the veterans respected me now. I know I really psyched myself up. I started to throw much better in practice. That week was the first time coach Landry started talking to me personally. He'd keep me late after practice and tell me some of the tendencies of the Cardinals, such as free safety Larry Wilson, and we'd work on certain patterns.

Coaches kept emphasizing that I must start reading defenses. They said Wilson was a great free safety, but that he had a tendency to go with the quarterback's eyes. And they felt since I was a rookie that he'd especially be doing this with me. So I practiced all week looking him off, glancing toward the sidelines and then coming back to the post route. The free safety was the only guy who could stop the post and everybody felt Wilson would bite for the turn-in route and be out of position.

This was a big game for the Cowboys, starting a new season after the disappointing loss to Cleveland in the 1968 playoffs. There were high expectations again and I kept thinking about what would happen if we got off to a bad start because of me. I knew I should never think anything negative but sometimes I'd catch myself doing this. I was also a little superstitious. My team had never won a game in the Cotton Bowl in which I quarterbacked all the way. At Navy we had lost to SMU and Texas and then there was the Baltimore loss. I had to put these things out of my mind.

Actually, the backfield had a completely new look. I was the quaterback: Garrison had taken over at fullback when Don Perkins retired; and Calvin Hill had moved in at halfback. Calvin had just been fantastic in preseason. They put him at halfback for the San Francisco preseason game and he gained over 100 yards.

But it *was* a new backfield and coach Landry talked all week about how the defense would have to be super. "You guys are really going to have to hold them," he said. "We've got a rookie quarterback." I didn't know what to think when he said that. But it was true. He also said he would call the plays. I had called them myself in the two preseason games in which I played but, as you know, I was to become accustomed to Landry calling the plays.

Coach Landry was very nervous. The team went to the motel where we usually stay before a home game. Landry likes to bring us together so he can keep us thinking football. Usually he says a few words to us, but this time he just stared at the wall. Me? I was getting a little cocky. By that time I was completely positive. I was standing next to him and I said, "Hey, coach." He didn't even look at me. "Hey, coach," I said again. "Do you realize just a year ago today I was the starting quarterback for the Pensacola Navy Goshawks against Middle Tennessee State in Murfreesboro, Tennessee? And just think, coach, now I'm starting in the Cotton Bowl for the Dallas Cowboys against the St. Louis Cardinals."

Coach Landry got this dirty look on his face and just walked away. He never said a word.

"It isn't the ideal situation going into the season with a rookie quarterback." Landry said a few days before the opener, "but I have a lot of confidence in Staubach. He's much different than somebody who has just come out of college. And I think he'll perform well Sunday.

"No, I don't feel he'll be running as much. But I would say the Cardinals had better be long-winded for a chase if it's a warm afternoon."

I remember that game as well as any I've ever played. Everybody was encouraging me before the kickoff.

"Don't worry," Chuck Howley told me. "Just go out and do the things you know how to do."

Well, Landry called the post to Rentzel about the middle of the second period. We had a second and five from our own twenty-five. As we broke the huddle I just kept thinking what I was supposed to do, what was supposed to happen, and wondering if Wilson would really take the fake. I knew Wilson was the guy I'd have to beat. As I dropped back I looked toward Dennis Homan, who was running a turn-in. I pumped once toward him and Wilson bit.

Rentzel broke free over the middle, coming from the opposite side. I turned and fired the ball as hard as I could. I thought I'd overthrown him. But he was there. He caught the ball about fifty yards downfield and took off for the end zone. The crowd and all our players were yelling, and so was I. I ran off the field and grabbed Lance. It had been a 75-yard touchdown play.

I was just like a kid. Everybody was patting me on the back and I knew coach Landry felt a little better, too. Our defense was fantastic, holding a passer like Charley Johnson and the Cardinals in check. The Cardinals also stopped us for a while and I got trapped a couple of times. But we had another chance at our own twenty just before the half. Homan faked a sideline and took off deep. I must have thrown the ball fifty or sixty yards in the air and he caught it in full stride. But Lonnie Sanders caught him from behind and we didn't score.

We led 7–3 in the third period and I was getting worried whether we'd score again. Calvin had been having a good day running. The Cardinals were trying to adjust and stop his wide sweeps, so Landry sent in a halfback pass. I handed off to Calvin, who started wide, stopped, and threw long to Rentzel. Lance had faked a block and then cut behind Wilson. It was a 53-yard touchdown pass and things were looking good again. The Cardinals were just about finished.

Late in the game we were on the St. Louis three. Les Shy ran the wrong way and I didn't have anybody to hand off to so I just tucked the ball and headed for the goal line. I faked a couple of guys and dove into the end zone. We won, 24–3. We all felt better. It was a good beginning. However, that beginning just about constituted my entire season.

Coach Landry didn't say much to me after the game. He just told me, "You'll do all right in this league. Don't worry about it." But Craig was really chomping at the bit. I knew he was coming back. I wasn't going to get a chance to play unless he was injured. But at least I'd gotten on some solid ground. I had done all right in a regular season game and I believed coach Landry at least knew he could depend on me.

Craig came back and got hot, hitting about 70 percent of his passes the next few games. Then he was hit by Claude Humphrey in our game with Atlanta and injured his right shoulder, which turned out to be a slight separation. We were getting ready for the Eagles the next week and Craig was hurting. He didn't throw all week. They told me in pregame warm-ups that I was probably going to play. But Craig was able to throw a little and started. Oddly enough, he had one of his best games, hitting thirteen of nineteen passes for 247 yards and five touchdowns. The Eagles had tried to use Leroy Keyes on Lance man-to-man and Rentzel just killed him, catching three of the five touchdown passes. After the game Tex Schramm and Clint Murchison told Craig he should have a sore shoulder every week.

Morton's shoulder was a factor the rest of the season. He would throw some in practice but he was never able to stay late and work on his timing. He showed a lot of courage and had a good year. I knew that his shoulder hurt but he'd get the adrenalin going and play. Looking back, I think they made a mistake by letting him come back so soon. Still, he had the great game against the Eagles and wanted to play so badly that they let him go. I think later the doctors also realized he should have rested longer. He had more problems with the shoulder but finished the season and had some good games near the end.

I was just there, mopping up. I don't think Craig was really worried about me taking his job. I accepted my situation. I was happy to be on the team, figuring I was in a pretty good position for a rookie quarterback.

The Cowboys finished with a regular season record of 11-2-1. What they were beginning to call the Cleveland syndrome got to us again when we played the Browns for the Eastern Conference title. Everything just came apart, much as it had in our two previous meetings with Cleveland. The Browns had beaten Dallas, 31-20 for the 1968 Eastern title and then beat us 42-10 during the regular season. There was also a feeling on the team that we just didn't play well in the rain. So, it rained.

We had a problem at right cornerback all season. Phil Clark had played there but he just got psyched out and so they used Otto Brown, a rookie. For the Cleveland game coach Landry tried to compensate. Mel Renfro was the free safety then, but when Paul Warfield was on the left side, Mel moved to cornerback and Otto to free safety. It got to be pretty confusing for them and Cleveland worked on that area.

We started out real well. Then a Cleveland punt hit Rayfield Wright on the leg while he was going back to block, and the Browns recovered. A lot of guys on the sidelines were psyched out about Cleveland anyway. I remember hearing somebody say, "Well, here we go again." Bill Nelsen had a good day quarterbacking the Browns and they won, 38-14. I came into the game late and did help us score a touchdown, throwing a TD pass to Rentzel. But it was unbelievable—we had lost to Cleveland again.

I think our kicker, Mike Clark, pretty well summed up

the afternoon. We tried an onside kick and Mike completely missed the ball. They started calling him "Onside" after that.

I have never seen anybody down so much in my life as coach Landry was after that game. We met in this room at Love Field the next day before our flight to Miami and the Playoff Bowl for the runnerup teams. He was ashen. He had always epitomized strength, even after losses. But not this time. He had so many hopes, so many expectations for this team that the loss really killed him.

Many people said they felt this loss probably hurt him more than those close, last-second NFL title losses to Green Bay in '66 and '67. He felt the 1969 team was a better team. And then to lose the same way to the Browns! He tried to tell us about his philosophy of life, how a person faced setbacks but became stronger from them. "We still have a good organization and a good team," he said, but his heart wasn't in what he was telling us.

The Playoff Bowl was a disaster. We hated to go. I don't think anybody really ever wanted to go to that Playoff Bowl and I'm glad it was discontinued. I played half the game and neither Craig nor I could get a touchdown. We got beat 31–0 by Los Angeles in a game that seemed to last a month.

I had been a part of the Cowboys' winning and now I was a part of the losing. The Cleveland game started great soul-searching in our organization, a microscopic look to try and find the missing link to an NFL championship. We were good, but not good enough. Why did we fall apart against Cleveland?

During the off-season coach Landry sent out questionnaires, asking our opinions on workout schedules, the coaches, and just about everything regarding the football team. The Cowboys would go through a period of change and reevaluation. I hoped my status would improve with this reevaluation.

13

Just One Race

On a shelf in Roger Staubach's office at home stands a large photograph of two small boys. They're probably two to three years old, their eyes are shining and their faces are pressed together. One is black, the other white.

I saw that picture one time when I visited the Scottish Rite Hospital and fell in love with it. Those kids are kissing each other and they couldn't care less what anyone thinks. Neither one has any idea about the color of his little friend's skin. He just knows he likes him.

That picture says so much. It particularly emphasizes that we must start with the children if we are to work sincerely to eliminate racial prejudice. In every walk of life the black, the Indian, the Jew, the Latin, the Oriental, and other minority groups suffer from prejudice in our country. And the people responsible for this had their racial attitude planted in their minds when they were much, much younger. This is where the situation must change, with the young people growing up.

Our little girls may hear an ethnic slur at school but they will come home and tell Marianne and me about it. We set them straight real quick. All of us are the same, we tell them. We're human beings. They have black dolls, and this helps make them aware there is no difference in people because of their skin color.

Athletics is one of the few areas where blacks have been given an opportunity and even that has not been equal. They have learned that people accept them as long as they are fine athletes. They are performing and people

160

want to know them and treat them as friends. But they find they still are not completely accepted as human beings.

When Willie Townes was playing for the Cowboys he was leaving a restaurant one day when some guy yelled, "Hey, Willie!" just like he and Willie were old buddies. He wanted Willie to come over to his table and meet his wife and son. The little boy was about the age of those kids in the picture and the man asked Willie to autograph a napkin for him. While Willie was signing it the little boy looked up at him from his high chair and started chanting "Eeny, meeny, miney, moe . . . catch a nigger by its toe!"

Willie looked at the guy and threw the napkin down. "Thanks," he said in a real sarcastic voice and walked out. He knew he was still the victim of the double standard.

When I was a rookie in training camp I lived in the room next to Wayman Docks, a black who grew up in a big family in Chicago. He was very intelligent, a deep thinker, and we talked a lot. He told me how he had seen his father persecuted for years and how so many in his family had suffered through life, had never been given an opportunity. This had churned inside him all of his life and he was very militant. He said, "When the revolution takes place, Roger, even though I like you, I will probably have to shoot you. You're white." That's tragic and it's sick but it shows you how we have made some blacks' thinking degenerate to the point of militancy.

I believe the militants who resort to violence are just as wrong and misguided as the bigots. The way to react to discrimination, I feel, is through the law. That's what Mel Renfro did when he sued a Dallas realtor under the Fair Housing Act. That happened in the fall of '69, my first season in Dallas, and I'm sure everyone on the team was behind Mel.

He is a relatively quiet guy who had earned tremendous respect and it disturbed everyone that Mel and his family had been treated so shabbily. They had looked at some new duplexes not far from our practice field and the club offices in North Dallas and were told they could lease one for a year if they paid down $650 to cover the first and last month's rent. They thought about it a couple of days and decided they wanted to live there instead of in a predominantly black area of Oak Cliff, where a lot of the black players lived. Oak Cliff, however, is a forty-five minute drive from the practice field. Mel's wife returned with the money but the realtor said there were no duplexes for rent, just for sale. Their suit charged the realtor with falsely stating the duplexes were for sale only. It was an obvious case of discrimination and the court ruled in Mel's favor. I was proud that he won but it was a shame he had to take those measures. The housing situation has improved some since but not nearly enough. I love Dallas, but I believe this is one area where it still must make tremendous strides.

For years the Cowboys' black players felt they were welcome to live in only certain areas of the city, such as Oak Cliff. Now they are spreading out some. Mark Washington bought a home in North Dallas and Calvin Hill and some others have taken apartments on that side of town, which is much more convenient. But a lot of other players, like Bob Hayes, Cornell Green, Jethro Pugh, and Rayfield Wright, have kept their homes on the other side of Dallas in the established black areas. I guess that seems a comfortable environment, as far as people feeling at ease with people, but this situation makes it more difficult to get together and enjoy camaraderie as a team. And it sure takes a lot of time if you go to visit someone. Rayfield and Andrea came to our house for dinner one night and we had a great time. But it took them an hour to get there and an hour to get home.

There is an underlying attitude that the blacks go one way and the whites go another but on our team I haven't noticed this creating any real problem on the field. Of course, Calvin spoke out about how the blacks don't receive the same commercial opportunities and fringe benefits—endorsements, appearances, courtesy cars—based on their performances as the white players do. It's a shame that they don't receive an equal shot. When Calvin became the first Cowboy to rush for more than a thousand yards he expected to be approached with some new opportunities in the off-season. Nothing happened.

Whites often feel so secure in their own surroundings that they never consider what has happened for generations before us. In training camp one night it was about eleven when I heard some music across the hall and went over. A few guys were sitting around in Mel's and Herb Adderley's room and they said, "Hey, come on in and have a beer." Well, at 2:30 in the morning we were still sitting there talking. They told about their ancestors who had been in the Civil War and what they had experienced and how it had continued from one generation to the next. I realized their family reunions never had been like mine, where you spend most of your time talking over happy memories. At theirs they talk about some of the most atrocious examples of prejudice that anyone could hear. All of this had been passed on to them and it bothered them, yet they still had open minds. It amazed me. I looked at it through their eyes and felt a lot of compassion.

It's tragic that the blacks and other minorities have fought in wars for a country which has not fulfilled the promises that the country stands for. It is getting better now and hopefully some day it will be a lot better. President Johnson did a lot to help the problems with the Civil Rights and the Voting Rights acts, but really those areas were covered when the Constitution was written. Read it, and you notice it guarantees equality for all.

In sports the blacks have had a better opportunity than in some other areas but it is still not completely what it should be. I'm sure there still are coaches who count the number of blacks on their team, whether it is football, basketball, or baseball. I definitely don't believe the Cowboys are that way. I know that Tom Landry doesn't care who is on the field, just as long as they are his best players. Whether he has an all black or an all white team, he is going to try to win football games. Also, he takes a very, very strong Christian stand. I would be shocked beyond belief if he ever expressed any prejudiced feeling against another person. That would go against his own philosophy of life.

I learned years ago that the Navy had prejudice just like everyone else. When I was a Plebe at the Naval Academy there was one black on our team, Daryl Hill, and the papers mentioned he could become the first black ever to play on the Navy varsity. But he stayed only one year and then transferred to Maryland. He left for various reasons but I think he was overly harassed by some upperclassmen. I think Daryl also had problems at the academy which weren't related to being black but it had to be extra tough when he had some prejudiced upperclassmen believing they had this Plebe as their own slave.

I was living in such a haze then that I never talked to Daryl about his situation. I just took things for granted. I honestly had no awareness of prejudice. In my early years at home it was instilled in me by my mother that there is no place for prejudice in a Christian life. But later I went through a period when I listened to a lot of propaganda about how blacks had everything they needed in their own schools but just wanted in white schools. Of course, that was a bunch of baloney but for a while I went for it. Then, thankfully, I came out of the haze and realized that what I learned as a child was right.

Dad would take business trips through the south and when he came home he told about black people being forced to sit in the back of the bus and use separate drinking fountains from the whites. Mother flew into a rage when she heard that. She couldn't understand people being prejudiced against other people, especially if they believed in God and Christ. She thought as I believe now, that if Christ ever came to Dallas he would go to West Dallas or South Dallas and spend time with the Mexican-Americans and the blacks, the people who haven't been given equal opportunity.

I went to a high school with an integrated student body. In fact, Purcell was located in a black area and I got to know a lot of black people in the neighborhood. I certainly didn't look down on them and they certainly didn't look down on me. There were problems in Cincinnati, though, just like anywhere else as far as whites calling blacks niggers and blacks calling us poor white trash. Just like there was anti-Semitism. I could see prejudice around me but I said, "Well, I'm not going to be like that."

I tried to understand why people were prejudiced. I really couldn't figure out a good reason for it other than a part of our brain cells are diseased as to how we feel about others. Again, this goes back to what you learned when you were growing up.

When I was a senior at the Naval Academy we did have our first black on the varsity. Calvin Huey was just the kind of guy you liked. He had a great personality, worked hard in football and was an intelligent guy. He was from Pescagoula, Mississippi, and he had some terrible stories about not being allowed in certain stores, restaurants, and clubs. Imagine the stigma you feel if you were thrown out of a place because of the color of your skin. But Calvin believed people were propagandized and brainwashed and they wouldn't change overnight. You must change them by slow process and example. Calvin changed a lot of people, just by being a good, solid guy.

When I graduated in June of 1965 my class of 801 contained only three or four blacks. That was a sorry ratio. There had to be more qualified blacks applying to the Naval Academy but they simply were not given the opportunity. You would hear the stories about their schools being weak and they couldn't pass the entrance exam but oftentimes that was hogwash. Evidently there were congressmen who were extremely selective in their appointments and they held down the number of blacks. Also, I don't recall any black instructors at the Naval Academy except possibly one my senior year. Of course, all of this has changed now, just as it has throughout the navy. When Admiral Elmo Zumwalt was Chief of Naval Operations he made the navy's greatest effort to eliminate all prejudice. But then the navy wasn't any different from society.

During my year in Vietnam I saw some terrible racial problems around our base at Chu Lai. We began to find some white sailors behind the barracks, all cut up. The doctor had to take 140 stitches to sew up one guy. Some blacks who had been treated badly and harassed by some whites just decided on physical violence to get even. The ones involved in the knifings were caught and two of them were under me. One man—let's call him Jones—and I had become pretty good friends.

He had been involved in an earlier incident, which was caused by some guys on a U-boat. Jones was on the beach, driving a big fork-lift and off-loading a U-boat. Some of the men on the boat started yelling at him, "Hey, nigger! You can move faster than that!"

Jones got enough and jumped off the fork-lift, which went into the water, and headed for the U-boat. He got on the boat and one of the guys knocked him off into the water. He just went crazy. I was standing by a shack where the guns were kept and he came running past me, soaking wet.

"Hey, what's up?" I yelled at him.

He didn't answer but charged right into that shack. I ran after him and when I got in there he was behind the counter and had broken the lock on an M-14 rifle case. I knew there was trouble so I dived over the counter on him. We were wrestling on the floor and he was yelling what he was going to do to those guys on the U-boat and I was trying to calm him down. Here I was, his officer, wrestling all over the floor with him. Finally, a chief came in and helped me corral him. We had to put him in a strait jacket. I found out what had happened when he cooled down and I reported the men on the U-boat. After that he got into trouble about the knifings and I couldn't help him.

Like a lot of young blacks he just reached his limit, taking all that humiliation. The prejudice and persecution the blacks have been submitted to has caught up with us. Some have come to hate a man simply because he's white and have reacted and joined militant groups.

Later when I was stationed at Pensacola Naval Air Station I met a tremendous guy named Chappie James. He's a general in the air force now and he's black. He had grown up in Pensacola where he had gone through some terribly tough times. Now he was back in his hometown to speak and everybody was listening because he was a hero. He told the black kids to keep working to make it, that things are changing. He was hopeful they wouldn't become violent or militant. A lot of people on the base had been talking about racial problems and he woke them up. He got them to think.

That's it. If people would wake up and open their minds we could really move ahead. You can't have any boundaries when you say you are not prejudiced. The "I'm not prejudiced but ..." philosophy has to be stamped out if we are to truly practice equality for all.

Like the little boys in that picture, you must feel it completely.

14

Super Spectator

I feel by the end of the summer Staubach will be battling Morton for his job. Morton did such a great job directing our running game last year, which was his strength after he got hurt, or else we would have used Staubach.

—*Tom Landry*
1970

Landry's special assistant
If I'm the quarterback I feel we'll walk off the field a winner, one way or another.

—*Roger Staubach*
1970

The season is not very long. Only six months. It would probably go by even faster if I were playing. The three weeks I played in 1969 against the Jets, Colts, and Cardinals, went by so fast they seemed like only one week.

—*Roger Staubach*

Coach Landry was telling us what it took to make a championship quarterback. Craig, Bob Belden, and I were sitting there during a meeting at the quarterback school in the spring of 1970. Coach Landry went over leadership qualities, reemphasizing that it takes a number of years for a quarterback to reach the point in experience and know-how where he can lead a team to the championship.

"There is no quarterback in the league with less than three years experience who has won a championship," coach Landry said. "Namath was unusual in that respect. He was the only quarterback to win a championship after playing just three years.

I was really burning. I spoke out and said, "Namath was only *in* his third year. Besides, how can you judge every individual by the same yardstick? If you do that I don't have a chance because I'm only in my second year. You've got to judge every individual separately."

Actually, Namath was in his fourth year but that wasn't the big point. I should have kept my mouth shut but couldn't. I was twenty-eight. What was the use if there wasn't an understanding that I at least had a chance to be No. 1, even a very slim chance? When the meeting ended coach Landry said, "Roger, I want to talk to you."

When we were alone he said, "You've got to understand my feelings about the development of a quarterback. The mental process is very important. You must be able to read and understand the defenses and utilize our offense to its fullest potential."

"I believe all that, coach," I said. "But I just feel right now I can physically make up for any mental shortcomings I have."

Actually, it was probably just prior to the 1973 season before I realized how important the mental aspects of football were. But I wasn't going to come out and say I didn't think they were all that important. I simply knew I never wanted to be relegated to the position where I had to sit back and know I had no chance whatsoever of playing. So I still wasn't in coach Landry's plans, though he did say I'd be playing more in preseason.

Something happened that spring before training camp that shattered me, I saw my father for the last time. My mother phoned me and said I'd better come home.

His kidneys had failed, there was a hardening of the arteries and he had become senile. Only his heart was still strong. My first year with the Cowboys he had been able to watch our games on television and knew I was playing some. But when I went to see him that last time he didn't recognize me at first. Then he grabbed my hand. I sent Marianne, the kids, and my mother out of the room and tried to talk to him. He was in a semiconscious state and all he could do was murmur. But something remarkable happened. Suddenly, he took my hand and said, "Son, I hope you do well with the Cowboys." Then he became incomprehensible again. So despite everything, he knew where I was and what I was doing. I often think about that when things are going rough for me on the field.

My father died that May of 1970 at the age of sixty-two. My mother sold the house and moved into an apartment, keeping her job at General Motors. She started visiting us in Dallas a couple of times a year and coming to some of the games. I'm sorry my dad did not live to see the time when I actually made it and was playing with the Cowboys.

Coach Landry's questionnaire had everybody buzzing that off-season. Players responded with anonymity, but it was obvious who I was. I hadn't been around long enough to have opinions about most things, so I just skipped them, I did write I wanted a fair chance to play, which I didn't believe I had received before.

The questionnaire resulted in some changes. Performance levels were set for everyone. If a starter didn't live up to his performance level he could lose his starting job. There was a feeling that some weren't working as hard as others. This eventually resulted in three starters being benched for the season opener because they weren't able to reach performance levels for one reason or another. Ermal Allen, who has a tremendous football mind, gave up active coaching and became a special assistant who scouted all teams, including us, and rated all personnel. Some players felt Ermal expected too much of them and the questionnaire could have had something to do with his change in jobs.

Players appreciated that coach Landry was honestly trying to get a better overall feeling of what the team wanted.

The questionnaire let us know Landry wanted to try to get closer to us, opening up a human side to his system. Since I've known him he has gradually tried to get closer to the players, to bring his understanding of us more into the open. He still seems to me to be somewhat distant, with an infallible tone, but he is trying. The men have always respected him for his tremendous mind, but they respected him even more for trying to become closer to them.

One of the new rules was that we had to wear our helmets, and our chin straps had to be buttoned at all times during drills. In an early scrimmage in Thousand Oaks I had taken my team to the 1-yard line, then fumbled the ball away. I let out some pretty strong words, yanked off my helmet and threw it to the ground.

"Gotcha! Gotcha!" assistant coach Jim Myers yelled, pointing at me like a bird dog. "That's $50!"

I was trying to figure out why the fine was $50 instead of the usual $25. Then Walt Garrison told me, "Well, your helmet bounced, hitting the ground twice. It cost you $25 a bounce." It actually cost me $25 and that was my third fine. Coach Myers had also gotten me the preceding year for missing breakfast. I didn't know I had to eat breakfast with the team. Ol' Staubach, the troublemaker.

Training camp started late that year as the National Football League Players Association and the club owners argued over the pension plan, exhibition pay, and other benefits. Negotiations reached a standstill as owners tried to break the association and so the veterans didn't report to camp on time. I had wanted to report with the rookies in order to get a head start but couldn't. So the rookies had an extra week to themselves and this helped them. We had a super rookie crop that year anyway with players like defensive backs Cliff Harris and Charlie Waters; defensive end Pat Toomay; linebacker Steve Kiner; wide receivers Reggie Rucker and Margene Adkins; plus a very talented running back named Duane Thomas. Duane didn't go into his shell that year and was friendly to everybody and even talked to the media. We were very impressed with his size and speed. He was later to become one of the more important factors of our Super Bowl drive.

I did play more in preseason. Craig was coming off shoulder surgery but looked good in the exhibition opener with San Diego. I came in for the second half, ran well and completed four-of-five passes. That was the only exhibition game we won. Things just weren't working out right. I guess there was still a hangover from Cleveland. Craig had some trouble with his arm and his knee was bothering him. His right shoulder apparently hadn't regained all its strength after the operation.

Los Angeles beat us as we broke camp, heading for Dallas. I learned a good lesson in that L. A. game. I played the second period and threw a long touchdown pass to Margene Adkins, who ran the wrong route but still got open deep. Margene had everything going for him as a receiver but he kept having trouble adjusting on routes and never could make it. That turned out to be the only touchdown he ever caught for Dallas. Later, just as the half was ending, I threw an interception.

"Why did you throw the ball?" coach Landry asked me as I came off the field.

"Wait a second, coach," I said. "I wanted to go for the touchdown."

"That's not the percentage thing to do. The percentage thing to do is run out the clock and wait for another chance in the second half. Now you've given them the ball and they can score by kicking a field goal."

Despite the fact that coach Landry had the wide open offense and was such a great innovator, he was still percentage minded. Percentages, percentages . . . the percentage thing to do. From past history it is not a good percentage to start a second-year quarterback. Landry is locked into percentages sometimes. He can look at percentages and know what will usually happen and what to do to counter it. I wasn't a percentage player. Craig was. Craig was really Landry's type of quarterback.

We lost a big exhibition game to Kansas City, 13–0 in Dallas. Everybody was up for this one because the Chiefs had formerly been the Dallas Texans. There still was a big rivalry and it was our first meeting. After that loss a lot of people were saying the wrong team left town. Craig was having some problems passing.

I played the second half of the final preseason game with the Jets, which we also lost 29–21. We got a couple of touchdowns while I was in there and I threw a TD pass to Dennis Homan. But we were 1–5 that terrible exhibition season and coach Landry was true to his word about the performance level.

Craig Morton, Ralph Neely, and Bobby Hayes were benched and Roger Staubach, Blaine Nye, and Dennis Homan were named starters. Morton's arm just hadn't come back. Neely had been moved from right tackle (due to the advent of Rayfield Wright) to guard and was having difficulty adjusting to the new position. Hayes, often a slow starter, started slowly.

"Craig is in a slump and Roger has been throwing well," Landry said. "So Roger will start. We decided to go with Roger because Craig was having so much difficulty throwing the ball and pressure was building up for him. When we graded preseason films Nye and Homan were the top performers at their positions."

"Craig just doesn't have the zip on the ball he used to have," one teammate said.

I was the starter but, as far as the situation, coach Landry wasn't handing me the job. I was, in effect, a lame-duck quarterback until Craig was ready to play again. But at least the door was open, if ever so slightly. I wanted to make the best of it. Once again, coach Landry simplified the offense for me at Philadelphia. I did all right, hitting eleven-of-fifteen passes, including a touchdown to Lance Rentzel. But Calvin Hill was the key. He ran well and we won, 17–7.

The Eagles were razzing Hill, who was to rush for 117 yards. They kept trying to upset him. Once after a ten-yard gain, in which he felt he should have gone all the way, Hill jumped up and slammed the ball to the ground in disappointment. An official, his back

173

turned, felt Calvin had thrown the ball at him and called a personal foul.

"Roger was great in the huddle," Hill said. "He held us together. When I got back to the huddle after that personal foul I was so upset I was incoherent. Roger calmed me down. I don't think I could have played if he hadn't."

"Key play in the game was Staubach's thirty-one yard touchdown pass to Rentzel," Landry said.

New York had us down 10–0 in the Cotton Bowl the following week. I just knew coach Landry was going to take me out of the game as we walked up the ramp to the dressing room at halftime. "Coach, please let me play the second half," I told him. He didn't say a word, but he didn't replace me either. Rentzel, on an end around, threw a fine touchdown pass to Bobby Hayes for forty-eight yards. We came back and won 28–10. I began to think I was on solid ground. I found out that you can never think that. Coach Landry replaced me the following week in St. Louis, and I didn't think it was fair.

I sensed that Landry felt he needed a quarterback with experience to ignite the team. I planned to take one game at a time and believed as long as we won with me in there he'd not replace me.

I suppose it was ironic that Larry Wilson's play would cost me my position. We got the ball and drove to the Cardinal fifteen as the game started. I faked an off-tackle slant to Garrison, turned and fired a sideline to Rentzel. It was one of the best passes I'd thrown all year and hit him perfectly, where he could have stepped out of bounds with a first down at the five. But Lance dropped the ball. It was third down and I threw again, this time to Pettis Norman. Jamie Rivers blitzed. I panicked and overthrew the ball. Wilson was just standing there in the end zone and the ball went right into his hands. St. Louis came right back and took a 3–0 lead.

Early in the second period we were moving again. I threw an in-route to Homan, looking at him all the way. Wilson, theoretically, should have stayed in his area. But

I'd forgotten Larry did just what they'd told me he would do. He watched my eyes, picked off the pass and that was the last of me. A year earlier, of course, I had looked him off and thrown a touchdown pass.

It was like a silent film, very animated. Roger Staubach left the field after the second interception and walked over to Tom Landry and Craig Morton on the sidelines. From the press box you could see Morton jump into the air and Roger sink into the ground. Morton would now enter the game. Staubach, his head low, stood on the sidelines alone in the crowd. With the Cowboys trailing 6–0 and eight minutes remaining in the second period, there had been a changing of the guard.

That was the first time in my career I'd ever been pulled. I kept thinking just one touchdown would put us ahead. Craig had some bad breaks and we lost, 20–6. But Craig was the man again. I never really thought of it being a situation where I lost my job. I knew coach Landry was just waiting for an excuse to get Craig in there. We played Atlanta in the rain at the Cotton Bowl the following week and won, 13–0. Craig didn't have a good day throwing (three-for-ten, thirty-seven yards, and two interceptions), but he operated a fine running game featuring Calvin Hill.

Minnesota killed us the next game. It was the worst beating in Cowboy history. The score was 54–13 and could have been worse. My arm had been bothering me that week. I had skinned it on the Astroturf a number of times and apparently some fibers had gotten inside and the arm had healed over. Suddenly, my right elbow started swelling and my arm felt as if it were burning up. I had a bad infection and could hardly move the arm at all. Dr. Knight drained my elbow before the game. But it was hurting and I didn't want to play. For the only time in my life I didn't want to play at all.

I was on the sidelines during the Viking game with my arm taped up thinking, "God, please don't let me play. Not

175

today." With the score about 34–6 Morton came limping off the field after throwing an interception. Oh no, I thought. Don't limp. Don't limp. "Roger, go in," said coach Landry. It was awful. I threw some interceptions too, and we got demolished. The only good thing was Duane Thomas. Walt was hurt and Duane replaced him at fullback. He was great!

I would say our loss to Minnesota was a team effort.

—*Tom Landry*

The Minnesota game marked the first time during the regular season the Cowboys had played on real, live, natural grass. Incidentally, the grass died.

The infection in my arm was so bad when we got back to Dallas they had to put me in the hospital for a week. It was extremely serious. Dr. Knight was afraid the infection might have gone into the bone and, if so, I could have been finished as a quarterback. Bob Belden was activated and I didn't even make the trip to Kansas City that week. Craig's knee was bothering him and I probably would have played against the Chiefs if it hadn't been for my elbow infection.

I watched on television as Dallas beat Kansas City 27–16. Craig did a good job, once calling an audible and hitting Bobby Hayes with an eighty-nine-yard touchdown pass. Duane was great again. Calvin injured his back and Duane was playing fullback with Danny Reeves filling in at halfback. A halfback draw was called. As the huddle broke Danny told Duane to swap places with him. Duane did and ran forty-seven yards for a touchdown.

I came back the next week but Craig was in control again. We beat the Eagles, lost to the Giants, and then returned to Dallas to host the Cardinals. This one was billed as an early showdown game. It was the Monday night television game so Don Meredith, who had become a big hit as a commentator for ABC, was there. St. Louis seemed about to run away with the Eastern Division and had to be stopped. We were 5–3 and needed to win in order to get back into the race. Craig was beginning to have some trouble with his elbow, though not to a great extent. Well, we got beat 38–0 in another one of the low points in Cowboy history. The game was a nightmare. People started yelling for Meredith to play. They'd look up at the broadcast booth and scream, "We want Meredith! We want Meredith!"

"No way. You're not getting me back out there," Meredith told the audience.

"I never thought I'd see a Cowboy team lay down like that," Meredith said the morning after. "It was obvious there was no leadership out there."

The flack hit. We were 5–4, finished. They were all down on us, the fans, press, everybody. Some people wanted Landry fired. Some said Craig ought to be out of there. I remember some of the headlines: "Cowboys Are Through . . . Dallas on Downhill Slide." It was as if the entire franchise had folded.

"Well, I've just never been through anything like that," coach Landry told us. "It was embarrassing to all of us. You guys didn't really want to win. Maybe it was my fault. I don't know. But it was the worst performance I've seen."

He was talking to us the day after the game. Ordinarily when he finished talking to us we'd go out and have a short workout. But he just said, "Let's go out and have a touch football game." We've been doing that ever since. I think the looseness was determined then. We were apparently out of the race and hated by our own fans. So we just decided to go out and have as much fun as we could. When you're 5–4 the pressure is off.

The players also got together and talked about our situation. Le Roy Jordan, Bob Lilly, and Herb Adderley were all strong factors in pulling the team back together again.

"Everybody was down on us," Lee Roy Jordan said. "Friends, the media, coaches, everybody. All we

177

had was ourselves. So we pulled together. We didn't have anybody else."

Herb was a beautiful guy. He had been on all the great Green Bay teams and he kept telling us about a winning attitude and the ability to come back after defeat. The guy just brought a great outlook from the Packers. To me he was very important in helping us get to those two Super Bowls. He was a fine cornerback one of the leaders on defense. And the defense became superb. It went twenty-three periods without giving up a touchdown, stretching into the playoffs. We've had great comebacks and great defensive efforts, but I don't think any ever compared to that year. I believe I almost became the starter again during that period. I felt I should have a chance to play. It wasn't that I was blaming Craig, but I just knew I could do something to help us start winning again.

"I had to make a decision: either start calling plays for Morton and take some of the pressure off him or go with Staubach," explained Landry.

Coach Landry decided to use Craig, calling plays for him. He felt Craig with his experience, could execute better than I could. Calvin was having some problems with injuries at that time. He had injured a toe and missed most of the final games of the 1969 season and, I don't know, the coaches might have been down on him a little. Anyway, we went mostly to a running game, utilizing Duane at halfback in place of Calvin. Jim Myers, the line coach and offensive coordinator, did a fine job with our running game. He's always adapted the blocking techniques to the changing defenses, giving the Cowboys a strong running game year after year. Duane really responded and our whole offense was geared to him. He was a natural, darting runner who always seemed to be able to find daylight. We beat Washington and then another big problem hit the team. As we were preparing to play Green Bay in the Cotton Bowl on Thanksgiving, Lance Rentzel got into trouble.

178

The *Oklahoma City Journal* broke the story prior to the Green Bay-Dallas game of November 26, that Lance Rentzel had been released on an appearance bond after being questioned in regard to indecent exposure on November 19 involving a ten-year-old girl.

A felony charge of indecent exposure was filed against Rentzel on November 30, four days after the Packer game.

On April 8, Lance Rentzel pleaded guilty to indecent exposure and was assessed a five-year probated sentence with the understanding he receive regular medical and psychiatric care.

The night before the Packer game coach Landry talked to the team. "Something has happened which is difficult to talk about," he said. "Lance will tell you about it." At that time most of us had no idea what was going on, though some of the players had heard the rumors. "I've made a mistake in my life before and now I've made a second one." Lance told us. He was crying and I felt terribly sorry for him. "The Green Bay game," he continued, "will be my last for the Cowboys." At that time I didn't understand all the circumstances but I knew whatever he had done that he was very sorry about it. Lance had been nice to me and I liked him. But he had apparently been involved in a similar incident in Minnesota before he was traded to Dallas in 1967 and I knew it was serious.

Lance Rentzel played against Green Bay. It was his final game for Dallas. Cowboy officials might have originally been hoping to cover everything up. But it broke in the local papers, was on television, and everybody knew about it. The players got together and voted Lance should stay on the team. We felt he was a part of the team and his problem was ours. We wanted him out there. There was a typical lack of communication between management, the team, and Lance. Management was saying it was best for Lance to voluntarily stay out. Looking back, they were probably right. Lance might have taken a lot of abuse and the commissioner could have stepped in and suspended him.

After we beat the Packers, Lance came back and thanked the team again. His face was lined and he didn't look too good. I'm sure everything had begun to get to him. His career, his life, everything was coming apart. He spoke to us that last time from the heart and said, "I just want to thank all of you guys for sticking behind me. I've decided, though, that it's best I don't play again until this problem is straightened out." I think Lance wanted to play again that season but was pressured out.

Reggie Rucker, a free agent from Boston College, moved in at flanker. Reggie and I were friends and worked out a lot together. Lance had helped him, too. I thought Reggie could make it as a receiver. He had all the moves. The only problem he had was a lack of concentration at times. He'd make a fantastic catch and then sometimes the ball would hit right in his hands and he'd drop it. I used to kid him. I even phoned his wife one day and told her to put a mirror in front of him every morning when he woke up. He could look in the mirror and she'd tell him to concentrate. Reggie did a good job for Dallas but the Cowboys traded him to New England the next year. I thought that was a mistake but they don't consult me on such matters.

The big game of our stretch drive was in Cleveland. It was raining, muddy and, well, it was Cleveland again and so all of the old Cowboy hangups hovered over the game. But this was just a different team and the defense wasn't about to let things go wrong. Mike Clark kicked two field goals and we won 6–2. Cleveland had one close threat but Charlie Waters knocked the ball loose from Gary Collins, who had caught a Bill Nelsen pass deep in our territory, and Chuck Howley recovered. I remembered Dave Edwards had a bad ankle but he intercepted two passes that day. And Chuck was having a tremendous year. He was our only all-pro. We roomed together on the road.

"Roger Staubach is the most positive person I've ever met," Chuck Howley observed. "You disagree with him about something and, well, it's as if he's ready to fight you."

It was beginning to look as though we'd be flipping with Detroit for the Wild Card spot in the playoffs. But St. Louis completely folded. Every piece of the puzzle fell into place for us in the final weeks . . . everything that had to happen, happened. St. Louis which had a two-game lead with five games left, lost to the Giants twice. Then Los Angeles beat the Giants on the final day of the season while we were beating Houston. Had the Giants won we'd have had to flip for the Wild Card spot. But we were in, Eastern Division Champions on the final day. The Dallas Cowboys had done a complete turnaround.

Craig threw five touchdown passes in that final game with Houston, but his elbow problem was still there and was to plague him throughout the playoffs.

"In the playoffs we didn't have much of a passing game because Craig was having arm trouble," Landry said. "We just continued to emphasize our running game. When we needed to pass we would just drop it off short and not try to go deep. We just felt our defense could hold anybody."

Detroit finished strong. The Lions were coming up again and many felt they could go all the way, including the Lions. They were very vocal about this. We worked out on Christmas Day because our first-round playoff game was the next day. Coach Landry was talking to us piror to our workout in the Cotton Bowl. The sun was shining just over his shoulder. He looked like the Messiah. When he finished talking to us, we knew we would beat Detroit.

Again, it was our defense. Duane ran well, which helped keep the ball away from the Lions. The Lions' regular quarterback Greg Landry, was completely bottled up but they put Bill Munson in for the final few minutes and he got hot. We led 5–0 but Detroit was on the move. I was on the sideline holding my breath. The whole stadium was quiet. Everybody was just saying, "Oh no, here we go again!" But then Mel Renfro intercepted a pass and it was over. I was yelling at the top of my lungs. The whole team went crazy—even coach Landry, who was jumping up and down and wringing his hands.

We had made the NFC title game against San Francisco, which was coached by former Cowboy assistant Dick Nolan. John Brodie, the 49ers' veteran quarterback, was having his best year so we were underdogs again. I hadn't been playing but I was really caught up in the new spirit, the whole scope of what was happening. We'd been criticized, written off, and we were playing for the conference championship.

Duane was great again. By this time he'd become the best running back in the league. Walt Garrison wasn't supposed to play. He had some cracked ribs, a bad ankle that was swollen twice its ordinary size and was really banged up. But Walt still started the game. He hurt his ankle again and they had to help him off the field. A few plays later he was back. Walt's like that. He has as much courage as anybody I know. His spirit typified the entire team. We won, 17–10 and were in the Super Bowl against Baltimore. Oh yes, I went in for one play. Craig got his bell rung. I handed off, and came back out.

Craig lost his voice just before we left for a week of practice in Florida. His elbow was giving him problems and he didn't work out the previous week in Dallas. The Super Bowl was just a few days away and there was a chance I might play. Coach Landry left it open all week, which was unusual. Here we were in the Super Bowl and he was thinking about changing quarterbacks. Craig and I were competing but we *were* on the same team. I got very upset with an article in *Sports Illustrated*. The article called us the "team without a quarterback." It wasn't fair. Craig had a pretty good overall season, finishing as the fifth leading passer. They were just looking for something controversial to write about. When writers talked to me in Florida I let them know what I thought about the article.

The Super Bowl had me excited. I was not only happy about the team, but I would also stand to make $25,000. We stayed in Fort Lauderdale. Each day an hour was set aside for interviews with the swarm of reporters covering the game. We'd stay in our rooms during the interview

182

times and they'd call us down to a big banquet room if any of the reporters wanted to talk to us. They kept calling me and it was embarrassing. I was the backup quarterback. I hadn't been playing and yet, they were interviewing me. I didn't say anything about coach Landry leaving the quarterback situation open because I didn't want to start any controversy. Nobody ever called Chuck Howley to talk, which was odd. A tremendous linebacker, he was the only all-pro on either team. I think it bothered him down deep but it was a big game and Chuck was always ready for a big game, no matter what. Craig got his voice back and was able to work out. So naturally he was named the starter.

It was some experience being on the field for the first time in a Super Bowl. With all the balloons, fanfare, people, bands, and everything else it was like a circus. There hardly seemed enough room to work out. We felt we could run the ball on Baltimore and use short passes. We *knew* our defense would do its job. And Super Bowl V was a defensive game, a most unusual one.

We moved the ball well enough to take a 6–0 lead on two field goals. Then Baltimore got extremely lucky on a tipped pass. Johnny Unitas threw the ball, it bounced off a Colt and ended up in John Mackey's hands and he ran seventy-five yards for a touchdown. The pass would have been illegal if it hadn't touched a Dallas player before Mackey caught it. An official said it was tipped by Mel Renfro. Mel said he didn't touch it. But Baltimore had a touchdown.

We just weren't moving the ball well offensively, though naturally Baltimore had a fine defense and it deserves a lot of credit. For the first time since we had started our stretch drive, our running game was being stopped. Still, our defense and specialty teams kept giving us the ball in good field position and we were controlling the Colts. We were leading 13–6 when Baltimore fumbled the second half kickoff. We had a second down at the Colt one. We were ready to put the game away. Duane went for the touchdown but Mike Curtis hooked the ball loose. It fell to the ground and there was a big mixup, mostly by the referee. He made a very premature call, giving the recovery to Billy Ray Smith of the Colts, who had yelled, "Our ball! Our ball!" Dave Manders ended up with the ball and said he recovered it. He was standing there holding the ball and started yelling and screaming. Dave was jumping up and down. Had we been given the recovery we would have probably scored and the game would have been ours. This play cost us the game. I read later where Billy Ray said he didn't really recover the ball.

Late in the game it was 13–13. We were driving for what possibly could have been a winning field goal, but Craig threw to Danny Reeves and the ball slipped off his hands. It was a catch Danny could have made.

"It was Roll Right—13," Morton recalled. "Danny was wide open and he'd catch the ball nine out of ten times. I was going to come back with the same play to the other side. Roll Left—13, which should have put us on the Baltimore 35-yard line. From there we would have kicked the field goal and won the game."

Mike Curtis intercepted the pass Danny tipped. Baltimore drove close enough for Jim O'Brien to kick the winning field goal with five seconds left. That was it: Baltimore 16–13. I remember all the team's frustration being personified by Bob Lilly. He jerked off his helmet and slung it the length of the field. I really felt for the guys like Lilly and Howley who had played well so long and yet, came up short again in the championship game.

There were eleven turnovers in the Dallas-Baltimore Super Bowl game.

"It was the greatest defensive game that will ever be played," said Don McCafferty, the Baltimore coach.

"Very few people understand. I think it was the greatest Super Bowl game ever played, even though we lost. Goshamighty, it was great defense," Landry declared.

"Tipped balls resulted in sixteen points for the

Colts. The close calls the officials were forced to make —all the unusual things that happened just mounted up. And they all seemed to work against us—whether our luck ran out at this point or not, I don't know."

I'm sure that goal line play still haunts Craig. It could have won the game for us. And I have found it is not how you play as a quarterback but whether you win. Had we won, I think coach Landry would have just said Craig was his quarterback and gone on from there. But we lost. I found out on the plane coming home I would get a real chance ... perhaps my first real chance to be the No. 1 quarterback.

I was sitting with Marianne when coach Landry came back to talk to me. He told me he wanted me to work especially hard during the off-season. "I think you can make your move this coming year," he said, adding, "If you're ever going to make it." I believe he had begun to believe that he could possibly go with me, and win. I knew it was now time for me to be No. 1. If it wasn't going to be with the Cowboys, I was prepared to go somewhere else. I couldn't wait any longer.

15

A Loss, A Victory

Presbyterian Hospital is a modern structure rising almost serenely in North Dallas near Glen Lakes Country Club, an antithesis. Inside the hospital you get a feeling of solidness, surrounded by spotless tile floors, pale walls of off-green tinge and air smelling of antiseptic. At Presbyterian life begins, ends, starts anew, and time stops as people run the gamut of human emotions. Outside people move into the day and golfers leave the tee.

Sometimes when I'm driving on Central Expressway I glance over and see Presbyterian Hospital and it all comes back to me. I guess tragedies in your life are always there, though time eases the hurt you feel inside. Some two months after the Cowboys lost to Baltimore in the Super Bowl, a great tragedy struck my family. I was excited about the prospect of being a father again and getting a chance, this time maybe a real chance, of being the No. 1 quarterback.

Marianne did not have any problems during pregnancy or birth of our three daughters and everything seemed to be going like clockwork in this fourth pregnancy. But she was about a week late delivering and hadn't been able to feel the baby kicking for a few days. She went into the hospital expecting a normal delivery. I was standing outside the labor room while the doctor examined her. A nurse came out and said, "The doctor wants to see you."

"I don't want to alarm you," the doctor said, "but there's been a serious problem here. We can't find the heartbeat of the baby."

I got a big lump in my throat and in my stomach. Marianne knew it was even more serious. The doctor continued, "It's like a thousand-to-one shot the baby is still alive when we can't hear the heartbeat. Of course, we've had situations where the heart is in a position where we couldn't hear it. But these situations are rare. Very rare. I just wanted you to be prepared for what we might find."

Marianne and I knew our baby would be born dead. We both tried to hold back the tears, but we couldn't. It was a lot harder on Marianne—probably the worst thing she's ever gone through. I left the room and went out into the hall. There was a waiting room filled with people. Some watched a television set on the wall and others talked in low voices. I went back into the hall. Nurses and doctors in scrub suits passed by but all I could feel was this terrible heaviness in my heart.

An hour passed and Marianne had a normal delivery. Amy weighed eight pounds and three ounces. She was perfectly shaped, but she was dead. They never did find out what caused her death. The cord was shorter than normal and apparently she strangled.

I identify with other people who have problems. Many things in Vietnam really bothered me. I'll pick up a newspaper and read about tragedy which strikes another family and it really gets to me personally. I feel for them because I know they're just people like I am and have the same hopes, desires, and feelings. But nothing bothers you more when something like this happens. The death of Amy tore us apart. We had been so happy, looking forward to the baby's arrival. We were both smiling and happy one day, and the next day I was standing by the grave site with a little box, just a small box, and lowering it into the ground. The words: BABY GIRL STAUBACH were put on the grave marker. We never even knew her.

Months afterward, Marianne would wake up at night and cry. Our children small as they were, felt it. They had been anxious to see their little sister and would ask about her. We simply told them Amy was in heaven. Sometimes when they say their prayers they ask God to bless Amy too. Amy's death diminished everything for a while ... football, everything.

If Roger's going to do it, he'll make a go of it this year. I said three years ago that this is the year he could make his move to take over as the starting quarterback, and let me tell you, he dies hard.

—*Tom Landry*

After this year there won't be any more of that stuff. I'll settle it once and for all. I'm tired of it. I've earned that spot through a lot of years.

—*Craig Morton*

I believe I'll get an equal shot this year. If I didn't I wouldn't even go to training camp ... I'll be ready to move on somewhere else the minute I learn I'm not the number one quarterback.

—*Roger Staubach*

Coach Landry did what he said he would—he gave me an equal opportunity in training camp. I told him I wanted to be traded if I didn't get an equal shot or didn't become his number one quarterback. Sure, I wanted to play for the Cowboys. Coach Landry and his organization had built a tremendous team. But I wasn't getting any younger and, if I was going to play, it had to be in 1971. I couldn't wait any longer. So the minute he said Craig was No. 1, I was ready to leave.

The attitude of the team was good in camp. We *knew* we were better than Baltimore and this time everybody was determined to take that final step to the championship. Preseason was especially serious for Craig and me. We weren't just trying to get our games together, we were competing. Craig had come back strong again after having off-season surgery on his elbow. I guarantee you his arm was sound again. He was determined, and I knew how he

188

felt. He had waited a long time for this job and he wasn't about to let it get away.

Craig and I both had good preseasons. I did have a bad first half against Houston, though, and Craig probably got the edge with two exhibition games left against Baltimore and Kansas City.

The game in Baltimore saved me. It was a good trip. I visited the Naval Academy and talked to the football team. They had a big scrimmage that day and came to Baltimore to watch us play the Colts that night. Craig had a good first half, but I got hot in the second half and threw a couple of touchdown passes. If I hadn't done well I think coach Landry would have started Craig the final exhibition game against the Chiefs. And if that had happened, he'd have gone into the season as the No. 1 quarterback. Landry knew Craig's arm was back and he was showing a new maturity. Yes, Craig was very determined, but so was I. Nobody had worked harder than I had during the off-season.

One criticism of Roger's passing was that he had a slow delivery. This was pointed out to him and he worked on it. When he came to camp in 1971 he had one of the fastest deliveries in the game.

—*Ermal Allen*
Cowboy special assistant

I did well in the Kansas City game, but a blood vessel broke in my leg. I finished the preseason with an edge over Craig in statistics and some other things coach Landry judges us by, but it was very close. He did announce, however, I would start the season opener in Buffalo but we would have a two-quarterback system. Then luck seemed to jump into Craig's corner.

The swelling in my leg got so bad coach Landry decided to start Craig. He had a great day as we beat Buffalo. So it was my turn the next week in Philadelphia. That didn't work out very well either, thanks to a cheap shot by Mel Tom, the Eagle defensive end. I threw my first pass of the season on the fifth play of the game. It went right to Bill Bradley for an interception. I was standing there and, suddenly, something was pulling me from behind. That's all I remember. I was out for the game. Again, Craig came in and did a fine job.

When I looked at the films, they clearly showed that Tom came up behind me, pulled me around and slammed his elbow across my head. It was very flagrant and made the whole team mad. Later Tom said, "I was just trying to block him." But films from the end zone camera showed he just drew back and slugged me. It ended up costing him a $1,000 fine by the commissioner.

It wasn't funny when it happened but everybody was kidding me in the dressing room after practice the next week. All the writers were there and I was saying, "I'd like to catch that guy some dark night and use some of my hand-to-hand combat on him." Everybody was laughing. But Steve Perkins, then of the *Dallas Times-Herald*, wrote a story about how I wanted to use my combat tactics on Mel Tom. I mean, he's like 6-7. I could use karate on him and he'd still kill me!

Opportunity wasn't exactly coming my way. Craig was leading the league in passing because of the two games in which I was supposed to be the quarterback. We heard rumbles around the league about how George Allen had built up the Washington Redskins, our next opponent in the Cotton Bowl. Coach Landry just told us, "We have a two quarterback system now but Craig will start against Washington. We need his experience and this is a big game."

Had the team kept winning and Craig continued to do well, I believe he would have remained No. 1. But we found out the Redskins were for real. Charley Harraway broke away early for a fifty-seven-yard touchdown. Mike Clark kicked three field goals but we weren't doing anything offensively and trailed 20–9 in the final period. I got in and we scored a touchdown. If we had gotten the ball back I think we could have scored again, but we didn't and lost 21–16.

The Redskins went crazy. Clint Murchison had said he

thought we were one of the greatest football teams. I guess George Allen put that on his bulletin board because the Redskins really jumped on that statement.

The lowest point of the season, and the most humiliating for me, came against the New York Giants the following week on Monday night TV. I started but we didn't do much the first half. I fumbled the ball away once at the 4-yard-line. Calvin Hill also fumbled one away. About the only positive thing I did was throw a touchdown pass to Billy Truax just before the half, giving us a 13–6 lead.

Coach Landry pulled me out at the half. We were leading and he pulled me! Reporters asked me about it after the game and I just said, "No comment." Finally coach Landry came over in the dressing room. "Coach, don't say anything," I told him. "Whatever you say, you'll never understand me. What you just did to me out there wasn't called for. You'll just never understand me."

I thought I deserved the chance to go all the way. I felt my play had picked up near the end of the half and I would have come back strong. I was very confused and discouraged. I didn't even know if I was going to practice that next week. I was thinking how coach Landry didn't believe in me and was waiting to get Craig back in there, just like always.

Duane Thomas had joined us the week of the Giant game. Calvin injured a knee when Spider Lockhart knocked him out of bounds and Duane was ready to play. It was just amazing. He had missed training camp, the first three weeks of the season, and then stepped out there and played as if he'd never been away. Duane became upset when the management wouldn't tear up his old contract after his fine rookie season and give him a new one. But management said it had a precedent and this was never done after one year of a three-year contract. It hadn't been done for Calvin the year before when he was Rookie of the Year. So Duane came out and really blasted the whole organization—Tex Schramm, Gil Brandt, and Tom Landry. He called Landry "a plastic man," said Brandt was "a liar" and that Schramm was "sick, demented, and totally dishonest." I remember the writers kidding Tex about this and he said, "Well, that's not bad. He got two out of three."

Anyway, Duane reported late for camp. So they just traded him to New England for Carl Garrett. I remember talking to Carl right after he got to Thousand Oaks. He told me how glad he was to get with a good line and away from that bunch in New England. He also told the *Dallas Morning News* and *Fort Worth Press* the same thing and they printed it. The trade was then nullified because Duane wouldn't take all of his physical and Carl had to go back to the Patriots. Can you imagine how Carl must have felt after what he said? I was sorry for Carl but was glad to see Duane back in the Giant game. And I was sorry about the turn my own situation had taken.

Craig started in New Orleans but the team was lethargic. New Orleans went ahead 17–0, before I got to play.

Roger Staubach entered the game with six minutes remaining in the third period. He threw touchdown passes for forty-one yards to Gloster Richardson and sixteen yards to Bobby Hayes and the momentum switched to Dallas, which trailed by only three. But Charlie Waters fumbled a punt in Saint territory when John Fitzgerald backed into him and New Orleans recovered, going out to win 24–14.

Texas Stadium finally opened with a lot of ballyhoo. It's a fine, plush, modern place with a partial roof which protects fans from the weather. One wise guy nicknamed it the Half-Astrodome. I like it, though I know the afternoon sun peaking over the edge of the partial roof can bother receivers and guys trying to catch kicks. I started the game there against New England. Steve Kiner, who once had played linebacker for us, was now with New England. Steve was quite an individualist, like Duane. He pulled a stunt one day when he was with us that I'll never forget. Coaches have parking places nearest the door to the dressing room at our practice field and the players use the parking lot. One day it was really raining and Kiner just pulls his old Volkswagen right into Landry's parking place next to the door. Coach Landry came in a little later, soaking wet. "I admire somebody's courage," he grunted.

The day of that New England game Duane ran fifty-seven yards for the first touchdown. I hit a couple of touchdown passes and ran for another score as we won 44–21. I thought I was in then. I had finished strong, almost helped us pull the New Orleans game out, and directed the attack against New England. That's when coach Landry made a decision that was the shocker of all shockers.

COWBOYS TO ROBOT SYSTEM

—Dallas Morning News headline

"I've decided to alternate our quarterbacks on each play and call the plays myself," Landry said. "As long as I'm calling the plays it's much easier for a quarterback to have the play early so he can go to the keys and determine exactly what he's going to do on a particular play in each situation.

"I don't have any reservations about my decision this week. It's a matter of pooling all the information and all the efforts of everybody—quarterbacks, coaches in the press box, me, everybody. I'll catalog the information I receive on the sidelines and decide whether a play is to be used or how to counter a move. I'm usually two, three plays ahead. The quarterbacks will have more time to think exactly what they must do and their alternatives.

"I'm very satisfied with Morton and Staubach. Quarterback has been the strong part of our team. It's just that sometimes a change picks things up. I just felt we must do something and that we needed everything we could possibly muster to beat the Bears."

When coach Landry told us he planned to shuttle quarterbacks on every play we nearly fell off our seats. First we were shocked, and then we just stared at each other. But coach Landry had said earlier that shuffling quarter-

193

backs was the ideal situation because you can discuss the play and go over the situation with a quarterback before he enters the game. He had done it before with Eddie La-Baron and Don Meredith in the early '60s and later tried it a little with Craig and Jerry Rhome when Meredith couldn't play.

But there are a lot of disadvantages. A quarterback likes to get into the rhythm of the game and get a feel for the plays, mentally and physically. Calling his own plays, he can set up situations and take advantage of them. But coach Landry, as usual, was determined. Craig and I talked about the situation during the week and finally just decided we'd try and make the best of it. It was difficult. You'd have a good play and then leave the field and cool down. If you had a bad play it was on your mind and you wanted to make up for it, but you'd be going off the field again. Chicago beat us 23–19. In the final minutes of the game, when we had a chance to win, he let Craig go all the way. I had the impression Craig was No. 1 again.

The Cowboys had a tremendous total offense of 480 yards against Chicago. But the team couldn't achieve consistency inside the 20-yard line. Landry drew harsh criticism but said, "I still think it's the best way. I know statistics always look impressive to losers but we shuttled quarterbacks and moved the heck out of the ball."

Coach Landry had to make a decision. The team was split over us, which could have developed into a problem, although I think they would have rallied behind whichever quarterback was picked. Indecision over the situation was also hurting Craig and me. I know I was afraid of doing something wrong and being taken out. I had no idea what coach Landry would do. Sometimes I thought he'd go with Craig because that's what he usually did ... but other times I felt he might want a change, he might want me.

Both our quarterbacks have played well. They've been a strong part of our team, which I've said be-

194

fore. But I will go with Roger just in case some of the indecisiveness about the situation is upsetting to our team. Roger will make some mistakes but I'm confident he'll do the job we need and keep improving.

—*Tom Landry*
at a press conference
announcing his decision

Actually I got an inkling about coach Landry's decision at a Las Vegas party the Cowboy wives gave for charity the night after we lost to Chicago. That was some day. It was that night that we found out Ralph Neely had suffered a broken ankle in a motorcycle accident. And people at the party were talking about George Andrie's "heart attack." George had chest pains that day and decided to go to the hospital for a checkup. He didn't make it. The pains came back and he stopped at a gas station, asking the attendant to call the hospital. They took him and found he had indigestion.

Ray Renfro came to me at the party, drew me aside and said, "Rog, you're going to be the starting quarterback. But god, don't tell anybody." Still, with coach Landry you can't be sure until you hear it from his own mouth. So I had some doubts.

I can't estimate the time which goes into making major decisions for a professional team. There are hours of films, discussions, statistics and I don't know what all. So it seems a little odd that it only took Tom Landry ten seconds to say the words that changed my career and launched me on that comet which was the 1971 season. It was, perhaps, the biggest decision of his coaching career. It certainly changed my life.

Coach Landry phoned me at home after the Tuesday practice.

The practice had been normal, with Craig running the first team. I answered the phone.

"Roger, I've made a decision," Landry said. "I've decided you are going to be the starting quarterback for the rest of the season."

"Coach, I really appreciate that. I won't let you down."

Well, that was it. He just hung up. I started yelling for Marianne. I was overcome with excitement. It was something I'd waited so long for . . . worked so hard for . . . and at last I had it.

I started feeling we could turn it around again and have a good season, but nobody could project what happened. We were 4–3, had lost Neely, Calvin was hurt again, and Duane was beginning to turn completely within himself. The Redskins were hot and everything seemed against us. But I was the No. 1 quarterback now. This was my team. My career had begun at last.

16

Streaking, My Way

Craig would have done basically the same thing for us Roger did. But I felt at the time the team would unite around Roger because of his great determination and dedication. Roger is the most dedicated athlete I've known.

—*Tom Landry*
after 1971 season

Roger Staubach just isn't a guy you can tell he can't do something. There's no such word as can't to him. You tell him that, or figure he can't do something, and he'll go right out and prove you're wrong.

—*Mike Ditka*
tight end

Despite my elation over being the No. 1 quarterback, I felt sorry for Craig Morton. You couldn't help but feel for him. Craig is a heckuva guy who's had a lot of bad luck with injuries. It's tremendous when a man can overcome two injuries and subsequent operations involving his throwing arm. After coach Landry had picked me over Craig I remember saying, "If I'd gone through what Craig has I'd probably be a cook on a ship somewhere."

Of course, since that time I've gone through a serious shoulder operation myself but that's getting a little ahead of the story. Still, I know coach Landry wanted to make sure Craig had every opportunity to keep the number one job and felt for him when he didn't get it. He had groomed

Craig to take Don Meredith's place. Everybody involved with the Cowboys always thought he'd have the job when Don retired. Then I popped into the picture. I think coach Landry became a little intrigued with my somewhat cocky attitude and my free-lance approach to the game.

St. Louis once again became a barrier in my career. I played my first real pro game against the Cardinals and I had also lost my starting job against them. And the Cardinals were our first opponent after I became the starter in 1971. I had to begin proving I was the right choice, but I don't think the team was in a good frame of mind. We were questioning ourselves, which isn't good. You can't just talk positive and be a winner, you have to believe it deep inside. Sure, everybody was saying, "We can win the next seven," but they really didn't think so. We needed a break to get us started.

"Our backs are to the wall now," coach Landry told us. "If we lose in St. Louis we'll be through as far as any championship is concerned."

It helped me a great deal knowing I was the quarterback, with nobody looking over my shoulder. I knew if I messed up I'd still be in there. My confidence was high because I'd done well against New Orleans and New England. As usual, St. Louis played well against us and we trailed 10–3 at halftime. I threw a touchdown pass to Mike Ditka, our tight end, but the game was tied late in the final period, 13–13.

We had the ball deep in our own territory, facing third and five. Coach Landry, shuttling Billy Truax and Ditka in with the plays, called a quick out route to Lance Alworth. Lance caught the ball, barely making the first down by a yard. Had we missed that first down and had to punt, the Cardinals might have won. I threw another important pass to Truax and scrambled for about a fifteen-yard gain. We moved into Cardinal territory but the clock was beginning to spend the last two minutes. On a third and six at the St. Louis 19-yard line, I threw for Lance again. He dropped the ball.

Everything rode on a field goal attempt by Toni Fritsch. Toni had been a soccer star in Austria. The Cowboys had brought him over to try kicking a football but he'd never been in a regular season game before. Mike Clark had been having some problems so Landry brought Toni off the taxi squad. Well, in his first regular season pro game, Toni just lined up as cool as can be and kicked a twenty-six-yard field goal to win the game.

Toni Fritsch was lining up for the field goal when Cardinal linebacker Larry Stallings started razzing him. "Look out there! Look out! You're gonna choke!" yelled Stallings. Dave Edwards, blocking for the field goal, looked at Stallings and said, "You're wasting your time. He can't understand English."

Toni Fritsch kicked the field goal with 1:53 left. "Et nothing," he said. "I play big crowds en soccer. A pro is a pro, yes or no."

Next, we beat the Eagles 20–7, and I had a good day passing (fourteen of twenty-eight for 176 yards) and running (ninety yards) and then we went to Washington to play the Redskins. This was our biggest game. We had to beat George Allen's team to win the East and you could feel the electricity in the air. Allen had built a truly fine defense in Washington. I know if you don't run the ball against the Redskins you're in trouble because the front four really tee off on a pass rush.

The first time we got the ball we moved all the way to the Redskin 29-yard line. Coach Landry called a deep in-route to Alworth. Lance was going across the field, to my right, when Redskin tackle Diron Talbert grabbed my leg. I jerked my leg away and looked down the left sidelines. It was a weird feeling. Nobody was there. Everybody was on the right side, where Alworth and the other receivers had gone. I took off fast as I could for the goal line, which wasn't all that fast. I scored and that turned out to be the only touchdown of a fine defensive game, which we won 13–0.

"The only difference between the two teams was Staubach," said Allen.

"No, we don't have any plays where Roger is supposed to run," Landry noted. "He runs enough as it is."

Near the end of the game I tried to scramble and Verlon Biggs grabbed my shoulder and threw me down. It hurt pretty bad but the important thing was we had beaten the Redskins and regained first place in the East. I didn't see a lot of Mr. Biggs that day, anyway, thanks to the amazing Tony Liscio. Landry had trouble finding a replacement for Neely at left tackle. Don Talbert injured an ankle and Forrest Gregg pulled a muscle. It looked like we might have to switch somebody over to tackle. Then he thought of Tony Liscio. Liscio had retired, so naturally he hadn't gone through training camp nor the first nine games of the season. Tony was just sitting in his real estate office the Monday before the Washington game and coach Landry phoned him, asking if he'd be interested in going to Washington over the weekend and blocking a Mr. Biggs.

"I don't think my legs would hold up," Tony told him, "but let me think about it a couple of days."

"Tony," coach Landry said, "I'll give you thirty minutes. I have to make a decision at left tackle."

Tony decided to play and was one of the key blockers in our drive to the Super Bowl. He did his job about as well as anybody we had. I think Tony and Duane Thomas must have set training camp back fifteen years.

We faced a short week, playing Los Angeles on Thanksgiving Day, which didn't give my shoulder much time. The soreness didn't let up during the few days before the game and I couldn't hold a football in my right hand. I didn't know if I could even throw until pregame warm-ups. My shoulder did loosen up a little in warm-ups after I'd taken some codene. So I managed to play, throwing a long touchdown pass to Bobby Hayes (fifty-one yards) and another to Alworth (twenty-one yards).

Ike Thomas ran a kickoff back eighty-nine yards for a touchdown to get us going. We were a little flat after the Washington game and needed something to pick us up. Ike's kickoff return was the answer. Lance Rentzel was also playing for the Rams. This marked the first time he'd been on the field in Dallas since his trouble. The fans treated him fine and we were all glad to see him again. We were also glad to see him fumble an end-around which gave us the ball. We beat the Rams, 28–21.

Calvin Hill was ready to play again, although his knee was still a little sore and had to be heavily taped. So there was a chance Calvin and Duane would finally be in the same backfield against the Jets. But the problems had begun with Duane.

Duane had started showing up on our charter flights without a tie, breaking one of coach Landry's rules. He hadn't completely withdrawn within himself yet but was very tense and irritable. He wouldn't talk to the media at all. This made some of the reporters mad, so they blew the whole thing out of proportion. Duane was doing his job well but he seemed to stay in a bad mood most of the time.

One day in practice Danny Reeves, a player-coach that year, told Duane he'd have to play fullback now that Calvin was back. "No, I'm not going to play fullback," Duane said. "Duane, go ahead," I told him. Well, he looked right at me with that cold stare and said, "You shut up."

It was just a lot of little things, like not wearing a tie and ignoring the roll call. Forty-six guys would answer the roll and Duane wouldn't. "You see me," he once said. "You know I'm here." I wasn't bothered about Duane breaking rules like that. I was disciplined and going to abide by them. But some players started to say, "Hey, he's getting away with this, why can't I?" It was a bad situation. Coach Landry compromised a lot for Duane. He was personally interested in Duane and also knew what an important part of the team he was. He tried to understand Duane.

I don't know what Duane's problems were. I know he grew up very poor, his parents died when he was in high school and he was moved around a lot. I'm sure he has been taken advantage of most of his life. He had trouble with management and some other problems, which I don't know enough about to comment on. But sometimes he

201

would still respond during games. After a big touchdown, I'd go up and hug him or he'd say, "Nice play." And he was alert. He would sit there in meetings just staring into space, and you'd think he wasn't picking up anything. But he was. He knew two positions—fullback and halfback.

Walt Garrison is a tremendous, gutty back, but he was slowed by injuries so Calvin and Duane played in the same backfield against the Jets and New York Giants. We were unstoppable, beating the Jets, 52–10, and the Giants, 42–14. Everything was working. I know Garrison really got to feeling left out. He was just sitting there on the bench one day and said, "I feel like the bastard son at a family picnic."

Our offense was breaking all kinds of records. The defense also had regained its old form. There was just a great feeling on the team. We had it going. We could beat anybody on any day. Nothing could stop us. We routed St. Louis in the final regular season game, 31–12. I did have one low point in that game. I threw my first interception in 135 passes. But we had won our division again and were to face the Minnesota Vikings in Bloomington to open the playoffs on Christmas Day. Everybody was talking about how super the Vikings were and how tough they'd be at home in what was expected to be sub-freezing weather. Myself, I just felt we'd do whatever it took to win.

I couldn't believe everything that was happening. I was the leading passer in the National Football League, made some of the all-pro teams and won the Bert Bell Award from the Maxwell Club as the NFL's outstanding player. I was even named to the Pro Bowl. This all left me in shock. I didn't even know if I would be starting at midseason and all of a sudden here came all these awards. I was proud of them, but I also knew I'd gotten them because of circumstances. I was just the quarterback on a super team. The Bert Bell Award should have been a team trophy.

Things *were* starting to jell for me. I was getting my game together. I loved being in the playoffs and facing a team like Minnesota, a team many felt was the NFL's best. Sure, there was pressure but that's relative. There's pressure just living in our society today.

It bothered me that I wasn't calling my own plays. I felt I had gotten to the point where I could run my own game. I just don't feel in complete control unless I do. But we had a winning formula going. And I was thinking . . . If somebody was going to call my plays for me I couldn't think of a guy I'd rather have doing it than coach Landry.

So many things were racing through my mind as the regular season ended. I wanted us to go all the way this time. If we didn't the season would be like other seasons. I also didn't want anybody thinking that what I had done in the regular season was a fluke.

We *were* a little worried about the weather in Minnesota. Some of the guys remembered playing in that ice game in Green Bay in '67. There'd been some cases of frost bite and they said it was nearly impossible to function. The Minnesota game being played on Christmas Day did cause some furor. I would have liked to play on another day, but didn't have any deep religious convictions about playing on Christmas. Christmas is a family day and represents the birth of Christ. But since Christ was no doubt born on some other day anyway, I didn't worry about it. I was too engrossed in the game.

There was snow on the ground when we got to Bloomington, but it wasn't too bad. We worked out on the University of Minnesota field on Christmas Eve. It was certainly cold and the snow was frozen around us, but the field itself was all right. It was about 25 degrees game day but very little wind, so it was a good football day. We remembered how Minnesota had humiliated us the year before but now we were very confident.

Bud Grant the Vikings' coach was having some quarterback indecision of his own, except he had used *three* quarterbacks—Gary Cuozzo, Bob Lee, and Norm Snead. Shortly before the game he decided to start Lee against us. I believe he felt under our heavy rush Lee might be more mobile. Our defense really controlled the Vikings. Minnesota was able to score only one touchdown and that was after we led 20–5 in the fourth period. The game already was out of the Vikings' reach.

We led 6–3 at halftime and came out really fired up in the second half. Cliff Harris intercepted Lee's pass in Viking territory and we moved to their 13-yard line. We'd been having a great success with an off-tackle play to Duane at fullback. We call it a Dive-37 Switch. I fake a pitch to the halfback, going wide, and the fullback slashes back in. John Niland and Dave Manders double teamed Alan Page and there was a huge hole. Duane ran right through, standing up for the touchdown.

Lance Alworth faked Ed Sharockman out completely to get our final touchdown drive started. Lance feigned a streak, getting behind Sharockman a couple of steps. Ed isn't very fast and thought he was beaten on a bomb so he took off downfield with everything he had. Lance curled back to the sidelines and Sharockman wasn't within fifteen yards of him. We got to the nine where we planned to hit Truax, who had to beat safety Paul Krause. Billy wasn't open so I scrambled all over the place. Then I saw Hayes get clear and threw him a touchdown pass. We won, 20–12. We had taken another step.

The toughest playoff game we had, including Miami in the Super Bowl, was the NFC title game with San Francisco in Texas Stadium. The 49ers were a good, tough team once again. They really stopped Duane, who had hurt them so badly the year before. Dick Nolan had obviously geared his defense for Duane using Landry's flex alignment and gap defense. I ran a lot myself. Calvin reinjured a knee and Walt came in and was actually our most effective runner. San Francisco double covered our wide receivers, which also confused me.

Fortunately, John Brodie and the 49ers were having just as much trouble with our defense. Brodie made a mistake in the second period, allowing us to score. He tried a screen pass deep in his own territory and it went right into the hands of George Andrie. George ran it back seven yards to the two, and from there we scored. George was coming to the end of his career. He'd had many good years playing end, next to Bob Lilly but he had back trouble and had been splitting time with Pat Toomay. But he got up for the playoffs.

Andrie's play allowed us to take a 7–0 lead. That's the way it stood in the final period, with the game hanging in the balance. Finally we mounted an eighty-yard drive in fourteen plays to score and win 14–3. That drive almost didn't get started.

The Cowboys faced a third-and-seven at their own 23-yard line as Staubach faded to pass. He failed to spot a receiver and started scrambling, back-tracking toward his own goal line. He was being chased from all directions and retreated all the way to his three. Then he ducked away from Cedrick Hardman's pursuit and headed back upfield.

Danny Reeves was covered by linebacker Dave Wilcox, who didn't know what to do. Staubach was coming towards them. If Wilcox went up to make the tackle, Staubach would drop the ball over to Reeves. If he stayed on Reeves, Staubach might run for the first down. Wilcox reacted toward Staubach, who then hit Reeves for a nine-yard first down pass to keep the drive going.

Hardman said later, "Staubach gave us a lot of trouble with his running. He's much niftier than Greg Landry."

And Tom Landry noted, "The big play for us came on that third-and-seven. If Roger hadn't made the first down we would have had to punt. San Francisco could have gotten the ball and won the game."

They were doubling our wide receivers on that third-down play which got our winning drive started. I was supposed to hit Danny as he came out of the backfield. Danny didn't appear open when I went back to pass so I started scrambling. Hardman was chasing me and he's awfully fast. I doubled back, cutting underneath him, and then started running back to the side of the field where Danny was. Reeves was over there yelling at me. He had no idea where I was going because I'd gone from right to left and back to the right again. I also didn't have any idea where I was going. But we completed the pass and went on to score and win.

San Francisco played a great game, especially Wilcox. But I'll never forget what Frank Nunley, another line-backer, said before the game: "I just hope Staubach does try to scramble." That's how hard-headed I was then. For some reason I was going to prove to Nunley I could run. I ran more that game than any in the playoffs (eight carries, fifty-five yards). I'm not like that now. I don't like to get punished by those linebackers any more. Still, I'll run if I see an opening.

Coach Landry had good insight into me. "Well, he'll keep running until he keeps getting hit and then he'll slow down. The more he learns, the less he'll run." I still like to run, I admit, but I've become more aware of the importance of laying the ball off to the backs when I get into trouble. You do that and you'll last longer in this league. But Landry never said anything directly to me about my running. We'd gotten that far and he wasn't going to try and change anything, not even me. I had some key runs that year I believe helped us win. He felt he had some control over me by calling the plays. But I'd execute the best I could and, if things weren't working out, I'd take off.

We had won the National Football Conference title again. We were back in the Super Bowl and it was a tremendous feeling. This was a different team. There was the feeling that this was *the* team, the best Landry had had. There wasn't a lot of emotion after our victories over Minnesota and San Francisco. I think we were being described as being "deftly clinical."

Calvin and Duane were both playing and Walt was ready again. That gave us three fine backs. Liscio looked as if he'd never been away and John Niland and Rayfield Wright were all-pro in the line. People had really begun to notice Rayfield. He'd done a fine job blocking Carl Eller in the playoff game, which is a good way to get every-body's attention. Blaine Nye and Dave Manders were both underrated. Dave never made a mistake on snaps. The

206

seams were always just right when he snapped the ball. We never fumbled a snap, a real tribute to him.

Our passing game had changed. Ditka and Truax caught forty-five passes between them and the Cowboys had been known as a team which never threw to the tight end. Pettis Norman, who had gone to San Diego in a swap for Alworth, had said, "Playing tight end for Dallas is like being another offensive tackle."

Alworth had lost some speed when he came to the Cowboys but he was a fine pattern runner, had great hands and made a lot of big plays for us. Everybody had talked about what a great blocker Rentzel had been, but the coaches were calling Alworth the best blocking wide receiver the Cowboys had ever had. Lance hadn't had to block in San Diego but the flanker's block is very important in our wide running game. "In San Diego," Lance said, "I used to go around the house telling myself, 'watch it, catch it, tuck it, run it.' In Dallas I growl at the cat, make faces in the mirror and kick the trash can. Blocking is something you have to make yourself do. I'm not a Mean Joe Greene but I'm a mean gnat."

Bobby Hayes was having a good year. He caught eight touchdown passes and averaged twenty-four yards a catch. When Bobby's right he's just great. He hasn't lost any speed and he can really turn it on.

In the defensive line, Bob Lilly had what might have been his best season. I know some of the opposing players said, when they looked at our films, they couldn't help watching Lilly. It's just amazing what he can do. Jethro Pugh had a good year and we felt he should have been all-conference. Larry Cole, George Andrie, and Pat Tomay gave us strength at defensive ends. Dave Edwards, Lee Roy Jordan and Chuck Howley gave us the best linebacking in the league. Mel Renfro once again was proving he was the class cornerback in football and Herb Adderley was helping us not only with his play but also his leadership. Cliff Harris in his second year was coming into his own at free safety. Cornell Green, a four-time all-pro at cornerback, had completely adjusted in his second year at strong safety.

207

We had an excellent, solid team, without any mental hangups. It was a tremendous feeling to get back to the Super Bowl, where we had left off one year before. We had the players, momentum, everything. This time we wouldn't let it get away. This time we would be World Champions and not be stopped just short. It wouldn't wait until next season. It would be this season. Now!

17

Super Team

The stigma had haunted the Dallas Cowboys like ghosts of Christmas Past. It always seemed there somewhere, ready to pop out . . . The Dallas Cowboys couldn't win the Big One. But this was a new team with a new quarterback. It was a confident team and New Orleans in mid-January of 1972 was a new place, a new time.

New Orleans, the Fun City of the South and the Sin City of the South, had become the nation's sports capital for Super Bowl Week. Some 50,000 visitors crowded into the night scene of Bourbon Street, where brassy, blue notes came from behind neon lighted doorways. The sounds of jazz, sad and old and new, intermingled with barkers outside strip joints and dark bars where ladies of the night sat under dimmed lights. It was as if Mardi Gras had come early . . . Hurricanes at Pat O'Brien's, Ramos gin fizzes, shrimp remoulade, bouillabaisse, seafood gumbo.

But it was here in this city that the Dallas Cowboys would lay to rest the stigma. They *would* win the Big One.

Naturally, it was a much different feeling for me than it had been at our previous Super Bowl in Miami. The year before I was happy for the team and caught up in the general excitement. But this time I was the quarterback. This time I would play and become a part of the outcome. I felt such great excitement within me that sometimes I thought I would explode.

There were two weeks between our NFC title victory over San Francisco and the game with Miami in Super Bowl VI. We worked out in Dallas a week, then went on to New Orleans, where once again we went through all the interviews and sidelights which are part of the Super Bowl experience.

Duane Thomas had caused some intrigue before we left Dallas. He didn't show up for a workout, causing some speculation that he might stage a one-man boycott of the game. Jim Brown had begun to handle Duane's affairs and we just weren't sure what he might do.

We, as players, became very concerned. Duane had been playing exceptionally well. Now we had a chance to take it all and wanted him to be there. Fortunately, he came back to work and went on to New Orleans with us. I never did know why he missed practice that day. I think he may have just been sick.

There is no question that you have an advantage if you've been to the Super Bowl before. You anticipate what is going to be happening around you, the almost circus-like atmosphere. We knew what to expect. We had momentum going for us and we weren't just talking about what we could do . . . we *knew* what we could do.

Our entire game plan was set before we went to New Orleans. I think coach Landry devised his best game plan ever. Everything was figured out just right for the Dolphins. Mike Ditka said, "The year before Craig was having trouble with his arm before our Super Bowl game with Baltimore. I don't think deep down we really had that much confidence in our game plan as far as passing. This wasn't Craig's fault. His arm was just a physical problem. Now we have complete confidence in everything and we've got two quarterbacks throwing well."

Our main objectives on defense were to take away the Dolphin strengths, wide receiver Paul Warfield and fullback Larry Csonka. Mel Renfro, as the corner back, had the main responsibility on Warfield but he would also get some help from the safeties. He was really up for it. I know he always wants to be at his peak, especially when he's playing against the best. The press was making a big thing out of the matchup.

Nick Buoniconti is a tremendous middle linebacker who pursues as well as anybody in the game. He has good speed and great quickness. We knew we had to run the ball in order to win and Buoniconti was the key. We planned to use countermoves, actually using Buoniconti's fine lateral pursuit to our own advantage. Our runners would start wide, getting Buoniconti on the move, then cut back inside the flow of the play. This would give our guards, John Niland and Blaine Nye, and center Dave Manders good angles to block or shield him off. Calvin Hill's knee was still sore but he could play, so we had all three of our runners ready. Basically, our passing game would be composed of short, play-action passes. Miami's linebackers dropped back deep to get into their zone coverage and I was supposed to hit the backs short. Miami's defense had some tremendous players besides Buoniconti—guys like Bill Stanfill, Manny Fernandez, Jake Scott, and Dick Anderson. There didn't seem to be a weak link.

We landed in New Orleans late Sunday afternoon, full of anticipation. The first look at our motel was sobering. It was right across the street from the airport and we could hear planes going over at all hours. We couldn't believe they would put us in a place like that. Some of the guys didn't particularly like it because the place was twenty-five miles from downtown. I didn't mind that, but those jets certainly bothered me. It didn't help matters when we learned a jet had once crashed into the motel shortly after takeoff, killing eight people.

"This is a cruddy place," Chuck Howley said. "We'll be so damn mad by gametime we'll beat the hell out of Miami."

The Miami Dolphins stayed at the Fontainebleau, several miles from the French Quarter. It sparkled with Old New Orleans atmosphere. Interviews with the players were conducted near poolside, where a

211

pair of trained Dolphins, Jimbo and Tinkerbelle, sometimes played catch with Bob Griese for the cameras.

Coach Landry gave us the night off after we arrived. Everybody went to the Quarter. This would be our last night out before the game. Walt Garrison and Margene Adkins had some disagreement that night and it erupted the next day right in front of my locker. They started flailing away at each other. It didn't last long and they apologized to each other. Margene is really quick but I'd hate to tangle with Garrison. He's a tough sonuvagun. Coach Landry made sure there was no more trouble like that, telling us he'd fine anybody who disgraced the team $5,000.

Problems continued between Duane and the press. On picture day everybody wore game uniforms and was supposed to be available for interviews and pictures at our practice field. Duane just found an empty section in the bleachers and sat down. Soon he was surrounded by a large group of the media but wouldn't talk. Finally, he said, "What time is it?" Somebody told him and he got up and went into the locker room. Then we got down to serious business, sharpening our game plan. Duane worked hard and we relaxed about his situation.

New Orleans is a fascinating place to visit for three or four days if you have nothing on your mind. But Sunday was what it was all about for us and I channeled all my energies in that direction. I'd gone out to eat some shrimp on our night off, then returned to the motel. The only other time I went out was to take my mother, Marianne, and her parents to dinner. There just wasn't time. Coach Landry, Craig, and I studied films in his room almost every night. "Miami is a zone team and you've got to hit the backs," he kept telling me. "You've got to hit the backs. Notice how the linebackers drop back pretty deep. So this leaves our backs open short. Hit them. Let them make the yardage." We also went over what type plays we'd be running in different situations.

The week had been humid and sluggish. But a couple of days before the game it rained, cooling things off. We were warned there might be rain during the game but bright sunshine greeted us on Super Bowl Sunday. There was only a slight wind and temperatures were in the 30s—perfect for football.

I felt confident and excited as the team busses headed for the Sugar Bowl. You must be confident at a time like that. You can't go in waiting for something to happen. You have to believe you're the best and make things happen. We did.

Over 80,000 people were in the stadium and a vast television audience was waiting to watch us play the Dolphins. We certainly knew Miami's capabilities. The Dolphins had won eight in a row, knocking off Kansas City and Baltimore in the playoffs. Most people thought Kansas City would win the AFC but Miami beat the Chiefs by a field goal in the longest game in history, that sudden-death overtime battle on Christmas Day which lasted 80 minutes, 40 seconds. I knew one thing. Once and for all we wanted to stop people from saying the Dallas Cowboys couldn't win the big one and I didn't care whom we had to beat to do it.

The team had a chip on its shoulder. Everybody seemed very short tempered. They were ready and you knew they were going to go.

—*Tom Landry*

Everything builds to this game. Starting in training camp it builds through October and November and into the playoffs. The last game is like the last chapter of a hair-raising mystery story. You wouldn't think of missing it.

—*Pete Rozelle*
NFL Commissioner

There was the same carnival atmosphere on the field

before this game as the year before in Miami. Al Hirt played his trumpet, pigeons were let loose to fly around the field and jet fighters passed over in formation as the national anthem was sung. Finally it all ended—the build-up, the pomp, the practices, the interviews, the planning, everything. It was time for the game.

Both teams started slowly but we got a break on the Dolphins' second possession. We had read all week where Larry Csonka and Jim Kiick had lost only one fumble between them all season. But Csonka fumbled a handoff from Griese which Howley recovered at our 48-yard line. We moved right down to the Dolphins' two, where we faced a third down. Coach Landry called a pass, which depended on my reading the safety and outside linebacker. Duane was swinging out of the backfield into the flat. If the safety and linebacker went with him, I was supposed to throw to Mike Ditka, who should be clear. If they went with Ditka, then Duane would be open in the flat with Tony Liscio moving out to block for him. I got confused. I didn't look at Mike and just threw the ball to Duane. The safety and linebacker stopped him so we settled for a field goal.

In the second period our offense started controlling the Dolphins. Duane and Walt would cut back for daylight, making good gains behind angle blocks. Alworth caught a big eighteen-yard pass as we moved all the way downfield to the Dolphin seven. Lance had told Landry before we kicked the field goal that the cornerback, Curtis Johnson, was favoring him to the inside, that he'd be open on a quick out pattern. I was to try to hit Alworth on the out, just inside the flag. But Johnson made a great play. He was right on Lance. I threw the ball as hard as I could, harder than I can remember throwing a ball at that short a distance. Johnson couldn't react quickly enough and the ball hit Lance. I don't know how he hung on to it but he did. We had a 10–3 halftime lead.

We felt Miami would adjust at halftime to stop our inside running game, which was tearing them apart. So coach Landry said we would start running wide. Again, he was right. We started making good gains outside. Our passing game also picked up. It was as though we'd grabbed hold of the momentum we'd ridden through the final part of the season and playoffs. Everything was working.

We just about finished the Dolphins by taking the second half kickoff, then moving all the way downfield for a touchdown. Duane made a beautiful twenty-three yard run and Bob Hayes ran an end-around for another good gain. We moved to a third down at the Miami three. As we went to the line of scrimmage and I started calling the signals, I noticed the play called would go right into the heart of a Miami overshift. So I audibled, changing the play away from their strength, to the weak side. I rolled out and pitched back to Duane. Dick Anderson, their strong safety, was the only guy who seemed to read the play. He charged in but Duane faked him out and scored standing up.

Our defense was beautiful. Once during the first half Bob Lilly broke through and caught Bob Griese, who had kept retreating while looking for a receiver, for a twenty-nine yard loss. Mel and the other guys were shutting off Warfield as well as anyone ever had.

Then, as the final period started, Chuck Howley, a guy who just has a knack for big plays, made another one. Chuck had been going out and cutting down the wide receiver on his side, Howard Twilley. Griese apparently felt he could send Kiick in Howley's direction and that there was no way Chuck could cut Twilley, get up and make the play. Well, he just underestimated Chuck. He went out and cut Twilley as Griese turned and dropped the ball over toward Kiick. Chuck was so agile and quick that he just jumped off the ground, grabbed the ball and started running down the sidelines. We were going crazy yelling for him. He had some blockers around him and it looked as if he'd go all the way. But he just ran out of gas and stumbled and fell on the Miami nine-yard line. It was just one of those things. Chuck was one of the most balanced and coordinated guys on the team. Was he ever mad! He came off the field, saying, "Nobody touched me. I just fell. I can't believe it."

Two plays gained only two yards. Then Landry called

the same play I'd blown in the first period. This time Miami reacted toward our back in the flat and I threw to Ditka for a touchdown.

Calvin lost a fumble at the Dolphin one or we'd have scored again later. There was some criticism after the game that we were trying to run up the score. Mercury Morris claimed the Cowboys were kicking sand in their faces. That wasn't true at all. You have to keep in mind that so many frustrating things had happened to the Cowboys. So many games had been lost on freakish things, that even with a couple of minutes left to play, we just kept on going. Coach Landry never believed we'd actually won until the final gun.

There were thousands of Miami fans at the game. They'd started out waving these white handkerchiefs, which is their custom. After we got ahead 24–3 you didn't see them any more. Herb Adderley looked up in the stands and said, "I know why we don't see those white handkerchiefs. They're crying in them."

Maybe we had looked unemotional in the two playoff games, but everything erupted as the Super Bowl ended. We were jumping and screaming on the sidelines. I guess the first guy to congratulate coach Landry was Craig Morton. He hadn't played a down but he was a part of it. All of us were. John Niland and some other guys picked Landry up on their shoulders and he smiled broader than I've ever seen him. Bob Lilly started jogging off the field to the dressing room and, suddenly, just jumped straight up into the air. "I felt like I could jump all the way out of the stadium," he said.

The dressing room was bedlam. We were hugging each other and put Clint Murchison and Tex Schramm in the shower. The press came in and you could hardly move. A platform was there for national television interviews. We'd go up, answer a few questions and somebody else would take over. Jimmy Brown had apparently told the network Duane would consent to an interview, the first he'd given all season. It didn't come off too well for the sportscaster, Tom Brookshier.

Brookshier was trying to interview Duane and Brown

was standing beside them on the platform. You could tell Brookshier was nervous. He asked, "Are you as quick and elusive as you looked?" Duane just said, "Evidently." There was a long silence and Brookshier asked, "Do you weigh more for certain games?" Duane looked at him blankly and said, "I weigh as much as I have to." It went on like that. I guess Brookshier felt pretty bad.

A writer came up to me in the dressing room, informing me I'd been voted the Most Valuable Player for the game by *Sport* magazine. Then I made a historic statement.

"Holy cow!" I said.

I know it was typical voting. Like most of the time, the quarterback gets the spoils or takes the blame. This isn't right but it happens. I'd done a good job (hitting twelve of sixteen passes for 119 yards and two touchdowns) but we had set a Super Bowl rushing record with 252 net yards. Duane or Walt could have won the award. I was just one of many who could have received it . . . Renfro, Lilly, Howley, and others. I was extremely proud of it, but I knew a lot of other people deserved it, too.

It took a long time for the dressing room to clear out. Howley looked around and said, "I sure don't remember it being this crowded in Miami last year."

We left no room for second guessing nor doubting. We had won the championship as thoroughly as anybody had. Nobody could say the Dallas Cowboys couldn't win the Big One now. Nobody!

When Roger Staubach left the Dallas Cowboy dressing room after the Super Bowl, he just had time to hug Marianne and his mother before he was engulfed by throngs of well-wishers and autograph-seekers. Two uniformed sailors had waited to shake his hand. Their handshakes were lost amid a hundred others.

Some six blocks from Sugar Bowl an elderly woman watched Staubach walking along the street, surrounded by the crowd. "My, who is that?" she asked. Told it was Roger Staubach, she said, "Why is a world championship quarterback walking?"

217

A little later, at a small gathering of family and friends to celebrate the victory, Mrs. Elizabeth Staubach told Father Joseph Ryan, "I am just overcome with happiness. I couldn't be more proud to be his mother. He's been successful in every area of life . . . as a human being, a husband and father and, once again, as a championship athlete."

We got together in my mother's hotel room for a little celebration. Mother seemed very happy and it made me feel good to see her that way. Then Marianne and I went to the team party back at our motel. The place didn't look so bad after the game and I didn't even notice the jets passing over. Everybody was ecstatic. A great weight seemed to have been lifted off the team. There was a band and Charley Pride, the country and western singer who lives in Dallas, sang for us. But one of the things I remember most was people coming up to me and saying, "This is something you'll never forget. A world championship. That's something to always remember." I believe that.

One of the writers at the party noticed the little finger on my right hand for the first time. "It looks like a pretzel," he said.

"I've dislocated it a few times over the years," I told him. "But it's bent just right, so I don't want to get it straightened out. I can grip the football better this way."

The finger is pretty crooked, bending out at about a 45 degree angle at the middle joint. We laughed about it. Everything was funny, happy. I tell you, a guy can win individual honors and games but there is nothing in sports comparable to a championship. Nothing!

Well, they officially declared me a square the next day. Marianne, my mother and I went to the *Sport* magazine luncheon. They told me that as the Super Bowl's MVP I'd won a sports car. The guy from *Sport* asked me which model I wanted. "Would you mind," I asked him, "if I picked a station wagon?" He looked at me a little funny and said, "A station wagon? Sure, sure that'll be fine." But he told all the writers I picked a station wagon. Ol' Staubach, the square. I didn't have anything against a sports car but we had three kids and could use the station wagon.

A lot of people were also getting the impression I was some kind of religious fanatic. I had thanked God for the victory over national television, which created the wrong impression for some people. I mean, I wouldn't have blasphemed God if we had lost. Some of the writers did a good job, telling about my religious feelings, but others didn't make it sound as though I meant it. God is the center of my life, through thick or thin, whether we win the Super Bowl or lose it. I just told everybody I had promised whatever I achieved in sports would be for His honor and glory. I wasn't ashamed about my faith and spoke out.

In one interview a reporter asked me what my ultimate goal was. "My ultimate goal is beyond this life," I told him. "It's going to heaven." Then I added, "All your passes are completed in heaven."

"What about defensive backs?" he said.

"Well, there are no defensive backs up there," I said.

Everybody used that quote. And all the headlines were coming out, saying things such as, "Staubach, the Square Quarterback." The things I was saying just weren't in vogue then. Neither was I, especially. I wore my hair short and didn't dress flashily. Apple pie, God, and American patriotism just weren't things people were speaking about in those days. That's changed now. There were anti-God movements then, but now it has run the cycle, and people more and more are coming back to religion.

When my mother got back to Cincinnati the people she worked for at General Motors had her desk decorated with newspaper pictures of me from the Super Bowl. They had written things on her desk like, "Roger is a winner . . . His mother is a winner." Her friends there told me later how happy she was.

Marianne and I flew to Los Angeles for the Pro Bowl that Monday night. I could have written a headline for that one—Square Goes to Pro Bowl.

18

What Goes Up...

The Dallas Cowboys received some 200 requests a month for Roger Staubach's appearance at banquets, business, social, and charity functions. A special secretary had to be hired to keep up with his mail.

"I keep waiting for Mike Ditka and Billy Traux to bring in the words," said Roger, speaking at a banquet following the Super Bowl.

"I never see Roger now," said Marianne Staubach. "It used to be, wait until after the season and he'd have more time. Now, this is worse than the season. I never see him. I bet Bob Griese isn't that busy."

They were playing the national anthem before the start of the Pro Bowl game in Los Angeles, a week after our Super Bowl victory. Just as the music started, a flock of birds was turned loose to fly around the stadium. Mel Renfro and I were standing beside the NFC bench behind Cornell Green. As the birds flew over us, one of them let loose and the stuff plopped right on top of Cornell's head. Mel and I started laughing. I've never seen Mel laugh so hard in my life. He was just shaking. National television cameras were panning our bench. We must have looked very disrespectful but we couldn't help ourselves. Cornell never moved, standing there all rigid with that stuff on top of his head. He had a lot of hair and we thought maybe he didn't even know what had happened. But when the music stopped he just calmly reached up and took the stuff off his head and threw it away.

The way that Pro Bowl game went, the birds should have used me as a target. I had worked hard in practice getting ready. It was a new experience for me and I wanted to show I was a good quarterback and could throw the ball well. There were, of course, tremendous receivers there, but I discovered that our receivers were just as good as any in the league. Dick Nolan of the 49ers was our coach. He named me as the starter with Greg Landry of Detroit the backup quarterback. And, naturally, I would call my own plays.

Greg had pointed out something to me as we dressed for the game, something which would come back to haunt me later. He just looked at me putting on my shoulder pads and said, "Don't tell me you're going to wear those in the game. Those are the worst looking shoulder pads I've ever seen. As much as you run, you'll get killed."

I was using typical quarterback pads. They were small but gave me more room to throw. Greg, who also ran a lot, was wearing the large pads running backs use. I didn't want to change. A guy gets superstitious about his equipment and, when things are going well, he wants to keep it just the same. So I just forgot what he told me.

Frankly, I'd just as soon forget about that game. Hopefully I can get back to the Pro Bowl one of these days and redeem myself. The players seemed to have a half-assed attitude about the game. There wasn't much blocking, and Buck Buchanan of the Chiefs just kept breaking through and creaming me. We simply weren't executing very well. I was extremely serious but the guys would just say, "Don't worry about this one. It's just another game." I ran fairly well—I had to. But I'd just as soon not talk about my passing. I hit only one of six and had two interceptions.

Greg came in and threw a touchdown pass and did quite well. A lot of the Kansas City players, such as Buchanan and middle linebacker Willie Lanier, had good days for the AFC. Jan Stenerud also kicked four field goals to help the AFC beat us 26–13.

I left Los Angeles for Philadelphia, where I received the Bert Bell award. It's presented by the Maxwell Club, which also gives a trophy to the outstanding college player each year. The Maxwell Award, however, isn't as prestigious as the Heisman Trophy in the college category. I know the Maxwell people sure hate to hear somebody referred to as an ex-Heisman Trophy winner. The banquet and award for being named the outstanding pro player were a tremendous experience for me. Some Navy people were there. So was my former Navy coach, Wayne Hardin, and my high school athletic director, Brother William Schroeder, who was a terrific inspiration during my athletic career. That was also the only banquet where I was honored which coach Landry attended. But that evening set in motion a very tough off-season, one I hadn't expected and was eventually to regret.

Sometimes I've heard the banquet circuit called the knife and fork circuit. An athlete usually gets caught up in it when he wins awards or plays on a championship team. People want to see him, meet him. I can imagine what O. J. Simpson went through after last season, with the fine year he had. I'd gone through it all on a lesser scale after winning the Heisman Trophy. But this was all unreal. There were constant demands for appearances with everybody feeling their particular affair was the most important. I made a promise to myself that, although I would attend these functions, I'd also try to use my time in the off-season for God's honor and glory by appearing at as many charity functions and religious activities as I could without accepting a fee.

I had never haggled over appearance fees, usually getting $100 to $200 before. But after that Super Bowl people were calling and offering $1,000 to $2,000 for personal appearances. I never signed with a speaker's bureau, though a number of them contacted me. Reputable agents charge ten to fifteen percent of a speaking fee, while others will do or say anything to make money.

I allowed myself to be harassed into going to a lot of banquets. I know I was away from home half the time for almost three months following the Super Bowl. One guy followed me from the Pro Bowl to Philadelphia, wanting me to speak at a banquet in Binghampton, New York. I finally just said, yes. Some groups tell an athlete he's won this or that Most Valuable Player award, hoping to get him to come to their banquet for nothing. They'll tell four or five players the same thing, then present the award to the one who attends. Some groups, such as the 101 Club in Kansas City, are reputable but for every legitimate one there are two that aren't. All the people you meet at these banquets are warm and hospitable but the time factor makes it impossible to attend all of them.

There are just all kinds of banquets. A hair spray company, for instance, might want you to attend a function in conjunction with a sports promotion. They really put the compliments on you. A guy could really get into trouble if he started believing everything people said about him at banquets.

One speech was scheduled for me in New Mexico. A man called through a speaker's bureau, saying the fee was $1,500. When I found out it was a fund-raising campaign for a prospective senator I turned it down. I made up my mind to stay away from political functions. But some New Mexico people phoned me saying I was already on the program and that, if I'd come, they'd specifically tell everybody I wasn't there for political reasons. I finally consented . . . and found out firsthand how some of those so-called agents operate.

The agent who originally phoned me had told people running the banquet that he was my representative, which was a lie. Then he charged them $2,500 for getting me. Of course, he told me the complete fee was $1,500. So he had finagled almost 50 percent for himself. The bad thing about this is that it reflects on you, though you might not even know about it. The people being tapped just figure you're the one who's charging the exorbitant fee. I can't emphasize enough the importance of dealing with reputable agents, and there are a lot of them.

After a while I got to thinking what a crazy merry-go-round I was on. Here I was accepting money for appearances and not doing what I had promised—making appearances and doing work for religious and charity organizations. So I just told myself, look, for every banquet or appearance you get paid for, do one free for a

223

good cause. I established priorities such as the Fellowship of Christian Athletes, the Boy Scouts, the Salvation Army and also became involved with Easter Seals. Naturally, I still had to turn down what I'm sure were some worthy causes and I hope people understand there just wasn't enough time. But for every one I turned down, I was also turning down one for a $1,000 speaking fee.

I've really cut down now. I made only a few speaking engagements after the 1972 season and did little following the '73 season, probably turning down at least twenty for $1,000 to $1,500 apiece. I try to make up for the money lost by working that much harder in real estate, thus limiting my appearances to charity functions. Fortunately, the real estate business has been good to me. I've worked for the Henry S. Miller Company since coming to Dallas, often making as much, if not more, money in a year than the Cowboys pay me. In 1972 I made almost $15,000 more than my Cowboy contract called for. A great benefit working in real estate is that it allows me to be home nights with my family and not on the road half of the time as I was after that Super Bowl victory.

I had just finished my original three-year contract with the Cowboys when we won the Super Bowl. My base salary had been $25,000 a year. The new contract was also for three years running through the 1975 season, and I received a substantial raise. If I qualify for all the incentive bonuses in a season it still amounts to well under $100,-000.

Endorsement offers also rolled in after our championship. Bob Griese and I had done a television commercial for Vitalis which ran during the Super Bowl. We made $5,000 apiece and it was fun, with each of us chiding and kidding back and forth. But later, I was sorry I had done it. The Super Bowl was very serious and here I was bantering with Bob on television. In retrospect this just didn't look good.

There were offers to do everything—shampoo my hair on television, shaving, endorsing laxatives, just everything. Some of the things I turned down frustrated my friend and attorney, Roy Coffee, who was very instrumental in some valuable contract negotiations, but I felt I had to make my own decisions as to the type of things I'd do. I didn't want to get into anything which might reflect negatively on football or myself.

One of the best working relationships I have is with Aurora, a toy company with family-oriented games. Charles Diker signed me for Aurora right before the Super Bowl. Aurora uses me in the right vein and, besides endorsing products, I'm also on their advisory board and do public relations work for them. I helped with terminology for their Monday Night Football Game, which has been a big seller. I also attend a toy fair in New York each year. On a national level I've also had a good relationship with Haggar Slacks, as well as Colorcraft. Regionally, I found that things went better with Coke.

Marianne, who was a couple of months pregnant, went with me to the toy fair that first year. We really had a good time in New York, going to see *Applause* and then out to dinner and dancing at El Morocco. While we were eating I got to thinking what a difference a year can make, a championship can make. "Do you realize," I told her, "that this time last year we'd been to a movie and stopped at McDonald's for a hamburger?"

I'll never forget that rat-race after the Super Bowl. Nothing has ever equaled it for me. But after almost three months of constantly being on the go, something happened which brought me back down to earth. I was in Greensboro, North Carolina, in late March, taping a commercial for Panasonic which would be for a syndicated show on the Heisman Trophy.

Marianne had some bleeding during her pregnancy. The doctor had been concerned at first but her problems seemed to have subsided and things looked all right. I was in that studio working on the commercial when a call came in from Dallas. Marianne had been taken to the hospital. She'd had a miscarriage. They had been trying to phone me at the motel and had a difficult time finding me. I was just sick. Here I was doing a commercial and Marianne was going through a thing like that without me. I

225

should have been there. It was very traumatic for her, having gone through the stillbirth with Amy a year earlier.

I got on the first plane back, worrying all the way about Marianne and doing a lot of soul-searching. The doctor assured me that my absence had nothing to do with the miscarriage. But I had been gone too much, neglecting Marianne and the girls. It wasn't worth it. Nothing was. I still do a few speaking engagements now and am away from home once in a while, but nothing like that off-season. My family is too important.

I thought we had one of our better off-season programs after we won the Super Bowl. It started in April and everybody really got involved. Players such as Roger Staubach, Mike Ditka, and Bob Lilly would often work twice a day, setting examples for everybody.

Roger and Lilly, I know, gave up a lot of opportunities to make money because of their involvement in the off-season program. They were looking at themselves as teammates first, then they tried to take what opportunities they could find without hurting themselves or the team for the coming year.

—Lee Roy Jordan

A number of very nice looking girls came to our practices during training camp in Thousand Oaks. We'd be practicing and then during a break, look over and check them out. (Just looking, mind you.) One afternoon a very statuesque girl stood out above all the rest. She had long red hair, was well built, wore a mini skirt, and a low cut blouse. You couldn't miss her.

As I was leaving the field one of the guys was talking to her and called me over. "Roger," he said, "I'd like you to meet Sister Teresa. She used to be a nun. You're a good Catholic, so I thought you'd like to meet her."

I couldn't believe a nun would look like that. She looked more like one of those sexy Hollywood types. So the next day I went over to her and asked, "Listen, you weren't really a nun . . . were you?"

"Why yes," she said. "Actually, I still am a nun. You see, I was at the convent for three years and now I'm on leave. I like football so I just came over to watch."

I swallowed the whole story, as ridiculous as it seems now. She was dating some of the bachelors on the team, going out and living it up. And all along I was acting very reverent around her and calling her, "Sister Teresa." That had to get the biggest laugh in camp that summer. There weren't many.

I had worked hard in our off-season program, running, lifting weights and throwing from April until we went to camp. I knew staying on top would be more difficult than getting there and wanted to make sure, if things didn't go right for us, I wouldn't be at fault.

We have this game we play. During certain passing drills, a receiver will get a point for dropping a pass and the quarterback gets a point for throwing a bad pass. The loser has to buy everybody Cokes. Yeah, Roger is the judge whether passes are bad or not. Ol' Roger never buys the Cokes.

—*Robert West*
rookie receiver

When the team got to Thousand Oaks something was missing. I'm not sure what it was but I felt it, just an unsteady feeling in the stomach. We worked hard but maybe we lacked some intensity and concentration. Coach Landry has said that there's just a natural letup after achieving a goal like winning the Super Bowl, and that could have been it.

The first big problem that solidified was with Duane Thomas. He almost completely withdrew again, not even taking his meals with the team. He'd check in at meals, then grab some fruit and take it back to his room. Herb

227

Adderley and Calvin Hill tried to talk to him but nobody got through.

I went by his room one day with a couple of apples and an orange. I'd heard he was sick so I wanted to check on him. "You want something to eat?" I asked him, offering the fruit. He wouldn't accept it. He wouldn't talk. He just stood there staring at me. I kept trying to talk to him, bringing up subjects that might interest him. But he didn't say a word.

"Do you want me to leave?" I asked.

"No, I like to listen to you talk," he said.

I noticed his bags were packed and asked, "Are you leaving?"

"No," he said. "I always keep my bags packed."

What happened with Duane was very disappointing. I had seen him a couple of times during off-season and he was communicative. One day we worked out at the practice field. "I'm going to rush for 1,500 yards this year," he said. "I'm going to run for 500," I said. "Are you crazy?" he asked me, smiling. "The way you run?" We both laughed.

Duane even called my house, looking for me one day. Another time I tried to get him to come over for dinner. He almost did but said in the end, "No, I can't do that."

I'm sorry about Duane's problems but he isolated himself more than ever when we got to camp, causing some unrest. It seemed he almost felt it would be against his grain to be with the team off the field. Something just made him extremely unhappy. He had broken off with Jimmy Brown and could have been having problems with management again. I don't know.

What he did at the College All-Star game epitomized his withdrawal. Before the game he just stood there, leaning against the goalpost, while the team came onto the field. He was very alone there.

He did practically the same thing after being traded to San Diego. The only game he was active for was when the Chargers played Dallas. In pregame warm-ups he went in the end zone, put his hands on his knees and stood there

228

for fifteen minutes, looking at the ground. I felt a change of environment might help him but it didn't.

After we had beaten the College All-Stars coach Landry got enough of the problem with Duane and told Tex Schramm to trade him. Duane had missed a couple of practices as tension mounted. We faced a big problem. Coach Landry had told us before the season that everybody would be treated equally with no exceptions. He meant this so when Duane didn't show up for practice, it was all over. Coach Landry went by to talk to him for a final time but apparently got nowhere. Again, some of the players tried to talk to him. I don't think Duane ever had anything against his teammates but was just going through a difficult time of his life. There was a lot of speculation that he was sick, on drugs, this and that, but I did not believe he was on drugs. Dallas traded him to San Diego for Billy Parks and Mike Montgomery. We missed his talent but there was also something else about him, behind his mask. There was a certain warmness, despite the way he acted and some of the things he did.

That College All-Star game was the last time Duane Thomas played for the Dallas Cowboys. Things also didn't work out for him in San Diego, and he was traded to Washington. I've heard he's much happier there and I hope he is. It would be a terrible shame if he didn't fulfill his potential.

I was having my own problems on the field. The preseason was important for me because I wanted to prove I deserved the honors I had received. I wanted to become more consistent.

There wasn't much team enthusiasm for the College All-Star game. The trip to Chicago from Thousand Oaks was very tiresome. We had to bus for over an hour to get to the airport and then fly all afternoon across the country to Chicago. We had nothing to gain from beating the All-Stars but a loss could have been damaging psychologically. They couldn't have beaten us unless there were a lot of goofy breaks but that happens sometimes.

I got knocked out in the second period. I wasn't doing that well anyway, though Gloster Richardson did drop a

229

touchdown pass. We had a lot of fine receivers in camp. We had gotten Parks and Ron Sellers in trades and Lance Alworth and Bobby Hayes were returning starters off a championship team. That dropped pass might have hurt Gloster because he was cut the next week.

Coach Landry didn't mention to the team he was going to cut Gloster, which caused another small riff. That was another example of not communicating. Landry didn't mean anything at all by it but just neglected to tell the team. Gloster had a lot of friends and Mel Renfro and Herb Adderley were especially upset. They didn't feel it was justified to let Gloster go.

We came back to Dallas to play Houston, then returned to Thousand Oaks to get ready for our game in the Coliseum with Los Angeles. I did okay after a slow start against the Oilers but something still wasn't right with me. On the surface things looked fine. I was the starter, coming off a championship season. But the team wasn't coming together and I became very anxious. I started pressing, running more than I should have, trying to make things happen. I became very intense about the situation. This all cost me one mid-August night in the Coliseum. It cost me more than anything that's happened to me in football . . . and almost ended my career.

19

The Off Season

I don't think a lot of people realize what a fine quarterback Roger is. I think he's not recognized as yet for being as good a passer as he is. With the sound coaching and good personnel he has around him I think Roger is in a position to really dominate the game as he plays more and more.

—*Bart Starr*

I don't suppose the good Lord ever created a more conscientious guy than Roger.

—*Sid Gillman*

Any problems the Cowboys have this year will come from key injuries.

—*Lee Roy Jordan*

Those are the worst looking shoulder pads I've ever seen. You'll get killed runing as much as you do.

—*Greg Landry*
a haunting refrain

Asked if he closed his eyes when Roger Staubach took off on his figure-8 scrambles, Tom Landry said, "No, I just sweat him out."

Southern California nights are still comfortable but they do get a little warmer in August. As I remember that Saturday night it was warm, with the day's heat still stored in massive Los Angeles Coliseum. A shirt-sleeve crowd, over

80,000, was filling the seats as we warmed up before we played the Rams in the *LA Times* charity game.

You usually lose the crowd in your mind when you're warming up. Its sounds are never intense but just a steady, constant hum in the background. I felt funny that night. I'm not sure how to describe the feeling but something just wasn't right. There was an uneasiness. I'm not a sooth-sayer but perhaps I just had a slight premonition and then let it pass.

I felt very intense about the game. Things weren't going right for me or the team and a lot was on my mind. I wasn't like an eight-year veteran, who just says, "Hey, this is an exhibition game, take your lumps and let it go at that." I wanted to make sure the team started moving the ball consistently.

We got off to a bad start and I began running, not even waiting for pass patterns to develop. I'd just take off. I was pressing. The game was tied 3–3 but Herb Adderley intercepted a pass and we were deep in Ram territory. We had third-and-nine at the Ram twelve. A pass was called and as we broke the huddle I said, "Come on now. We've got to do it. We've got to score!"

I took the snap, dropping back to pass. A defensive line-man broke loose on my left. I ducked and he went over me. I rolled to my left and Mike Montgomery, sensing I might run, knocked down the linebacker on that side, Isiah Robertson. I took off for the first down. Someone was coming from my right to cut me off . . . a white jersey, middle linebacker Marlin McKeever. I didn't want to go out of bounds, I wanted to score. I ducked my head and drove into him with my right shoulder. A severe burning sensation jarred me before I ever hit the ground. As I moved to get up my shoulder was hurting and just hanging there. Something bad had happened. I had dislocated my left shoulder a number of times but this was worse. Much worse. The shoulder hadn't just popped out. It was loose, hanging by a thread, and I had absolutely no control over it.

I got up, holding my right arm against my chest, trying not to move my shoulder. As ridiculous as it sounds, I

232

remember thinking, it must be broken. . . . I hurt it while scrambling. I've got to get back into the huddle and call another pass. Then I'll stay in the pocket, get hit, and leave the field. Everybody will think I got hurt while in the pocket. I couldn't stand to hear the I-told-you-so's about getting hurt when I scrambled.

But I left the field. Deep down, coach Landry was probably thinking, "I knew it! I knew it!" Still, he didn't say anything. They took me to the dressing room. Dr. John Tomec, who had worked with the team during camp, examined me. He knew right away. "It's badly separated," he said. "I'm afraid that's it for this season."

I was hurting, disgusted, sick. All I had worked for, all I had done was finished by one play. I took Codene on an empty stomach on our flight back to Dallas that night. It made me sick and I vomited. My whole career might be finished. I knew that any time doctors have to operate on a quarterback's right shoulder, that could be it. Sure, your shoulder will be all right but you might not be able to throw as before. The pain might not go away. Once again, I started thinking about people saying, "Well, I knew that would happen if he didn't stop running."

Marianne watched the game on television. Wire service reporters asked her what she was thinking about when I went down. The College All-Star game, in which I'd been knocked out, was fresh on her mind so she said, "I was just hoping he hurt his head again and not his shoulder." This made headlines across the country. Between that statement and coach Landry calling the plays for me, people got the impression I was some kind of brainless jock who couldn't think for himself.

There was a problem the next day. Tex Schramm wasn't sure I should have an operation. Dr. Marvin Knight, Dr. Pat Evans, and another orthopedist were there. "There's no question, we should operate immediately," said Dr. Knight. "This isn't a defined area which could heal. The damn thing is really separated. We have to operate immediately." Schramm finally said, "Go ahead."

Coach Landry was there to see how the operation went and how soon he needed to trade for another quarterback.

233

(No, not really.) He was there to comfort Marianne and stayed for the entire three-hour operation, which I sincerely appreciated. When I woke up the first guy I saw was Dr. Knight. "Everything went well," he said. "We fixed it and cleaned it out good. You'll be fine. . . . You'll be throwing again." I thanked God and Dr. Knight for the way it worked out. Just a very slight mistake and I could have been an ex-football player.

> No, I have no doubts Roger will come back. The same competitive spirit which made him go for that goal line will make him come back.
>
> —*Tom Landry*

I received numerous cards and heard from a lot of people while I was convalescing. Marlin and Sue McKeever sent flowers. One card got my attention. It was signed Sister Teresa.

There was nothing I could do while the pin was in my shoulder, holding it in place. I stayed away from the practice field, not wanting to hang around and just talk. Gradually, I realized you're paid to be a football player and that's it. If you can't play you're of no value. The coaches had a job to do so they never called. I didn't hear from many of the players either. Chuck Howley, Dave Manders, and Lee Roy Jordan took Marianne and me out to eat a couple of times. Bobby Hayes phoned and, of course, Calvin Hill phoned a lot and came by. That was about it.

I began to feel sorry for myself. There I was in the thick of things one day and an outcast the next. I read a lot of books, watched television, got grouchy. I learned how to shave and eat with my left hand, though one writer told me I really hadn't accomplished much until I could use chop sticks with my left hand.

Danny Reeves, the backfield coach, was activated and became backup quarterback. Danny also was a great halfback until he hurt his knees. I knew Danny could handle the job. He had a great football mind and we were a lot alike as competitors, both terrible losers, whether the game was ping pong or football.

Dr. Knight kept the pin in my shoulder four weeks, longer than normal. He knew I'd push myself the minute the pin came out so he wanted to make sure my shoulder was ready. I'll never forget when he pulled the pin out. There was a crunching sound and I almost fainted.

I went to work a mile a minute, working out on the practice field and at Dr. Ken Cooper's Aerobics Activity Center, which is run by a friend of mine, Russ Harris. It was amazing how atrophy had set in and my conditioning had deteriorated. But with Russ pushing me, the extra workouts at the Aerobics Center made a big difference in my coming back so quickly. At first I moved my arm in a circle, then gradually started lifting light weights. Our trainers, Don Cochren and Larry Gardner, worked with me, helping rehabilitate my shoulder. I kept my extra running to myself. I didn't want anybody thinking I was a fanatic.

I was amazed how much conditioning I had lost during my four-week layoff. I pushed myself to get back into shape, taking my frustration out on the track. Sometimes my chest would feel as though it were going to burst but I'd tell myself, beat the Redskins, and run that much harder. I had it in my mind all along I was going to play that season, though a lot of people had written me off. And I also knew the injury wasn't about to keep me from running when the opportunity presented itself. You can't back away or be shy about something like that. You have to go ahead and play your game. The only concession I made was to start using the bigger shoulder pads, which Greg Landry had suggested at the Pro Bowl.

Nine weeks after the operation I was throwing again in practice. My shoulder hurt but just being able to throw the ball did a lot for me mentally. I had to get used to the pain, which never went away that season. But I knew if I could get the strength back in my arm I could stand the pain. A lot of tissues in my shoulder hadn't completely healed and you could press your fingers in there and find the weak spots.

I made the trip to Baltimore in mid-October but didn't suit out. The weather was cold and I threw some on the

235

sidelines and got depressed. My shoulder hurt so much I thought it would take forever to heal.

Coach Landry activated me the following week before we played in Washington. This might have bothered Craig. He had been working his tail off out there and then I was back. But Landry looked at the situation realistically. Sure, I wanted to play and some people felt I should, but Craig was his man. The team felt the same way, knowing it would take me a while before I could do the job again. Washington beat us, 24–20 and I felt my chances to play were good the following game with Detroit. But Craig had a fine night, which solidified his position. All I did was watch.

The team was 5–2 but still not right. It wasn't Craig's fault but the defense didn't have the same intensity as the year before and some inner problems had developed. Coach Landry had angered some players the way he replaced Herb Adderley with Charlie Waters at cornerback. Herb had helped us get to two Super Bowls but coach Landry just pushed him aside without saying much about it to the team. Herb was the type of guy who would get beat but he'd also come up with a big play when the chips were down. Charlie was very aggressive and a better tackler. Maybe he deserved the job. I'm not arguing about that. I just feel coach Landry should have said something to the team about Herb. He eulogized Herb in the newspapers and I think he could have avoided some of the discontent if he had been more personal with the team.

Coach Landry and his staff also couldn't decide on the starting wide receivers, playing musical chairs with Lance Alworth, Bobby Hayes, Billy Parks, and Ron Sellers. Lance and Bobby had been starters on the championship team and were very unhappy about the situation. Craig had more success with Ron, so he played more than the others and made a number of big plays for us.

I still can't believe Bobby Hayes didn't make a touchdown that season. Bobby started slowly with a lot of little nagging injuries. Then he got in there and dropped some key passes. When this happened he started pressing, which I can tell you from my own experience isn't good.

The coaches seemed to have lost some confidence in Lance as a receiver so he was used mostly as a blocker. Personally, I felt he'd lost some speed but could still make the big catch. He had been a great receiver and resented the fact they didn't include him more in the passing game.

Billy Parks was something else. He had all the ability in the world but wouldn't always use it. Some days he just didn't want to play football. Coach Landry and Sid Gillman, who had coached Billy in San Diego before joining the Cowboy staff, kept trying to pull a consistent effort out of him. I couldn't stand to see Billy goof around in practice. I couldn't conceive why he'd do it. Some days he'd work hard and others he'd just say his leg bothered him and stand around.

Billy and I were good friends but we'd argue a lot. At that time I was for Nixon and he was a McGovern man. Billy was a sensitive, completely idealistic guy with a lot of deep feelings. He'd have given the shirt off his back to anybody but, as a professional football player, he just didn't have the killer instinct while he was with Dallas.

Billy Parks was completely involved with those he befriended. At times he would feel bad when he started in place of Lance Alworth, whom he liked. Once he was supposed to start the Green Bay game but said he didn't feel like playing. Tody Smith, a close friend, had been deactivated that week and Billy was emotionally upset.

Prior to the San Francisco game in Dallas on Thanksgiving Day a special program was held in which Melvin Laird, secretary of the navy, inducted recruits. Billy, anti-Vietnam and anti-military, had to be restrained in the ramp as the Cowboys waited to go onto the field.

Billy and I agreed on some things, such as the plight of black people. But once I asked him to join Calvin and me in a project to help blacks in West Dallas during Christmas. He disappointed me when he failed to respond. I

237

wonder if he has done anything except talk about these problems.

Gillman and Reeves were also clashing. Danny made no bones about the way he felt. Sid had been hired as a special assistant after a long head coaching career in San Diego. When Danny was activated Sid took over duties as backfield coach, leaving Danny in limbo when I came back. Sid, of course, was a very respected coach but he didn't know our system as well as Danny. Danny resented some things Sid wanted to change and often contradicted him, keeping guys in the backfield thoroughly confused. Coach Landry made a mistake letting this situation continue. It eventually led to Danny quitting. Danny, with his great football mind, would make a fine coach. He's now in the business world but I hope he gets back into coaching some day.

Tody Smith, another guy with tremendous ability, was also unhappy. Tody was a tough, aggressive defensive lineman but didn't want to play Landry's coordinated defense, preferring to free-lance more, as he had done in college. There had been problems with him in training camp. He left for a while and was fined.

When I think about all of our problems that season I believe the team did better than could be expected.

Me? I was just there, doing more observing than playing. I did get very upset when we played San Diego. We had a 31–0 lead so Landry told me to warm up. I waited. San Diego scored a couple of touchdowns. "You won't be going in now," he said. I was mad. I thought, he doesn't even believe I could have held a 32–0 point lead. I know I took it all the wrong way but I was ready to play again. We finally won 34–28.

We outscored the Cardinals 33–24 as I watched again. Finally, I got in for the first time against Philadelphia, a team we beat 28–7. I was lost. Everything was confusing and I was just seeing flashes of things I should have seen clearly. It was like being a rookie all over. My arm was stiff, and hurt, but at least I had gotten my feet wet.

Doug Scovil, my quarterback coach at Navy, was on the 49er staff and came over to me on the sidelines before our Thanksgiving Day game. "How do you feel?" he asked.

"I feel good. I hope I get in there today."

"I hope so, too," said Doug, "I hope we get so far ahead you'll get a chance to play."

I laughed, "Thanks! That's a good way to look at it! You'll get so far ahead even ol' Staubach will get to play."

Well, the team fell apart against the 49ers and I did get to play. Linebacker Skip Vanderbundt dealt Craig a lot of misery, picking up one of his fumbles and running it for a touchdown and then intercepting a pass and returning it for a score. We were getting beat so badly Landry put me in. I was lousy.

People were really coming down on Craig and I think this hurt him psychologically. He had been doing a good job and we all knew it, yet he was booed in the 49er game and some of the press started criticizing him. This made the whole team mad. Sure, I wanted to play but Craig had done well and I was pulling for him. He reacted like a man when I got the job the year before and I wanted to be the same way.

The team picked up again and Craig led us past Washington, giving us a 9–3 record and a probable spot in the playoffs as the wild card team. We led the Redskins 28–3 at halftime and finally won 34–24. That was our trend all season: get ahead and hold on.

Alworth was used in that game to crack down on the outside linebacker, which helped our wide running game. Lance, coming in motion back toward the ball, would veer over as the ball was snapped and block Jack Pardee. It was a completely legal block. But, typically, George Allen said after the game the block was vicious and illegal. Allen was using that as a ploy to get his team fired up for us if we played again in the playoffs. He didn't want our victory to have an adverse psychological effect on his team so he tried to convince everybody we'd won because of something illegal. Ironically, Charley Taylor cracked back on Chuck Howley, tearing up his knee. Taylor's block was a lot more questionable than Alworth's.

The loss of Howley hurt, though D. D. Lewis stepped in

and did a fantastic job at weakside linebacker. D. D. just hadn't played that much. But this reminded everyone again how our team had changed from the one which won the Super Bowl.

Some observers felt Landry and his staff had pushed for changes too soon. Others believed the Cowboys were replacing some starters just in time.

Players were replaced, others injured, but nine new players were in the regular line-up as the season ended. On offense Morton had replaced Staubach and Alworth and Hayes were relegated to part time duty, dividing time with Parks and Sellers. Tony Liscio had retired, leaving left tackle to Ralph Neely. Duane Thomas had been traded so Calvin Hill was the top running back.

Defensively, Bob Lilly spent some of the latter part of the season on the sidelines, nursing a sore back. In some, Lilly would make only a brief appearance, giving way to Billy Gregory. Waters completely took over left corner from Adderley. And finally, Lewis moved in for the injured Howley.

The team which represented the Cowboys in 1972 playoffs was far from the same team which won the Super Bowl.

Our last regular season game with the Giants hurt us in the playoffs. Everything went wrong for Craig and we trailed 20–3 at the half. I came in and we really turned it around, putting exactly zero points on the board and losing 23–3. Coach Landry was extremely worried about the way we finished the season. Our 10–4 record was good but we had no momentum and, for the first time in seven years, the Cowboys weren't going into the playoffs as a conference or divisional champion. Washington had won the NFC East. We were the wild card and had to play the 49ers in Candlestick Park two days before Christmas.

I was throwing better the week before we played San Francisco. I felt about 90 percent of the strength was back in my arm. If I got the chance, I was confident I could help this time.

When Billy Zeoli, a regular speaker at our team devotionals, talked to us the morning of the 49er game, his topic was, "Never Give Up." That also turned out to be the theme of our game.

Shortly after we took the field to warm up, Doug Scovil came over to me again. "How are you feeling? I hope you get in there today," he said.

"I'm feeling great," I told him. "I just hope I get a chance to play."

This was practically the same conversation we'd had before the Thanksgiving game. But as he started walking away I said, "Doug, if I get in there today, I'm going to pull it out."

It could have been the hangover from the Giant game that coach Landry had feared. We just didn't have it. Lilly's back trouble had had him in the hospital part of the week. He tried to play but couldn't. Vic Washington ran the opening kickoff back ninety-seven yards for a touchdown. We were behind before the game was hardly started. Then things started going against Craig.

Late in the first period Morton's blocking broke down and he was running for his life. Safety Windlan Hall hit him and he fumbled to defensive end Tommy Hart at the Dallas 15-yard line. The 49ers scored in six plays. In that same period Craig threw long for Billy Parks and the old Cowboy nemesis, linebacker Skip Vanderbundt, intercepted at the Dallas 32-yard line. San Francisco scored in five plays.

When we were behind 21–6 in the second period I thought coach Landry would put me in. But just as the half ended Alworth beat all-pro cornerback Jimmy Johnson on a post and Craig hit him for a twenty-eight-yard touchdown. We were back in the game although we'd done very little.

But in the third quarter Calvin lost a fumble to San Francisco at our 1-yard line and the 49ers went ahead

28–13. We knew the game had all but slipped away. Craig had one last chance. He threw a bomb to Hayes but Bobby let the ball slip away at the goal line. It would have been a tough catch but a possible one.

Dallas was behind 29–13 with 1:48 left in the third period when Tom Landry told Roger Staubach to go in.

"I felt I had to do something to change the mood of the game," explained Landry. "We hadn't been doing much for three quarters and Roger has a way of turning things around. I decided to use him."

Landry told me to warm up. I didn't see Craig's reaction but everybody said he was obviously mad and disgusted. Yet, he came over and talked to me about the situations I might face. "I have confidence in you," he told me. "You can win."

The way I started didn't look as if I could do much of anything. I completed a twenty-five-yard pass to Parks on a post. Then the bottom started falling out. Cedrick Hardman got by Neely on a play action and when I turned around, boom! On third down I fumbled while scrambling and San Francisco recovered.

On one of his first plays, Staubach was trapped by a lineman and kept his feet. He was going nowhere but he wouldn't fall down. Another 49er hit him and he kept his feet, though his helmet was jarred sideways on his head. Finally, a third 49er plastered him and down he went. You could read the unbelievable determination and fury all the way from the press box. He was obviously disgusted that three linemen, outweighing him by over 550 pounds, could bring him down.

Something also was happening to the 49ers. They were growing very conservative, more or less trying to sit on their lead. Our defense picked up. Calvin broke loose for forty-eight yards to set up a field goal. At least we felt the final margin of defeat might be respectable.

The 49ers still weren't worried. "Hey, now you guys know how it feels to lose!" Dave Wilcox kept yelling across the line of scrimmage. Some of the other players were laughing on the sidelines and many of the fans had already left. I heard later they were whooping it up, yelling and giving each other the victory sign.

Dallas, trailing 29–16 got the ball at its own 45-yard line with 1:53 left to play after Jim McCann punted only thirty-two yards off the side of his foot. San Francisco, knowing the Cowboys had to pass, launched an all-out rush at Staubach. Roger hit three passes in a row, two just ahead of the blitz, moving Dallas to a first down at the 49er 20-yard line.

Bruce Taylor is a good cornerback. We felt before the game Parks could beat him on the post. I was calling my own plays but during a time-out coach Landry said, "The post to Parks will be open."

Billy made a tremendous move and I hit him. He scored with 1:10 left. We were behind 28–23 and I felt, at least, we had achieved something. Frankly, I still didn't think we could possibly win because we'd have to recover an onside kick. Chances of that were a thousand to one. But when I came off the field, there was electricity around our bench. Everybody was jumping up and down and yelling. They thought we could win and I got caught up in the optimism.

San Francisco loaded its front line with receivers and defensive backs, anticipating the inevitable onside kick. Toni Fritsch approached the ball and, just as he started to kick, he slung his right foot behind his left and nudged the ball sideways to his right. This seemed to momentarily confuse the 49ers.

"The other team," Toni said, "they don't know which way comes the ball."

The ball rolled to Preston Riley right in front of our

bench. A backup linebacker, Ralph Coleman, crashed into him and the ball squirted loose. Mel Renfro dived on it. I couldn't believe it.

I was really nervous as I went back onto the field. The 49ers had to wake up now. They'd be ready. The crowd was dead quiet. I knew we could win!

We had a first down at mid-field with 1:03 left to play. I worried about the clock but as I dropped back to pass, I saw a huge hole up in the middle. I didn't even look for a receiver but started running and got inside the 30-yard line.

I called a corner route to Billy. Taylor was right on him but Billy caught the ball, balancing on the out of bounds mark, then stepping out at the ten. Now, I knew the clock was no problem. I called a "62 Wing Sideline," planning to throw to Parks, our hot receiver. Sellers, in at tight end on passing situations, told me as we broke the huddle, "Look at me. They're not covering me over the middle. I'll be open. I can beat Hall on the hook."

There was no time to look for Parks. San Francisco had an all-out blitz. I saw it coming and quickly threw the ball to Sellers. He caught it right in his stomach for the touchdown and started jumping up and down in the end zone. I just exploded inside. So did everybody else. Larry Cole was doing cartwheels onto the field. I'd never seen anything like it. Craig Morton caught me and started hugging me before I ever got off the field. I turned back and saw Wilcox's helmet bouncing about fourteen feet in the air. The 49ers were like ghosts. We scored twice in the last minute and a half to win.

Dick Nolan met coach Landry at mid-field just after the game ended. "I don't believe it," he said. "I just don't believe it."

"That's the greatest comeback we've ever had," said Landry.

Our dressing room was bedlam. I had been almost left alone by reporters after our games but now they all crowded around me. Finally, one asked me about Washington the following week. "The Redskins have to beat Green Bay first," I said. "That game could go either way.

So I don't know who we'll be playing. I don't care either."
There wasn't any question in my mind that I'd be starting.
I was wrong. Newspapers in Dallas the next day quoted
coach Landry as saying he wasn't sure whether he'd start
Craig or me. At first I couldn't believe this. Then my perspective returned. I had played about 13 minutes of a
playoff game. Craig had played the entire season. I realized logically I might not be playing.

The quarterback debate was on again. I must have had
fifteen calls from reporters, not one of whom said Craig
should be starting. Coach Landry kept everybody in sus-
pense until Thursday after practice, then called Craig and
me over.

"Craig, you've performed well all year," he said. "You
put us into the playoffs. But I've decided to go with Roger,
which is certainly no reflection on you.

"The primary reason is that Roger brought us into this
game. I saw us put things together in those last few
minutes of the 49er game like we haven't all season. I believe we have momentum going now. If what I saw was
right, then Roger will continue this trend against the Redskins."

Again, I felt sympathy for Craig. He just walked off.
But I had to start getting ready for Washington. When I
got home that night and opened the door, Jennifer, who
was then six, came running up. "Daddy, Daddy, have you
heard the good news!" she screamed.

"I think I *have* heard something about it," I told her.

Our NFL championship game with Washington had everything—two good teams, different philosophies, controversy. I thought we had things going for us again. I was
sure in my mind we'd beat Washington.

Coach Landry planned to beat the Redskins with our
running game, the same approach we'd used so effectively
in Dallas. We also put in a new passing game for third
downs when we had to throw. We would use four wide receivers—Parks, Hayes, Alworth, and Sellers—at the same
time. This confused me and the receivers. Half the time I
know Billy was just out there running around in never-
never land, confused with the new formations.

Washington was really fired up. The Redskins, their fans, everybody was just vibrating before the game. Billy Kilmer, who had a great day, said later it was the best game the Redskins played that year. We got behind 10–0. Then I bootlegged against the flow and ran twenty-nine yards to set up a field goal. To give you some idea how thoroughly Washington shut down our running game, outside of that run we only netted sixty-seven yards rushing. Later Fritsch missed a short field goal and we were behind 10–3 at halftime.

We talked about how to improve our running game at halftime. But when we came back out Calvin started wide and Pardee broke through and threw him for an eight-yard loss. Jack was one of the finest linebackers I've ever seen. He was very smart, seeming able to stare into our huddle and know exactly what we were going to do. He kept getting the Redskins in just the right defense to stop us. I was glad to see him retire.

We just missed on everything we tried. We'd come up a yard short on key third downs. Calvin overthrew Walt Garrison by inches on a halfback pass which would have been a touchdown. But we still felt we could win with a break. We got it! Kilmer fumbled in the third period with the ball rolling deep into Redskin territory. First Cornell Green seemed to have the ball but lost it. Lee Roy had it and then appeared to sling the ball toward the Redskin goal line. Finally, Jerry Smith recovered for Washington.

Our defense played well enough to win but Washington was able to just keep pecking away at us with field goals. Kilmer threw two touchdown passes to Taylor and the rest of the Washington points came on Curt Knight kicks.

Twice Taylor caught bombs on streak routes down the sidelines. He ran straight downfield and under a fifty-one-yard bomb behind Waters to set up the first touchdown. Then in the final period he raced behind Mark Washington to catch a forty-five-yard touchdown pass. Waters had suffered a badly broken arm attempting to return a punt and Washington had replaced him.

I completed only nine of twenty passes. I was the culprit. I've studied films of that game a hundred times. I don't think I was doing something bad so much as I just wasn't making anything happen. Our 26–3 loss to Washington that year was the first game I could remember where, win or lose, I wasn't a positive factor for my team.

Maybe Craig could have done better. He might have keyed quicker but I'm not sure how much difference he could have made, considering the Redskins took away our running game. As far as the general public, I don't believe Craig could have taken another loss, whereas in my own case, the loss swung a lot of public sentiment toward Craig.

I left Roger in because we didn't move the ball at all. If we had been in a different situation, moving the ball but having the breaks go against us, I would have put Morton in. Roger didn't have a good game. But under similar circumstances I'd go with him again.

—Tom Landry

I felt terrible about the defeat but then I read what some of the Redskins were saying and it burned me up. Diron Talbert said coach Landry should have gone with Morton. "Staubach was rusty," he said. From what I've heard since then, Allen was worried about me because of my unpredictability and the fact I'd had some success running against Washington. Still, they did a lot of talking. I don't ordinarily get into verbal battles in the newspapers but I said publicly, "Next time they'll have to kill me." What happened that day in Washington and what the Redskins said stayed with me that entire off-season.

20

One to Remember

Washington had unseated the Dallas Cowboys as Eastern Division champions, marking the first time in seven years Dallas hadn't won a conference or divisional title. Redskin and Cowboy officials and players had not kept hard feelings about each other secret.

Many felt the Cowboys had shown definite signs of decline in 1972 and expected the pattern to continue. Roger Staubach, disappointed in the playoff loss to Washington and upset about Redskin players saying he was rusty, said, "They'll have to kill me next time."

"That's the kind of attitude we need to face the challenge this season," said Tom Landry.

"There should be hard feelings on both sides," said Redskin defensive tackle Diron Talbert. "That's the way the Redskins and Cowboys ought to feel. If Roger didn't feel like that he wouldn't be the competitor he is. Hell, there's a lot of emotion in this rivalry. No one should be playing in a Dallas–Washington game if he can't play with a lot of emotion."

Inside the Cowboys, Landry planned to let Roger Staubach and Craig Morton call their own plays in preseason and, hopefully, settle the quarterback issue once and for all.

I had anxious moments about my shoulder during the off-season of 1973. After my operation the pain just hadn't gone away. When I threw I'd feel an ache and sometimes a sharp pain. I worked with weights on my right arm and shoulder and had all the strength back but the pain was affecting my delivery. It killed me when I tried to throw in March. Finally, I just decided to lay off completely for a while. Strangely enough, when I came back and started throwing a few weeks later the pain was gone. My shoulder was back to normal and I'll always be thankful to Dr. Marvin Knight for the job he did.

I devoted myself during the off-season to making up for our playoff loss to Washington. Most of the players felt the same way. Our sights were set on beating the Redskins, which I think hurt us in the end. We thought only about beating Washington, not winning the Super Bowl. I believe we learned after last season that your ultimate goal must be winning the Super bowl, as ours had been our championship year, and not just beating one team. But George Allen had changed our situation. No longer could the Cowboys walk through their division into the playoffs. From now on we'd have a dogfight on our hands with Washington just to win the division.

There was a lot of unrest during the off-season. We were shocked when Ron Sellers was traded to Miami for Otto Stowe, a wide receiver we knew nothing about. Players such as Jethro Pugh, Mel Renfro, Lee Roy Jordan, Dave Manders, and Bob Lilly, were very vocal in their unhappiness over contracts.

One of the truly great players in Cowboy history, Chuck Howley, had retired. Some players felt if management had offered any encouragement Chuck would have played another season. Chuck was thirty-seven but had come back strong from knee surgery, running a 4.9 in the forty-yard-dash during the off-season.

You couldn't keep the guy down. Before we played Baltimore in 1972 Chuck had a bad hamstring pull. We had gone out to eat the night before the game and coming out of the restaurant we had to chase a cab. Chuck could hardly walk, much less run. Well, the next day he played to stay in shape and be ready in case something happened and had a fine game as usual.

Chuck certainly could have played another year but apparently he wasn't sure he wanted to try. He finally agreed to stay in shape and be ready in case something happened to D. D. Lewis at weakside linebacker. The club faced another problem if Chuck had decided to play again. D. D., who was certainly capable, had been waiting around for four years to take his place and wasn't content to sit on the bench another year. So I'm sure Chuck and the coaches had a lot to consider.

I was beginning to feel that the players were ready to go after Washington but management wasn't. Our players had contract problems but apparently Washington players didn't. We kept hearing about all the money the Redskins were making. This didn't help the situation.

Frankly, I was very concerned as we reported to training camp. A number of players had hinted they might not show. Lee Roy made the first important concession. He hadn't signed his contract but came to camp and said, "I'm putting all this off-season stuff out of my mind. I want to help the Cowboys win the Super Bowl and I'll do it whether I play out my option or not."

Lee Roy and I roomed together, adjoining Craig's room. Just as the veterans were reporting Craig walked into our room and said, "I'm leaving. I've had enough. I can't work out anything with Schramm on my contract so there's no reason for me to stay around."

At first I said, "Yeah, you want me to have to do all the passing here and throw my arm out. Then you'll come back in fresh and really be zinging the ball." But he was serious and left.

Newspapers were full of stories about our state of chaos. Then something else very strange happened. Lilly flew from Dallas to Los Angeles, where he was to be picked up and driven to camp. On the way he became depressed over the state of mind the team was supposed to be in and, after landing in L.A., he got on another plane to Las Vegas, then returned to Dallas, determined to retire.

This put everybody in a panic. Lee Roy and I phoned him. A lot of other players talked to him, too. We asked him to come back, telling him we needed him. I've never seen Schramm move so fast. It was probably the first time in his life he really went after a player. Tex jumped on a plane to Dallas to see Lilly.

"Anytime a Bob Lilly quits, you're damn right I'll go after him," Tex said.

Lilly finally consented to at least come to camp and see the situation for himself. "The attitude is a lot better than I've heard," he said. "I want to play on this team."

Reporters were calling our training camp "The Shambles." One day Mike Ditka, who had retired and become our receiver coach, started kicking a blocking dummy all over the field. When somebody asked him what he was doing, he said, "Oh, I'm just kicking some of the shambles out of the way."

John Fitzgerald and Dave Manders were supposed to be in a big battle for starting center. But there was no battle. Dave didn't show, saying he had officially retired. John's a tremendous player and a great blocker, but Mandy is the best snapper in the league on punts and field goals. All the time I had played with him the ball always came to me just right. We'd never fumbled a snap. He retired because management wouldn't give him $2,500 more in his contract. "I'm about to find out how much clout I have," I told a friend. "I'm going to tell Tex I want Mandy back."

I asked Tex, "How can you lose people over a few thousand dollars when we're all working and trying to catch Washington?"

"We've got guidelines we must go by," he said. "We have players in certain categories who are paid accordingly. We also must keep individual salaries in proper perspective to a player's contribution to the team. If you pay one player higher than the bracket he's in, then you should pay everybody else more.

"Overall, I feel the Cowboys are paid well," Tex said. "We don't have a lot of guys paid extremely high but, on an average basis, they're paid as well as anybody in the league."

He didn't give Mandy the extra $2,500. I found out how much clout I had. But I was worried about so many players being upset. I've never had any contract problems, though I probably could have gotten more money if I'd really tried. Still, quarterbacks are usually paid more money, plus they get more commercials and outside deals so I felt I wasn't in any position to try and get the guys to sign for less money than they wanted. Then I came up with an idea. I told one of the players at the meeting, "You know what we should do? We should just throw all the money into a pool and divide it by forty. That way everybody's making the same and we can just go out and play." Of course, everybody laughed but I was half serious about the idea.

Craig came back a week before our first exhibition with the Los Angeles Rams. He felt he had reached a verbal agreement with Schramm. So the competition was on again. I certainly felt we should battle for the job, that neither of us deserved to have it handed to him. Craig and I have an astonishingly good relationship, considering we were always fighting for the No. 1 job. I can honestly say I was pulling for him to do well every minute in 1972. I believe he felt the same way about me in 1971. But I don't care what anybody says, when you're in competition with somebody it's human nature to feel negative about him.

We don't socialize off the field because our life styles are so different. I'm married and he's a bachelor. Our outside interests obviously are going to be different. But we have a mutual respect. Both of us had also expressed our feelings to coach Landry about calling our own plays and he consented to let us, at least in preseason.

Craig had gotten behind when he walked out of camp so I got to start against the Rams. The Coliseum was where I'd been injured so I wanted to make sure I didn't flinch. I ran the ball when I felt I should without any hesitation at all. And the team came together. It put all problems aside and played very well against the Rams, winning 24–7. Otto stepped right in and eased everybody's minds. I had worked with him some during the off-season and noticed how explosive he was off his break. He had a great year for us before he suffered a broken foot at mid-season. I think Otto will become one of the game's great receivers. Some of the rookies, such as Rodrigo Barnes, Harvey

Martin, and Drew Pearson, looked good and the veterans all played hard.

The team seemed happy again, and hungry, which hadn't been the case after our Super Bowl victory. Lilly came into my room when we got back to camp and said, "You know, this team has character."

I was happy about the way our team was coming together but, of course, I was worried about my mother's illness and hated the suffering she was going through.

Neither Craig nor I knew where we stood as we came down to the final two exhibition games in Dallas against Kansas City and Miami.

Roger Staubach completed seven of nine passes for 111 yards in the Cowboys' 27–16 win over Kansas City, whereas Craig Morton went five of ten for sixty-four yards, suffering two interceptions.

However, Morton was very instrumental in helping the Cowboys come back in the second half to beat Miami 26–23 on Toni Fritsch's field goal with three seconds left. After entering the game with Dallas trailing, 23–13, Craig hit on thirteen of eighteen for ninety-nine yards and a touchdown. Roger had completed four of eight for sixty-five yards and a touchdown in a losing first half cause.

For the preseason Staubach's statistics read forty-two completions in sixty-seven attempts for 671 yards and five touchdowns while suffering three interceptions. Morton's totals wre thirty-five of fifty-two for 399 yards, three touchdowns and three interceptions.

Broadcasters had mistakenly said on national television that the Cowboy quarterback issue would be settled by the Miami game. Coach Landry had given no indication whatsoever of this. Craig had come into the Miami game and done well but I had the edge for the preseason as a whole. Still, Craig felt he should get the job after the Miami game and so did some of the fans.

Cowboy fans were split over us, though the only feedback I got on the situation was what I knew through the media. Since I've been with the Cowboys I've only received three negative letters. But I read letters fans had sent to the *Dallas Times-Herald* that dragged me over the coals.

Once again, some people were saying Coach Landry favored me because we were both very active in the Fellowship of Christian Athletes. Coach Landry had nothing to do with my joining the FCA. Bruce Bickel, the FCA's regional director in Chicago, got me interested when we were teammates at the Naval Academy. I believe coach Landry likes my complete dedication to football but he also knows Craig is more in the mold of what he feels a pro quarterback should be. I've worked more on the mental aspect of the game the last couple of years, spending more time studying films, and I believe this has helped me some in his eyes. But actually, he's probably had more personal contact with Craig than me. There's no way coach Landry would let his feelings for anybody influence his football decisions. He makes the ones he believes are best for the team.

Our paths have crossed socially in FCA work and also work for the Paul Anderson Youth Home. But we've never even had dinner together. I did play eighteen holes of golf with him once. I bet he didn't say fifteen words to me.

We've disagreed numerous times but I have a tremendous amount of respect for the man. He doesn't have a close relationship with anyone on the team. However, I know he can be a very personable man because I've heard him speak and watched him with young people. He's a Christian who not only speaks the word but lives by it.

The man is a football genius. It's no accident that the Cowboys have been so successful, making the playoffs eight straight times. It hasn't always been a wealth of talent that has gotten them there. I believe the success has come due to coach Landry's ability to utilize the talent he has and put together a group of individuals as a team. There's no way in a job like he has that all the players are going to like him. But even if he had picked Craig instead of me last season, and then traded me, I still would have left Dallas with a great respect for him.

I really thought I might be leaving. Coach Landry phoned me, asking me to meet him at the practice field a few days after the Miami game. "This is it," I told Marianne, as I left the house. I had made up my mind I wanted to be traded if I wasn't the starter. Craig was thirty and I was thirty-one. Neither of us had that much time to be sitting around on the bench. As I drove to our meeting I wondered just what all it would take for us to move. Maybe in the final analysis I would have gutted it up and remained on the bench another year. But in my heart I wasn't absolutely sure I could feel positive about Craig if he was playing, and that wouldn't have been good for the team.

Coach Landry and I talked for an hour. He went over my positive points and my negative points. He asked me how I felt about the situation. "Coach, I've given this all a lot of thought," I told him. "I think you need to make a decision and stick by it. If you aren't going to start me I want to be traded. If I have any choice in the matter I'd prefer you traded me to Atlanta." Atlanta was a good aggressive team and, at that time, the quarterback situation there was far from solidified.

It was difficult to read him as we talked. Sometimes I felt he wasn't sure. I knew the man had been around Craig for a long time and certainly felt for him. Craig had come back to camp with a lot of determination. "You're going to be the starter," he finally said. The conversation ended.

Coach Landry asked Craig over to his house that night and told him. Craig immediately said he wanted to be traded as soon as a deal could be worked out. He felt he had won the job and still wasn't satisfied with his contract, so I know he felt pretty low.

For the first time I could hear some people booing me in Texas Stadium, which I hated like everybody else does. Everybody has loyal fans who stick by them but there are others who want somebody new at the slightest provocation. I wasn't the new wonder anymore. I know I'm at the point in my career now where fans will really get after me if I don't do my job, just as they got on Craig and Don Meredith before him. No matter what a player says, the fans' reactions play a great part in his feelings and attitude.

Dallas fans really rode Meredith, which was unfortunate. I have a lot of respect for Don as a quarterback. If Dallas had beaten Green Bay in those two championship games—and it certainly wasn't his fault they didn't—Don would have gone down in history as one of the game's great quarterbacks. People pay their money so they have a right to boo, though a guy's not out there messing up on purpose. He's trying to do his very best.

On the surface I had every chance I wanted now. I was starting again, healthy again, and coach Landry had decided we'd go into the regular season with me calling my own plays. But I still had the feeling Landry wasn't completely sure he should have gone with me over Craig. Some of the fans were upset and all these things added together made me awfully nervous as we went into our regular season opener in Chicago. I certainly hadn't received an overwhelming vote of confidence.

About all I can say about the Chicago game is that we won . . . with help. I didn't throw well, hitting only nine of twenty-two passes. I think I was pressing too hard, trying to prove I should be No. 1. I did manage, however, to complete my famous butterfly touchdown pass to Otto.

The ball apparently slipped in Staubach's hand as he threw for Stowe in the end zone. It looked like a shuttlecock going through the air in a badminton match. Stowe turned completely around, jumped up and caught the ball for a twenty-one-yard touchdown. Staubach also threw an eighteen-yard touchdown pass to Bobby Hayes but he suffered two interceptions. In his defense, four of his passes were dropped.

The game was tied 17–17 with a little over three minutes remaining. I felt we'd probably get one more chance to score, though we'd have to drive the length of the field, as the Bears lined up on fourth and one at their own twenty-nine-yard line. Coach Abe Gibron decided to gamble. Bobby Joe Green was in deep punt formation but the snap went to the short man, Bob Parsons, who tried to run for the first down. Billy Joe DuPree was right there, dumping him for a three-yard loss. We quickly moved into position for Toni's eleven-yard field goal and won the game 20–17.

"I don't remember if anybody blocked me on the play or not," Billy Joe said later. "If they did, I was just bumped. I got on that cat just as he got the ball. He had to pay the price."

I felt if I didn't improve the next week against New Orleans I should start dusting off my old Navy uniform. And I wasn't even around for the finish. Somebody hit me on the head during a scramble, knocking me out late in the third period. Craig came in and did a fine job, winning the week's most valuable player award from the media.

Dallas was leading 26–3 when Staubach, who had completed ten of fifteen passes for 124 yards, had to leave the field. Morton came in, completing five of seven passes and helped Dallas finish off the Saints 40–3.

"Craig did a great job," coach Landry said. "This doesn't surprise me. We know what kind of quarterback he is and we're thankful he's on the sidelines ready to play."

I was a little worried Craig wouldn't stay on the sidelines if I didn't improve. I knew I had to relax, stop worrying about whether anybody thought I should be No. 1 or not and do the job I knew I could do.

Our 45–10 victory over St. Louis was a tremendous boost to my spirits. My mother was able to watch the game and I seemed to be back into the groove again. The team was 3–0, a full game ahead of the Redskins who had been upset by St. Louis. Our next opponent was Washington, the team we'd been waiting nine months to play again. I didn't even get my chance to die on the field.

257

We took a 7–0 lead in the first period, thanks to a fine play by Otto. Working against cornerback Pat Fischer, Otto ran straight downfield for eight or nine strides, faked a corner route and then cut sharply inside toward the goalposts, beating Fischer by several yards. Otto has tremendous explosion off the break and I overcompensated, leading him too far. But he hurled himself through the air and made a diving catch for the touchdown.

Calvin Hill was running well behind good blocking. The way we were moving the ball I thought we'd blow the game wide open. I took some pretty good blows and was having problems. I had injured my leg but felt I could still do the job. We moved in close twice more in the first half but each time I got trapped on third downs, increasing the yardage on Toni's field goal attempts to thirty-eight and thirty-nine yards. Each time he kicked too low, causing the field goals to be blocked in the line. So instead of 13–0 we only led 7–0 at the half.

I wasn't having a great game by any means but Washington had a fine defensive team. We still had our lead when I began having spasms in my leg in the third period. I had to leave the field for one series to have my leg massaged. When I came back in I missed a key on third down and was trapped.

As I came off the field Mike Ditka was yelling, "He missed the key! He missed the damn key!" Coach Landry was mad, too. He felt I'd been hit and was too fuzzy to play. "I'm putting Craig in," he said. I lost my temper completely and started yelling at Ditka, "Thanks Mike, you sonuvabuck! You helped me get put out of the game! We're leading . . . Look!"

Mike is a very fiery guy, whether he's coaching or playing. His attitude is a big plus for our team but he shouldn't have been yelling out like that. He later apologized. Sure, I was a little fuzzy for a while and my leg hurt. But the fact was Landry felt Craig had more experience and wouldn't make the mistakes I was making. I just died on the sidelines as Washington came back and won the game.

Sonny Jurgensen's passes to Charley Taylor had brought the Redskins back to tie the game 7–7. Then late in the final period Dallas faced a third and nine at its own 9-yard line. Under a heavy rush, Morton was an instant late releasing the ball on a turn-in to DuPree. Safety Brig Owens, seeing the play develop, ran in front of DuPree, intercepted the ball and scored from twenty-six yards out with 2:33 to play.

Motron brought the Cowboys back within a yard of tying the game. On fourth down at the Redskin four Craig dropped the ball off to Walt Garrison, who was stopped a yard short of the goal line in a wrestling match with safety Ken Houston.

Dallas had outgained the Redskins 269 yards to 174. But the Redskins had won the first showdown.

Coach Landry told the press he took me out because of my leg. Here I had said they would have to kill me and everybody was thinking I couldn't play with a little Charleyhorse. I told him I didn't want my teammates thinking this so I clarified the issue, telling the newspapers that I was taken out because Landry didn't think I was doing a good job. I still get a little mad when I remember that game. If we had been behind it would have been different, but we were ahead.

The team was down. Everybody felt we had outplayed Washington. We were drained emotionally when we went to the coast to play the Rams, who were undefeated. Los Angeles jumped on us before we knew it, taking a 34–14 halftime lead. Harold Jackson had a tremendous day, the best day a receiver had all year.

Harold Jackson, a 9.2 sprinter, dazzled the Cowboy secondary by catching touchdown passes of sixty-three, sixty-seven, seventeen and thirty-six yards and making another forty-four-yard catch to set up a field goal.

The Cowboys were obviously flat, emotionally and physically. They had lost to Washington on Monday, then faced a short week before playing L.A. on Sunday. Behind twenty points at the half they could have easily folded. Roger Staubach, who was to finish the day with fifteen completions in twenty-five attempts for 173 yards, started extremely slow but threw two second half touchdown passes to Stowe in a dramatic Cowboy comeback.

Dallas pulled within six, 37–31, and was on the move again with two and a half minutes left when Staubach threw his third interception of the day.

Just as I let the ball go on my last interception, defensive end Fred Dryer broke through and grabbed my foot. So the ball sailed over Billy Joe's head right into the arms of Al Clark. I didn't have a good day but it was the game coach Landry apparently decided to go with me win, lose or draw. He could have pulled me at halftime with justification but didn't.

Our cornerback Charlie Waters took a lot of the blame for those bombs to Jackson, though actually he had sole responsibility on only one of the touchdowns. Announcers on national television were blaming him for everything, which was unfair. Charlie, of course, turned out to be a good cornerback, though nobody even thought he'd be able to play last season. He had a lot of problems with the arm he'd broken in our NFC title loss to Washington. While it was in a cast, he was trying to put on his shirt one day and rebroke his arm. Doctors then decided to put a steel rod down through his shoulder to hold the bone together. The bone just wouldn't heal properly and they felt that was the only possible way he could play. His weight was down to 165 and he spent two and a half months in the hospital. Yet, he got himself into shape and came to camp ready to play. He was kidded a lot about that rod. Guys yelled, "Clang!" whenever he'd make a tackle.

Our team showed a lot of character, the way it came back against Los Angeles. I probably called my best game the next week against the Giants. We had a good running game and mixed our plays well. I only threw eleven times (completing eight) and we won 45–28.

Mike McCormack, who had been an assistant with George Allen in Washington, was the new Philadelphia coach. The Eagles had really picked up. They had quarterback problems ever since Norm Snead was traded, but McCormack had traded for Roman Gabriel. It was the biggest deal that season as the Eagles sent the Rams Jackson, Tony Baker, and two future No. 1 draft picks for Roman. They beat us 30–16 because they wanted it more than we did. We moved the ball well but I just wasn't coming up with the big play to get us across the goal line. We also lost Otto for the season. He was having a great day, with five catches the first half. Then as the second half opened one of the Eagles fell on the back of his foot, breaking a bone. I threw more than ever, thirty-nine times (completing twenty-four). We got behind 24–7 and had to throw, which I didn't mind, but Gabriel had a good day and we lost.

So we'd been wiped out by Harold Jackson and Roman Gabriel, principal figures in the big trade. Everybody was posing the question, just who got the worse of the trade? The answer was Dallas.

So we were back at our old familiar stand, 4–3 at the halfway mark. But the attitude was good. The team had never quit, even in games which seemed hopelessly lost. It hurt us losing Otto but first Mike Montgomery and then Drew Pearson stepped in at flanker and took up the slack. Our attitude going into the second half of the season against Cincinnati was that, whatever happened, we would make everybody pay who played us.

I'd rate Cincinnati's defense right up there with Washington's. We didn't move the ball consistently against the Bengals but we had our big play offense going and won, 38–10.

Calvin returned home to the scene of his collegiate triumphs when we played the Giants in New Haven at the Yale Bowl, though there was some doubt whether he'd be able to play. His knee was swollen and he didn't work out the week of the game. Calvin showed a lot of courage last season, playing with the sore knee and taking all the beating he does. But he played and rushed for ninety-five

261

yards. Our defense and specialty teams won the game, getting six turnovers. Assistant coach Gene Stallings had just taken over the specialty units and you could tell a world of difference. Specialty teams put us in scoring position for all but three of our points in a 23–10 victory.

The evening before the game Calvin stood outside the team bus, talking with a policeman. It was dark and we were all tired and anxious to get to the hotel. Calvin stayed at the front of the bus and we followed this policeman all over the campus, with Hill acting as tour guide. We were all yelling at him that we didn't care anything about going on a tour of Yale but he just kept talking.

Garrison had a lot of problems last season. He suffered severe head and neck injuries in preseason, missing a lot of time. Walt had bad headaches for about six or seven weeks after the injury. Robert Newhouse moved in at starting fullback and did a good job. But Walt took over again in late October and just went wild as we got revenge over the Eagles, 31–10. He was the game's leading rusher with eighty-eight yards on thirteen carries and also caught three passes for sixty-five yards and scored two touchdowns.

The big play he made was on a screen pass. I faked a fired pass, a quick throw off the run fake, then pumped and turned toward our tight end as if to drop the ball over to him. Then I came back to Walt on the other side. Our backfield coach, Ed Hughes, had just thought up the play that week and it worked to perfection. Walt caught the ball, broke two tackles and gained fifty-three yards to set up one of our touchdowns. I threw three interceptions that day but we won, which was the most important thing.

On Thanksgiving Day we played the Miami Dolphins, a team which had never beaten us. I threw an interception to set up the Dolphins' first score.

On the Cowboys first possession Staubach threw for Hill, running a crossing pattern with Garrison over the middle. Garrison, coming out of the backfield, was supposed to clear out the area for Hill.

Staubach released the ball just a little too quickly and it bounced off Hill's shoulder pad and into the arms of all-pro safety Jake Scott, who ran twenty-nine yards to the Dallas nine to set up the first score.

Paul Warfield got a note of revenge on Mel Renfro for the Super Bowl. He beat Mel on a deep pattern and took a forty-five-yard throw from Bob Griese for the Dolphins' other TD. Miami led 14–0 at the end of the first period.

We got it together for one tremendous touchdown drive, ninety-four yards in sixteen plays, and used up 8:31 of the clock. There was 14:10 left to play and we seemed to have the momentum. But Charles Leigh returned the ensuing kickoff fifty yards to erase our advantage and put us back into the hole again. We lost 14–7 and the Dolphins had the ball on our one as time ran out.

I put mother back into the hospital just before the Miami game. We knew she wouldn't last the season. Coach Landry called me in for a conference the following week, before going to Denver to play the Broncos. He spent fifteen minutes talking about mom, then hit me with his plans to call the plays again by shuttling our tight ends, Billy Joe and Jean Fugett.

"Your play calling has been good but we haven't won the close games and seem to be missing some big plays," he said. He knew the situation with my mother was critical and wanted to take some of the pressure off me. Marianne told me I was immediately more at ease.

"In no way do I mean to imply Roger isn't capable of calling the plays," Landry said. "He's as capable of doing it as anybody in the league and has done a good job. I just feel if we pool all our resources and I call the plays it is the best way for us to go."

Through Staubach's request, the media never mentioned his mother's illness until after the final game. Neither did anybody on the Cowboy staff so most all the general public was unaware of the situation.

We had been using play-action all along but really used it against Denver, utilizing rollouts so I would have more mobility. Coach Landry felt I had been getting trapped too much and wanted me on the move. Denver was making its strongest bid ever for the playoffs. Snow was expected but didn't start falling until after the game. Considering it was Colorado in December we were lucky. Unfortunately, our luck didn't hold during the game. Bob Lilly picked up a fumble and did the splits when he was tackled, tearing a muscle in his upper leg. For all practical purposes that finished him for the season and Bill Gregory, a fine young player, moved in at defensive tackle.

Roger Staubach, fourteen of nineteen for the day, combined with tight end Jean Fugett for both Cowboy touchdowns in the 22–10 victory. On the first touchdown, a six yard pass, Roger faked a trap, kept the ball and looked. Fugett feinted a step outside, then cut sharply back across the middle. On the goal line the Cowboys had both tight ends in the game so 5-7 cornerback Calvin Jones drew coverage. Staubach lofted the ball over Jones to the 6-3 Fugett for the score.

In the fourth period, with Dallas leading 13–3, Staubach faked to Hill and keyed linebacker Ray May as he dropped back. If May blitzed, it meant Fugett was probably loose, once again moving across the middle. If he did not blitz Roger would look for flanker Drew Pearson, also moving across the middle but deeper than Fugett. May blitzed. Roger saw him coming and, instead of dropping straight back, he moved to his right away from the blitz and quickly threw to Fugett, who legged out the final twenty yards on a twenty-seven-yard touchdown play.

"Roger did a tremendous job on the play," said Landry. "May was all over him."

The NFL system of breaking ties in divisions is very confusing without my trying to confuse you anymore. Fortunately, we only need to get into the second tiebreaker. If two teams finish with identical records the team which beat the other worse in head-to-head competition advances to the playoffs as that division's champion. We trailed Washington, which had beaten us by several points, by a single game as the teams prepared for their final regular season meeting in Texas Stadium. So in order to take over the driver's seat in the East we needed to beat the Redskins by more than seven points.

Our coaching staff felt we could be most effective against the Redskin rush by using play-action, roll-outs and bootlegs which would move me outside the thrust of their charge. On passing situations George Allen's front four just forget everything and come after the passer. His theory is they might get beat on an occasional bootleg but, under normal circumstances, they'd stand a better opportunity of getting to the quarterback. We gave them a completely different look on the bootleg. We faked an inside trap with Calvin going into the line, then I would keep the ball and roll out on the bootleg. On key third downs and short yardage I'd go ahead and run. If my way was blocked I'd pass. No, coach Landry didn't mind my running on third-and-short yardage, as long as I fell down or stepped out of bounds before being tackled.

I believe our 27–7 victory over Washington was the finest game Dallas has played since I joined the Cowboys, even better than the Super Bowl victory over Miami. We were ready. The fans were ready. Our fans had kept hearing about how loud and active the Redskin fans were so they wanted to give Allan's team some of its own medicine. Hoping to rev things up even more, Texas Stadium officials lifted their ban on banners. So they were streaming all over the stadium . . . "They Shall Not Pass Jordan." . . . "We Love Craig Morton."

We got a big boost in the first half when Curt Knight, a good kicker, missed three field goals.

Rookie end Harvey Martin knocked Sonny Jurgensen loose from the ball and linebacker Rodrigo Barnes recovered for Dallas at the Redskin 35-yard line just before halftime. With split end Bobby Hayes going deep and clearing out the area, Fugett sneaked back underneath the coverage, and Staubach found him with a twenty-four-yard pass to set up Toni Fritsch's nine-yard field goal, which was all the scoring in the first half.

I could feel it coming. The crowd was going crazy. So were the players. We were really knocking the Redskins out of there. Our defense was great and we were all yelling at them, "Look at those guys. They're fantastic." Our offensive line was tremendous. John Niland was handling Diron Talbert and Neely was taking control of Verlon Biggs. Rayfield Wright, Blaine Nye, and John Fitzgerald were doing great jobs. I agree with some critics that most games are won in the line. They can make all the difference in the world. Calvin was super, as he had been all season, going over 1,000 yards for the second straight year.

Free safety Cliff Harris joined middle linebacker Lee Roy Jordan in jarring Charley Harraway loose from the ball, which Mel Renfro recovered at the Redskin 39-yard line in the third period. Staubach combined with Pearson for thirteen and fifteen-yard completions and, on third and four from the Redskin five, Roger rolled deep to the weak side, ducked his head and plunged into the end zone. Roger had keyed on linebacker Chris Hanburger. If Hanburger came up to make the tackle he would have thrown to Newhouse. Hanburger went with Newhouse and couldn't come up in time to keep Roger out of the end zone.

Staubach took the Cowboys seventy yards in eight plays and seventy yards in ten plays for the other two touchdowns, finishing with sixteen of twenty—five for 223 yards passing. He ran three times for eighteen yards.

Washington's only touchdown came on a blocked punt which Ken Stone picked up and ran twelve yards for a score. With 10:31 left to play Dallas had a twenty-point lead.

The end told it best. Dallas stood at the Redskin two-yard-line in the final minute. Instead of attempting to score the Cowboys let the clock run out as the two teams looked at each other across the line of scrimmage.

Even when we won our big games, such as the victory over Washington, I didn't feel like celebrating. Each time when I'd leave the stadium and try to soak up our victory the reality of my mother's situation would hit me. She died four days after the Redskin game.

We went on and beat St. Louis to end the regular season. We had taken another step, regaining the division title against Washington, which had been our big goal that season. We found this didn't count for much in the playoffs.

21

Short Again

The day before Dallas played Los Angeles the Minnesota Vikings beat the Washington Redskins, the NFC's wild card team, 27–20. Minnesota had won the NFC Central Division with little difficulty, coasting through its final few regular season games with the title already in hand. Coach Bud Grant was later to say this was probably his best overall team. The defense still had noted players such as Carl Eller, Alan Page, and Jim Marshall and the offense was certainly better than ever with the return of Fran Tarkenton, the addition of John Gilliam at wide receiver and a sensational rookie halfback named Chuck Foreman. The Vikings were elder statesmen of the NFL and approached the playoffs with a now-or-never attitude.

Many observers felt the Los Angeles Rams, a team which had come together under new coach Chuck Knox, should be the NFC's favorite to make the Super Bowl. Though the defense wasn't expected to be especially strong, it held together well all season. And John Hadl, who had toiled eleven seasons in San Diego, had been reborn as a quarterback. Under his leadership the Ram offense became the highest-scoring unit in the NFC.

However, the Dallas Cowboys were at home and well schooled in the playoffs, so the game was virtually a toss-up. The teams played on a gray Sunday afternoon in Texas Stadium before 64,291 live fans and a national television audience. Minnesota awaited the winner.

We hadn't forgotten what had happened earlier in Los Angeles when the Rams beat us and Harold Jackson ran wild. So our defense especially concentrated on slowing down Jackson. If we could keep him under control we just didn't believe the Rams could score that much on us. Offensively, we thought we could run the ball and also be successful passing against their young secondary.

I'm not sure whether the Rams were jittery or what when the game started but they lost the ball each of the first two plays they ran. Lee Roy Jordan intercepted John Hadl's pass on the first play from scrimmage and our defensive end Pat Toomay jarred Larry McCutcheon loose from the ball on their next one and Mel Renfro recovered. So our defense gave us the ball at the Rams 26- and 35-yard line and we scored each time, though I wasn't around for the second touchdown. On these particular series I was fortunate to twice run for first downs on third down plays. The second time I ran twelve yards to the Ram eight but cornerback Charlie Stukes caught me across the neck with a forearm, stunning me momentarily. I left the game for a few plays but then came back to hit Drew Pearson, who made a great catch for a touchdown.

I used the smelling salts but my head wasn't completely clear the rest of the game. I knew what was happening and where I was but it was like being in a partial fog—reacting mechanically more than anything else. Coach Landry could tell some of my reactions weren't right but stayed with me. "Roger, are you clear?" he asked once. "Do you have cobwebs?"

"No, coach," I said, "I'm fine. Just fine." Then I'd go over and hit the smelling salts again.

We had a 17-0 lead. Sometimes when you get a big lead and have the kind of defense we do, it's easy to relax, become conservative and sit on your advantage. That's what we did. Our defense was stopping the Rams yet David Ray was kicking some long field goals, the last of which early in the final period cut our lead to 17-9.

Then on one of the most unusual plays I've seen we lost Calvin Hill and the Rams made a game of it. I handed off to Calvin going wide to his right. He looked upfield before he really had control of the ball and dropped it. He started to pick it up and kicked it. Then Calvin, Ralph Neely, and Ram defensive end Fred Dryer all dove for the ball. I walked over to the pileup and Calvin was writhing in pain. His elbow was all crooked and Dryer was afraid to move because he might hurt Calvin even more. They finally got them untangled. Calvin's elbow was badly separated, it finishing him for the season. He was one of the real keys to our offense and now we were without him.

When I got to the sidelines, Landry said, "We've got to open this thing up."

"We sure do," I agreed.

LA had recovered Calvin's fumble at our seventeen and scored. Now it was 17–16 with 10:28 to go. Our situation looked bad. It got worse. We decided to come out throwing as we put the ensuing kickoff in play at our 21-yard line. I faked a draw and then threw for Bobby Hayes, but he dropped the ball. On second down I was trapped. Dryer and another Ram defensive lineman, Jack Youngblood, were congratulating each other because the Rams were taking control of the game. The crowd was quiet as we prepared to face a third-and-fourteen at our own 17-yard line. If we had to punt the Rams, who definitely had momentum, would have good field position.

Coach Landry sent in a deep sideline pass to Hayes. Drew Pearson was supposed to run a turn-in on the play. Earlier I had told Drew to change routes and run a post on the same play, though I hadn't paid any attention to him. But he later told me, "Listen, I was wide open against the defense on the post." As we broke the huddle I remembered and told him, "Run the deep post again, not the turn-in."

I kept looking at Hayes as I dropped back into the pocket. Free safety Steve Preece seemed to freeze momentarily, thinking I was going to Bobby. Then I turned back and caught a glimpse of Drew, angling across the middle a step or so ahead of cornerback Eddie McMillan. I fired the ball as hard as I could. McMillan had made a good play. He was close to Drew and didn't have inside responsibility. But Preece, who did, was out of control as he moved toward Drew. Drew caught the ball between them. McMillan stumbled and Preece couldn't recover in time to stop him. Had he stayed in his area he'd have probably made the tackle, stopping us from a long gain. But Drew just kept going for an eighty-three-yard touchdown. I hadn't been tackled on the play so I saw the whole thing. Then I looked over the ground to see if there was a flag. There wasn't and it was like a bomb going off.

Our whole team reacted. The bench emptied and we all ran toward Drew. Calvin, his arm wrapped tightly, was one of the first to reach Drew in the end zone. That play brought us out of our sleep. Later we kicked a field goal to win 27–16.

I can't say enough about Drew Pearson. He was a free agent from Tulsa but when the team signed him he came to Dallas and went to work. I probably worked out with him more than anybody and it paid off for us later. Drew had a good attitude and was determined to make the team. I'm not sure where we'd have been without him at flanker after Otto Stowe and then Mike Montgomery got hurt.

After that touchdown, Drew was jumping up and down. He just said, "That's it! That's it! The ultimate feeling!"

We were in trouble before we ever started against the Vikings. Our running game was crippled. Calvin was out and Walt Garrison had no business trying to play. He had a broken clavicle and couldn't work out the week before the game. Our first year running backs hadn't developed so the only guy we had to carry the ball was Robert Newhouse. Robert, probably our best break-away threat, moved in for Calvin and Walt, of course, tried to play. Everybody did his best but we just didn't have it as a team. Personally, I played what was probably my worst game as a pro.

Washington had been able to run against Minnesota so we didn't see any reason we couldn't. On films, Minnesota's defensive ends Jim Marshall and Carl Eller were coming up field, which would have all but eliminated our roll-outs and bootlegs. But the Vikings changed tactics for us, having their ends crash. I wished we had used the rolls and bootlegs because I think I could have gotten outside the way they were playing. Anyway, Minnesota almost completely shut down our inside running game. The Viking defense was playing like crazy and we could do little.

Minnesota was able to run the ball against Dallas in the first half like nobody had all season. The Vikings concentrated on middle linebacker Lee Roy Jordan, who was finishing his best year. They tried to get Jordan moving, then fold block or area block him with one of the guards and the center. The Vikings' running game dominated the first half.

Dallas was obviously lacking offensively. It missed Hill's inside power and consistency, something the running game had depended on all season. Newhouse did a fairly good job, considering he hadn't played halfback that much. Garrison couldn't lift his arm. He was practically eliminated as a receiver and runner.

Oddly enough, Dallas trailed only 10–0 at halftime. Then Golden Richards' electrifying sixty-three-yard punt return for a touchdown could have swung the momentum in the third quarter. But Tarkenton came right back to hit flanker John Gilliam with a fifty-four-yard scoring bomb. Luck was not on the Cowboys' side. Strong safety Cornell Green was supposed to give Mel Renfro inside help on Gilliam but was slow reacting. Green had been knocked woozy on the previous play and couldn't remember what had happened.

The game was a comedy of errors the second half as Minnesota suffered four turnovers and Dallas six, including four interceptions off the arm of Roger Staubach. Two bounced off receivers and were intercepted. Another was a desperation bomb. But the key was a sideline pass which cornerback Bobby Bryant stole and ran sixty-three yards for a TD as Minnesota won 27–10.

I don't completely fault myself on all the interceptions, but certainly I do on the one Bryant picked off. I saw that one in my dreams after the game. I threw for Bobby Hayes on the sideline. I was a little slow getting it off and looked at Bobby all the way. Bryant had no deep help but gambled and went for the ball. When I saw him make his move I wanted to reach out and bring the ball back but couldn't.

Roger wasn't as sharp as usual . . . But the Vikings played a great defensive game. They were really coming off the ball and moving . . . I think overall Roger had an outstanding season, which is even more impressive when you consider the mental strain he was under.

—*Tom Landry*
after the Minnesota loss

Roger is still young for a quarterback and will do nothing but improve each year. When you look back he's led the league in passing his only two seasons as a starter and quarterbacked us to our only Super Bowl victory. He ranks with the best quarterbacks in the game now but we feel his potential has not been reached.

—*Tom Landry*
offseason, 1974

22

The Real Winners

Father Louis Guntzelman is one of Roger Staubach's closest friends, a Cincinnati priest who has known him since his high school days. He married Roger and Marianne and he has seen a most unusual life and career develop. But he is proud that Roger always has held firmly to what he believed when he was a schoolboy.

"Before fame and tragedy came he already was a person of deep, personal religious conviction." Father Guntzelman said. "He constantly looked beyond the horizons this world sets, yet all the while being a very normal and popular person. Many a talk we have had about eternity.

"Someone once said, 'Faith in God and an afterlife is a deep mystery. A mystery not like a wall against which you run your head, but an ocean into which you plunge. It is not night; it is the sun, so brilliant that we cannot gaze at it, but so bright that everything is illuminated by it.'

"Rog has taken that plunge, sees by that light."

My future reaches far beyond football, of course, and this is what really excites me. Christianity is the most important part of my life and I'll always speak out about it. I am fortunate to have been blessed with certain talents and skills and they are the reason I have become a public figure, in a position to attract attention and be heard. I would be rejecting God's love and blessings if I didn't use my opportunities to the utmost, to talk about my faith, why it is precious to me. To enjoy something beautiful like this to the fullest, you must share it.

It's frustrating for me to see people with a sphere of influence shrugging it off, never trying to understand and to grow as human beings. I've seen famous people in the entertainment business, people whom millions are anxious to see and hear on the TV talk shows, who are so involved in self-satisfaction that they never see what the world really could hold for them and what they could do with it. They just say, "Oh, I'm not into this God thing yet."

Well, I'm glad that I am, because that is where it's at.

My parents always treasured their religious faith and from the time I was very young they tried to give me what they thought I needed spiritually. They hoped that when I matured and became of age I would continue to embrace these values on my own. I have never regretted what they did. Not only were they my first teachers, they were my best ones. They lived the life they told me about and therefore it had meaning for me.

Now I believe, but not because my parents told me so or because God is a security blanket. I believe on my own. Faith is a mystery, all right, but somehow in his own way God provides his Word for man and touches the mind and the heart of the believer, enabling him to accept the Word. God is the one who takes the initiative. We accept or reject it. If we do accept it, we cannot just give it lip service. It means a life commitment. We must grow in our faith. As we do, our lives become more Christ-centered. With faith we can accept anything life has to offer through good times and bad.

It was difficult for Marianne and me to accept a stillborn child. We didn't understand why that was in God's plan. It was very difficult to understand my mother's situation, why God let her suffer.

So many times I have faced a problem and my mind was locked in on one solution. I thought there just couldn't be another one. Then suddenly someone showed me another way and my mind just opened up like a new flower blooming. I believe some day God will open up our minds and we will understand these tragedies and problems. In

275

the meantime, we must fill this void between doubt and understanding with faith in God and his plan for us. Thankfully, there is prayer. It's critical in the world today, calling on the Holy Spirit for strength and help. It's been so important to me when I had to overcome disappointments.

I've been asked many times about my Christian faith. Today people like to categorize you as a liberal, conservative, moderate, radical, or fundamentalist in Christianity as well as politics. But I have to say I'm not sure about my category as a Christian.

I do know this: I believe in Jesus Christ as the son of God. He is the redeemer of our sins and the savior for all mankind. He is my Lord and I believe he loves all of us with a constant and intense love. I believe in the Bible as his Word but I am very concerned when fellow Christians start using it so strictly, allowing little interpretation to judge the worthiness and the chance of salvation of all other people. It disturbs me when the fundamentalist Christian says the Jewish person is not saved because of ignoring Christ. I believe that all people have a chance for salvation, based on their own situation and God's all-fair judgment. However, I feel very fortunate to have a personal relationship with Christ. Through him I will attain my salvation by believing and returning the love that he offers me.

Christ and those who bear his name as Christians are the answer to the world's problems and theirs is a beautiful life. Christ and his religion often are pictured as doom and gloom, a do-not religion, and I am not concerned about people who picture it this way. Christ is joy. He is life. He is love. He is peace of mind. He is everything good. He gives us the ability to look beyond our shortcomings into eternity.

Those who claim to have left Christ or the Christian religion probably have never met him. You don't leave a good thing. That's why it is funny to hear some people say that what keeps them from being religious is their love of the good life. Had they really known Christ they would

276

see that he especially knows how to love. He helps us find and enjoy the good life.

It seems like we Christians don't realize the dignity of the job we have. Christ in the Scriptures calls us his followers, the light of the world, the salt of the earth, the leaven in the dough, the city on the mountaintop. And he wants us to perform that role in society every day, not just one day or one hour a week. The song in *Godspell* has it right when it says, "You are the salt of the earth and without salt it has lost its flavor; it ain't got much in its favor."

"What always has struck me about Roger," said Skip Orr, his longtime friend and Naval Academy teammate, "is how he can put everything in perspective—the good, the bad, the sad. Unconsciously when I'm facing a problem, I find myself asking, 'What would Roger do?' He really is exceptional. He has been thrust into the national spotlight and he's been there a long time, but he still has his sense of values and priorities."

When the Cowboys played Miami in the Super Bowl I had promised that it would be for God's honor and glory, whether we won or lost. Of course, the glory was better for God and me since we won because the victory gave me a greater platform from which to speak. But I found I wasn't giving him much glory. I was just looking after me. I was on a treadmill, just rushing around preoccupied with a schedule which centered on me.

On one particularly hectic day I was supposed to go by Children's Medical Center in Dallas and see a nine-year-old boy who had leukemia. I got to thinking, "Man, I just can't make it today." I had been out of town for a couple of days and wanted to pick up a new suit. I couldn't wait for that new suit. It seemed that looking good in it was more important than anything else.

It was a Friday afternoon and after the busy week I had had it was a temptation to call the hospital and postpone my visit a few days. But I finally made it that afternoon. I took a highlight film to show the little boy and he was so excited it was unbelievable. He was terribly sick yet, amazingly, he was alert and coherent. He knew who I was and had been waiting for me to come with the film. He had missed the entire Cowboy season but while he watched that film he relived all the big plays.

I felt very good about the visit when I left. Monday morning I called the hospital. The nurse told me he had died Sunday night.

It was like someone hitting me on the head. I asked myself what my priorities really were. Were they all for myself, or was I going to try to give to others the best that I could?

I tried to get back on the right track. I started spending more time with activities which didn't involve just me. I tried to give time to projects which weren't related to money, comfort, and prestige for myself.

In one talk I mentioned the field position of life. In football it's great to have ideal field position. As a quarterback it enhances my chances of moving our team to a touchdown. After that Super Bowl game I kidded Chuck Howley about how he intercepted Bob Griese's pass and made a long run down the sideline, only to fall a little short of the goal line. I told him, "You could have scored, but you just wanted to give the offense good field position. You wanted your old roommate to be the hero." Of course, I went in and threw a touchdown pass to Mike Ditka and got all the credit. But Chuck had done so much to make it easier for us.

Well, when God puts us on this earth he gives some of us good field position and others he doesn't. The bloated Biafran baby dying of starvation doesn't have very good field position, but those of us who do should realize it, and do something to help those who don't. It's tougher for those who don't have it but if they still try to do something with their lives God will reward them some day, just as he will punish those who have it and do nothing with it.

The one who is going to get us across the goal line is Christ. But it won't happen unless we live the life he talks about and use our talents, energies, and abilities in his behalf. If you make it across, though, you find the greatest reward of all, eternal happiness.

Ours is a very dynamic, fast-paced world. It can become terribly hectic. Sometimes your mind seems to spin when you consider everything that is happening. It seems that it's just one thing after another, that you just can't enjoy peace of mind. To me, there is a very simple solution to these problems. If you have a relationship with Christ, he will give you peace of mind. If only we try to live beyond the earthly life we're involved in every day there won't be problems like Watergate, war, adultery, prejudice, and crime. If we look beyond this we can withstand anything in our own lives because we are living for God and not ourselves.

Bruce Bickel was a Navy teammate, the back-up quarterback Roger's senior year. He introduced Roger to the Fellowship of Christian Athletes and both have been dedicated to its growth since. Bickel is regional director for the FCA in Chicago and Roger contributes to the program whenever he can.

"Roger possesses a consistent honesty and desire to remain sincere in his faith in God," Bickel said. "It has been exciting to watch him grow in his personal relationship with Christ and to see the strength it has provided him—and others."

The FCA is really fantastic. I believe in the FCA goal: "To confront coaches and athletes and through them the youth of the nation with the challenge and adventure of following Christ and serving him through the fellowship of the church." I try to help any way I can, speaking to high school Huddle Groups and at the annual banquets, attending summer conferences, and contributing financially. Through the FCA I hopefully give an example of the ideals that I express. Through it, young people have an opportunity to develop a stronger faith. And if they do they'll be better prepared to face life.

I hope that the years ahead will find many people taking a broader view of religion. I believe they have taken a narrow view partly because they distrusted our humanity. I don't think the things of this earth are evil. We can make them so, or misuse them, but when used properly they can contribute to our happiness and the glory of God. I can't see how drinking, eating, dancing, and enjoying the things of this earth can be wrong.

So many people make religion seem like a "shall not" religion. I believe religion is a "do" religion, a religion of love, so I welcome the disappearance of the over-occupation with sin and the greater accent on loving, caring, and doing for others. There are some who say that if you have a beer or a glass of wine occasionally that you're not a Christian. That is ridiculous. Christianity is just living and enjoying the fruits of this life in moderation according to Christ's example. And it isn't wrong to have some money as long as you use it properly and don't let it possess you.

If you allow Christianity to encompass every phrase of your life you can live it to the fullest. It can't just be part of your portfolio, like your investments. You must have it in your business life, your political life, your social life. You can't just bring it out at what seems an opportune time. Christianity as a crutch just doesn't work.

When it comes to religion, I am not a scrambler. As an athlete I have gone somewhat against the grain. In baseball I tried to steal home without getting the signal from the third base coach. In basketball I probably shot too much. And in football I am a running quarterback, free-lancing and doing things I am not supposed to do. I have been tabbed a gambler on the field and that is the way I have been as an athlete. But I pray to God I will never gamble with my immortal soul.

Christianity is part of my make-up. I wouldn't go into a game without wearing my helmet and my shoulder pads. (Particularly my shoulder pads.) And wherever I go I want my faith with me. All the way.

One of the most impressive qualities which Marianne sees in her husband is perseverance. "If Roger believes something is worthwhile," she said "he'll stay with it. No matter how much time it takes he'll stay with it until he does it."

Father Joseph Ryan, who has known Roger since his Plebe year at the Naval Academy, remembers Roger's first golf game. "He hit six straight balls into the water," Father Ryan said, "and the other players were hurrahing him. But typical of his determination, he kept hitting until he got one over."

Roger has projected this determination in his faith in God. "He has tremendous faith," Father Ryan said, "and he gets great strength from this. While he was at the Naval Academy he not only served at Mass but during Lent he led ten or twelve midshipmen in reciting the Rosary in his room. Nobody batted an eye. Roger was comfortable. He practiced what he preached."

Maybe you saw that cartoon of the playboy and the family man. On one side was this guy with a big bottle of champagne and three beautiful girls. On the other was a man with a couple of children and only one woman. He looked like he was leading a very dull existence. The playboy looked over at him and said sarcastically, "Boy, what if there isn't a God?"

The playboy was implying that the family man would be shortchanged in life and its pleasures, while he felt he was taking full advantage of them. Realistically, however, he was probably enjoying only sexual pleasure and therefore missing a lot. His was a superficial set-up. All women were the same to him and he had the frustrations of a hit-and-miss relationship. In contrast the family man had security and peace of mind, the sense of fulfillment that a happy, growing relationship produces.

I am a family man, of course. After we won the Super Bowl several interviewers asked me about my personal life and I answered them with my own spiritual values. As a result I felt I was classified as a guy living in a world that just wasn't with it, a spiritual world that was sterile and boring. But I know I live in a full, rich world. Sex and good times are a part of that world but I enjoy them exclusively with my wife. Marianne gives me all the love, understanding, strength, and comfort I could want. We have three daughters who bring another dimension to our love and our growth. No matter how low I feel I can spend a little time with them and realize how lucky I am.

They don't give much thought to my awards around the house, although they found the Heisman Trophy made a good hobby horse. They figure I play football and that's part of it. Because I am a player, they like to go out in the backyard with me and toss the football back and forth. They really get a kick out of that. They think they are really pleasing me, and I enjoy it because I want to do things with them. They will grab the ball and act like the kids they see playing football in the park. It is funny to watch them because no matter how they try to act they are still little girls. And that is what they should be.

"When I take them to games occasionally," said Marianne, "they usually are more interested in the halftime show and what they eat than anything that happens on the field. Their biggest thrill at a game was after Roger's shoulder separation. He was with the team on the sideline but he wasn't playing and our seats were right behind the Cowboy bench. That probably was the best game for them because they yelled at him and he turned around and waved. When he is involved in a game they scream their lungs out but he can't hear them."

That was the year Michelle and Stephanie started calling me Roger the Pocket Passer. They still do. They heard people kidding me about getting hurt while I was scrambling, that I wouldn't be Roger the Dodger any more but a pocket passer. Kids will keep you loose, that's for sure.

I don't like neighborhood kids coming to our door to ask for autographs because I feel that when we're at home it should be a private time. But still I sign them and then they go and tell their friends. "Hey, he's home and signing autographs today!" Then the parade really starts.

One day when this was going on, our girls eased out the

back way and came around to the front door. They rang the bell and when I opened the door there they were with paper and pencil, asking "Can we have your autograph?" They like to tease and that's good. We are close and they feel comfortable doing it.

What scares me more than anything is the thought of not spending enough time with them. It's important to give children love and let them see love between their mother and father. That gives them security and it gives them a better chance of becoming successful and loving others when they are outside the home.

I think it gives them confidence, too, to come to you with problems. Kids are often so insecure that they join the wrong crowd and go astray if they don't feel free to go to their parents with their problems. This is especially true in the area of drugs. Love for your children can overcome anything.

We believe religious education is important, but we don't overdo it with them. We want them to realize that it is the center of our lives. Hopefully it is going to be the center of theirs as they grow in their Christian education through the Catholic church and the example we give them at home. As far as they are concerned, God has overcome the tragedies they have seen—our stillborn girl and my mother's death. They talk about their little sister Amy in heaven. It was a tremendously emotional experience for them but now they understand it in a pleasant way. We worried about how they would react when my mother was dying in our home but we had conveyed to them how we believed in God, heaven, and eternity and they understood. My mother gave them strength, too. They would sit on her bed and talk to her. She was so thin and feeling so much pain but she would sit up and talk to them. She would tell them that Grandma was going to heaven soon. When she was gone, God and our religious faith got them over the tragedy.

Marianne and I both learned love and trust as children and we believe that has strengthened our life together. Marianne also came from a close family although a much larger one. She is the oldest of five children—three girls and two boys—and I know that she missed her family in the early days of our marriage. Some nights she would start crying out of loneliness for her family. She had spent all of her life close to home and now we were moving around in the service. But she adjusted to navy life, just as she adjusted when we moved to Dallas. She was rather leery of life in professional football because it is the entertainment business. It's a faster pace and some people change as a whole new world opens up to them. The divorce rate probably is a little high. But she had confidence in me that I wouldn't change, that I wouldn't disclaim my life and my values.

Now she has found that a football life isn't so bad. She doesn't like the insecurity of football. She knows that anything can happen and suddenly your entire career is changed. But the schedule does allow you more of a home life than the average person realizes.

Everyone thinks you are away from your family so much but aside from those weeks in summer training camp it is a great family life. Our games are on Sunday afternoons normally so that means if we play on the road I am gone only a day and a half, from Saturday morning until Sunday night. It's not like baseball and basketball. Those guys are gone constantly.

During the season I am home a lot at night. After the children are in bed I go into my office and study game films. Some nights Marianne will come in and watch for a little while, just to be together. We both enjoy this closeness.

I'll always be thankful, also, for the way Marianne and the girls help bring me out of my dark moods. My second year with the Cowboys I started the first two games while Craig Morton was having arm trouble. We won both games but I felt coach Landry was just looking for the first opportunity to put Craig in. The third game was at St. Louis. I got off to a bad start and pretty soon he had Craig in there. That was probably the worst I have ever felt in a football game. Marianne knew how low I would be so she brought Jennifer, Michelle, and Stephanie with her to meet me at the airport that night. The weekend really had gone badly for her while I was gone but she didn't let me know that. She just wanted to make it easy on me. So there she was with the girls all dressed up nice, greeting me just like we had won the Super Bowl. Still, as we rode home, I was in a bad mood. Naturally, the girls noticed it and they were puzzled. To them this should have been a very happy time. Finally, Jennifer asked, "Why does daddy have a sad face on?"

That broke me up. I started laughing and began to realize again how much I had going for me.

I wish I could say I've never let a game get me down since but I'm not that way. I want to win and I want to play well and a bad day does make me feel low. After we lost the NFC championship to the Vikings Marianne and I came straight home from the stadium. The girls saw how miserable I was when I walked in the door. Michelle, who's the most emotional of the three, rushed up to me and yelled, "Daddy, you won that game! They just announced on TV that the other team cheated and you won the game!" She was so serious about it. She wanted me to be happy.

I stayed in my lousy mood, however. I just sat there, staring at the TV. Finally, Jennifer brought me a letter she had written. "I love you, daddy, and I'm sorry you lost the game." Then she wrote "I love you, I love you, I love you. . . ." When you experience something like that you remember that the family is what really makes the world. Football is secondary. My greatest All-Star team is with me all the time.

I don't feel like I've arrived, by any means—either on the football field or in my personal life. There's still a lot of room for improvement and I have many personal goals and ambitions yet to be fulfilled. However, with the strength and support I've received from my family and my faith, I believe I have at least achieved a first down, and I still have a lifetime to go.

23

Roger Revisited

One year after original publication of this book Roger Staubach paused to reflect on the highs and lows of what proved to be another unusual period in his life.

The 1974 season was never really in focus for the Dallas Cowboys. The new World Football League struck hardest at Miami and Dallas, signing Calvin Hill, D. D. Lewis, Jethro Pugh, Rayfield Wright, Pat Toomay, Craig Morton, Otto Stowe, and Mike Montgomery to future contracts. Although Hill would be the only player ultimately to change leagues, the disruption and distraction of the signings was evident.

The National Football League Players Association and NFL Management Council clashed in their most heated arguments over the so-called freedom issues and the usual division of money. As training camps opened the NFLPA called a strike, saying there would not be a season unless their demands were met. Players boycotted camps and walked the picket lines, wearing T-shirts which said, "No Freedom, No Football" and showed a clinched fist—the sign of revolution. Fans grew extremely tired of NFL politicos, of the mercenary aspects of football.

When the final gun had sounded for the 1974 season the Dallas Cowboys had an 8–6 record, failing to make the playoffs for the first time in nine seasons. Roger Staubach got off to an extremely bad start and experienced his worst year.

"Roger went through a very frustrating season," said Tom Landry. "It wasn't so much his fault as it was just a team attitude from the very beginning. Quarterbacks tend to reflect a team."

"After that season maybe we should change the name of this book," sighed Roger. "Call it: *Fourth Down, Lifetime to Go.*"

On Thanksgiving Day in Texas Stadium I thought we'd finally done it, that the fans had completely turned against us. I'd had a bad first half and we were behind our big rival in the east, Washington, 16–3. In the third period I scrambled out of the pocket and Dave Robinson came over to hit me. That was the last thing I remembered until late in the game.

I was out on my feet. They apparently helped me to the bench and I just sat there, not really knowing what was happening or where I was. I got my senses back near the end of the game. I remembered we had been behind 16–3 and when I heard all the fans yelling and screaming, I thought, now they've turned on us. They're yelling for the Redskins! We've hit rock bottom.

Of course I found out later what had happened. Clint Longley had come in when I got knocked out and brought us back with a fantastic passing show. I walked over to coach Landry and said, "I'm ready to go back in, coach." He just looked at me. I don't blame him. I was standing there when he sent in what turned out to be the winning play.

We had a second and ten at midfield with 35 seconds left and no time-outs. It was a desperation play, one in which coach Landry hoped Clint could hit Drew Pearson over the middle and, somehow, Drew might split the defense and outrun the secondary for a touchdown. Washington expected the play. The Redskins were in their Nickel Defense in which defensive back Ken Stone replaces middle linebacker Harold McLinton.

But just before the huddle broke Drew told Clint, "I'm going to fake inside, like I'm going across the middle, and then turn back and just take off deep." When Drew started inside Stone went with the fake and then he slanted back downfield, getting a step on Ken Houston. Clint threw a

287

perfect touchdown pass. We won, 24–23. It was the first time Clint had played in a regular season game. He wasn't trying to read the defenses or anything. He was just dropping back and hitting the open man. Blaine Nye called it "a triumph of the uncluttered mind."

Clint also helped my old friend, Diron Talbert, end up with his foot in his mouth. Before the game Diron said, "If Staubach runs you like to get a good shot at him and knock him out. Everybody tries to get a scrambling quarterback, putting him in the arms of somebody who's going to hurt him. If you knock Staubach out you got that rookie Longley facing you. That's one of our goals. That rookie is all they have behind Staubach now." I don't really need to comment anymore on this. Clint did the talking with his arm.

When Clint threw that touchdown pass to Drew it was like a cannon exploding inside me. Everybody was screaming and yelling on the sidelines. Clint pulling that game out was the highlight of last season. My contribution was getting knocked out. It didn't really bother me what Diron said. This is a contact sport and you take your licks and just hope they aren't serious. I never consider getting injured when I go on the field.

There weren't a lot of high spots in '74. You might say the bubble burst. It was the first time I've been booed by hometown fans like that. I didn't like it but I can accept boos. Any athlete, no matter what he says, doesn't like to get booed. You're playing out there first for your team and then the fans. You like to have their support. People who don't think fans are a part of a team's success are wrong. But I deserved some of the booing and that was just the way things are.

I've given it a lot of thought and the fact I couldn't prepare properly for last season affected my psychologically. I've had an ankle problem since college and it finally caught up with me. Dr. Marvin Knight had to perform surgery on it June 1, 1974. He removed the bursa and cleaned the Achilles tendon, which had started to corrode. I think this was caused by all the cortisone I'd taken over the years. I firmly believe if you have worked hard preparing you can overcome a lot of things which go against you. There are just no shortcuts or easy ways to prepare for a season. Through the years the off-season workouts and the knowledge that I have worked hard during the off-season have had a very positive effect on me. I couldn't do that this time because of my ankle problem and subsequent surgery.

I'd had a lot of trouble with the ankle near the end of the 1973 season. But I rested it after we lost to Minnesota and it felt a little better. Then when I was invited to the Superstar competition in Florida the ankle went out completely. Dr. Pat Evans, one of our team physicians, tried everything to avoid surgery. He put a cast on it for a couple of weeks, hoping complete rest without movement in the ankle might help. Nothing worked.

After surgery the idleness bothered me. I'm not the type of person who can sit around. I tried to move around too soon, which helped spoil our vacation. I'd taken my family to Bishop's Lodge in New Mexico, just outside of Santa Fe. The cast was off but my ankle got so bad I had to go to the hospital emergency room for treatment. I spent most of our vacation in bed.

It took three monhs before they could stop draining the ankle but many other things happened, too. The problems between the NFLPA and NFL Management Council was a strain on everybody. I went to the association's convention and, man, was I discouraged. I talked to Ed Garvey, an attorney, and the NFLPA executive director, and other association officials and was led to believe that our demands would be drastically changed once it came time for training camp; that they were only to be used as a bargaining tool. Some of them were ridiculous.

The NFLPA presented the owners with fifty-seven demands. Some were logical; others were not. The players demanded, in effect, complete freedom of movement. They wanted no curfew with training camp and practice sessions shortened. A player who got cut in training camp was to be paid the full salary of his contract, plus a sum for social adjustment.

The good demands were camouflaged. Basically what the NFLPA is trying to accomplish is good because, through the years, I don't think the owners have always been fair to the players. In many cases they've been downright selfish. But I didn't like the form our stand was taking. It seemed to me the association was trying to revolutionize football instead of taking steps to improve it. My teammates and the association knew how I felt about the hard core approach but now, as I look back, I should have gotten more involved behind the scenes and tried to help change things.

The association realizes it made a big public relations mistake. We came out with the demands and just threw them into the owner's faces. We should have gone in there very humble, telling them the NFL had been good to us all, providing us with opportunities which we appreciated. Then we could have presented some logical demands we felt would have streamlined the league.

I think a big problem in the association was that Garvey tried to split groups, even into the blacks and whites. Many blacks felt they were seeking social upheaval. Blacks haven't been treated very fairly in our society over the years and so they certainly could relate to taking such a stand—a revolutionary stand. It was as though we were going into a kind of black separatism. The association even came out with the clenched fist to signify what we were doing. That's the symbol of a revolutionary country. Sure, there are areas in society that need changing but to equate it to professional football isn't apropos. Garvey and the NFLPA officials led the players to believe this was necessary.

NFLPA demands were released to the press so naturally the owners turned the more ridiculous ones against us. I told everybody concerned that I'd go along with the strike as long as I believed what we were doing would eventually turn out for the best. But the more that happened the more disenchanted I got. I kept in touch with the association, talking to Bill Curry, the president, and Garvey. They kept telling me this or that was going to happen but, in the end, none of our demands had really been changed.

I worried and talked to a lot of people about the situation. I left a loyalty to some of my teammates, who believed so strongly about the association's stand. But I also knew I was going against what I felt was right. Some of the Cowboy veterans were filtering into camp, crossing the picket lines. As a quarterback I'm looked upon as a leader so I felt it would cause a big commotion if I reported. But I finally decided that going to camp was the right thing for me to do because our demands hadn't changed. I reported before the third preseason game with Houston.

Shortly after I reached camp Garvey declared that he'd "have hated to have been at Pearl Harbor with Staubach." He later said his statement was misconstrued and sent me a telegram of apology. But I think his original statement was an example of the kind of leadership he gave the association. Players eventually reported to camp so the association took a beating, humbling itself.

I'm still a dues-paying member of the NFLPA and was involved in some 80 percent of its licensing programs in 1974 and '75. The association is necessary, though some owners were trying to break it up. Perhaps the leadership needs to be changed. Personally, I was surprised Garvey was still the director when the '75 season opened, although I knew he had strong support from a number of players.

But the NFLPA shifted to a more low-keyed approach, which is good. Hopefully the situation can be worked out in the background without the negotiation problems dominating the football scene as it did before.

Our team wasn't really together during the early part of the '74 season. A lot of players used the WFL signings and the strike issues as an excuse not to work out before camp. Club officials were worried, too. Tex Schramm had called me in during the height of the WFL signings and said, "You're coming to the end of your contract and I'd like you to sign a new one." I had another year but the organization obviously wanted some positive publicity. We didn't haggle too much. I negotiated myself and then had my attorney look over the contract, which was for four years, running through 1978. It's competitive to what the

291

other quarterbacks get, though certainly nothing like we're led to believe the Jets pay Joe Namath.

Training camp is mostly a lot of hard work, but I do remember one incident which livened it up—or rather, livened me up. I was just about asleep one night when I smelled perfume. Somebody sat on my bed. I opened my eyes and this beautiful girl was there . . . right in my room in the players' dorm. My heart must have jumped into my throat. I jerked the covers up to my chin, leaped out of bed and yelled, "Hey, I'm married and have three kids! What are you doing in here with me!"

"A couple of guys had sneaked the girl into Roger's room," said Golden Richards. "We were standing in the hall watching when she went in and sat on his bed. It was one of the funniest things I'd ever seen. His eyes got big and he sat right up."

"I wished they'd sent her into my room," sighed an unidentified teammate.

My training program took another bad turn against New Orleans, our fourth preseason game. I was tackled, suffering a couple of fractured ribs. I didn't know I'd been injured that badly until practice the next week. I was trying to call signals and move around but it got to be a little much and I talked to Don Cochren and he took me to the doctor for x-rays.

"He was out there trying to practice with his ribs like that," said Cowboy trainer Don Cochren. "He couldn't talk loud enough to call signals. But that's Roger for you."

Staubach missed the final two preseason games. Craig Morton, who had signed a WFL contract later to be voided, took over but had problems. The team's problems seemed to be captured in the final preseason game with Pittsburgh. The Steelers won 41–15 and fans in Texas Stadium booed loudly.

When you've been a very successful team such as the Cowboys, the preparation and work you must go through to retain that success isn't as important as it was the first time. Problems became more significant and you take them onto the field with you. We couldn't bring our team together, though there were false hopes when we opened the regular season by beating Atlanta, 20–0. The Falcons were one of the favorites in their division but didn't turn out to be very strong. Then the tailspin started. We lost four straight games and I had an unbelievable string of nine interceptions in a three game span. I'd gone through the entire 1971 season with only three interceptions.

The Eagles are a young team, on the upswing, and their spirit was high when we visited Philadelphia for a Monday night game. We weren't doing much offensively but we took it to them physically and they were very listless when they came out for the second half.

Dallas, leading 7–0, moved downfield to what appeared the clinching touchdown over the listless Eagles. But Doug Dennison, attempting to gouge his way into the end zone on short yardage, fumbled. Cornerback Joe Lavender picked up the ball and ran uncontested 96 yards for a touchdown.

Early that season the Cowboys just didn't have the drive or character to overcome such misadventures. The Eagles came alive and won in the final seconds, 13–10, on Tom Dempsey's 45–yard field goal.

I've never been a part of a team that was so dominant in a game and still lost. Everybody in our organization was down the next few days as we prepared to play the New York Giants in Texas Stadium. It rained all week, making matters worse. Coach Landry usually recovers from adversity as quickly as anybody I've seen. He didn't after the Eagle game. Coaches say players are apt to get down but the coaches can get just as low as the players. I had hurt my knee in the Eagle game and just couldn't bounce back mentally. I showed absolutely no leadership, no drive. In probably the worst game we've played in recent years, the Giants beat us, 14–6. I had two interceptions and, though naturally we didn't know it at the time, Bobby Hayes caught his last touchdown pass as a Dallas Cowboy, a 35–yard throw just as time ran out.

Bobby lost his starting split end job to Golden Richards that season and, as you know, he was traded to San Francisco as training camp began for '75. I hated to see him go, though it was probably best for him. Plans were for Golden to start again and it isn't good to have a guy who had been a star riding the bench. It was sad the way things turned out for him with the Cowboys, the Bobby Hayes who had caught all those touchdown bombs from Don Meredith, Craig Morton, and me.

Bobby began to lose some of his confidence in 1972 when coach Landry used four wide receivers—Bobby, Lance Alworth, Billy Parks, and Ron Sellers. He also dropped a few of Craig's passes. Sellers was doing a good job and Craig just seemed to have more confidence in him.

I hated it that Bobby was upset in 1973 because he felt I was only looking for the flanker—first Otto Stowe and then Drew Pearson. But we're a flanker-oriented offense, using the split end to mostly clear out areas. I did have some options at times but Otto and then Drew were doing a fine job.

Bobby just didn't work hard enough adjusting to the changes in the defenses, the zones, and combination coverages where you must control your speed and work to get open. With the advent of the zones it was difficult to just take off and run past somebody unless they made a mistake. It really ended for Bobby in '74 when Golden became the starter. Golden had worked his tail off getting ready for camp. Bobby doesn't work out a lot during the off-season. He came in heavy and just never caught up.

Most people felt the Eagle game was pivotal for our season but I think it was the fourth one against Minnesota.

The Vikings, defending NFC champions, came to Texas Stadium undefeated. After Staubach and Richards combined for a 58–yard touchdown pass the Vikings cranked up and took a 20–7 lead after

294

three periods. Staubach threw an unbelievable four interceptions in those first three periods—two were tipped—and it was amazing the score wasn't worse. Boos, heard during the loss to the Giants, increased.

Minnesota, with its fine, all-out rush led by Alan Page and Carl Eller, is a club you just don't get behind and expect to beat. Knowing you have to pass, the Vikings really tee off on you.

But Dallas, going completely against the book, came back. Staubach was on target again and the Cowboys took a 21–20 lead with 2:26 left as Calvin Hill bore over from the eight.

Fran Tarkenton cranked up the Vikings, taking them 68 yards in 11 plays to the Cowboy 10. One play during the series lives in Cowboy infamy. Trying to pass. Tarkenton was hit by Harvey Martin and fumbled. Dallas recovered. The ball was called dead, though films and still pictures showed later it obviously was not. Ten seconds were left on the clock when the ball was snapped to holder Paul Krause as Fred Cox advanced for a 27–yard field goal try. Cox didn't hit the ball true and it took off to his right. It seemed to sail directly over the right goal post, neither inside nor outside. Back judge Stan Javie paused momentarily before he made his call. Then he signaled the kick good. The Cowboys fumed for weeks over that call. "If you're playing well you don't get in the position where victory and defeat depend on an official's call," said Tom Landry.

Craig Morton had signed with the WFL and so we weren't competing for the No. 1 job. If we had been in competition I definitely think coach Landry would have put him in against Minnesota, benching me. Had Craig gone in and done well what would coach Landry have done? He might have gone with Craig. I was very aware of the boos in the Viking game but they turned to cheers in the fourth period. Had we won the Viking game, beating a top team in a big comeback, I think it might have straightened us out for the rest of the season.

The situation with Craig ended in late October, just before we went to New Haven to play the Giants. Craig told me he was through in Dallas and forced the issue by not showing up for practice one Monday. The next day he was traded to the Giants. I'm sure it weighed on his mind that he should have been playing when I went sour early in the season. He played against us that week and did a good job, though we won, 21–7. I tried to find him after the game but he had already gone to the locker room. He'll put a lot of points up for the Giants. I talked to some of his teammates during the off-season and I know they have a lot of confidence in him. It seems odd not to see him at the locker next to me but I'm glad he's getting a chance to play and run a team.

St. Louis was the hot team in our division for the first half of the season. Don Coryell has done a fine job and the Cardinals are to be reckoned with now. After the Cardinals had handed us our fourth straight loss I was more determined than ever to straighten myself out. I'd thrown all those interceptions and was pressing. If we'd been winning the interceptions wouldn't have bothered me that much but they were contributing to our losses. I had ten interceptions the first five games and 15 for the season, the same amount I'd had in 1973 when I led the league in passing. But there's no getting around the early ones cost us, helping put us in a hole we never really got out of.

We had two games with Washington in November. The Cardinals were playing great but we can't forget our rivalry with the Redskins or George Allen. We went into RFK Stadium with a 5–4 record but still had hopes of a wild card spot. The Cowboys had a 5–4 record in 1970 and made it to the Super Bowl.

There is no place quite like RFK Stadium when the Redskins play. Fans go into a frenzy, the earth literally shakes. Allen has his players feeling ten feet tall when they play the Cowboys.

"The Cowboys and Redskins are one of the best rivalries in NFL history. It's like a championship game everytime we play," said Allen.

"Yeah, I'd rather beat the Redskins than anybody. It's a clash of systems, styles, coaches, what you believe in," said Dave Edwards.

I was a part of it, I watched it, but I still couldn't believe what was happening. Washington just killed us. The Redskins were scoring like crazy and we couldn't do anything about it. Ken Houston returned a punt 58 yards for a touchdown. Billy Kilmer threw a 31-yard touchdown pass to Roy Jefferson. When one of the longest halves of my life ended we were behind, 28–0. The Redskins' crowd was the loudest I've ever heard. You get behind like that and most people just expect you to play out the string. We talked at halftime and decided we were going to come back and at least let the Redskins know they'd been in a game.

Calvin Hill and Walt Garrison began to run well. Staubach, playing with an infected right arm due to fibres of artificial turf, began scrambling, coming off hits and doing the things he does best. The Cowboys went 82 yards in 12 plays, 80 yards in eight plays and the score was 28–14.

Dallas needed a break. It came. Mark Washington blocked Mike Bragg's punt and Dallas recovered at the Redskin four with 5:39 left. The Cowboys had finally started using tight end Billy Joe DuPree in the passing game and he made a diving catch of Staubach's 4–yard pass to draw the noose tighter, 28–21.

The Redskins seemed hypnotized, stunned as Dallas got the ball back and drove to the Washington six with just over two minutes left. Two running plays failed. A pass failed. Dallas had its final chance with fourth and six.

The lights had come on in the stadium late that afternoon and that crowd got very quiet, as though it had died. That fourth down play is one I'll never forget. I don't remember many specific plays, maybe one in high school and another one in the Army–Navy game.

Walt went out in the flat to the left and Drew ran a quick down-and-in. I saw Houston run out in the flat for Walt and this told me Bass was on Drew man-to-man. There was no way he could watch Drew so I came back to him. There was a little hole in there and Drew had a step. I tried to just lay the ball in there and when I let it go I knew it was a touchdown. My pass was low and a little behind him but he dove. The ball hit off his right shoulder pad, bouncing to the ground. Our last hope for the play-offs went with it.

"The pass could have been better but it was catchable," observed Tom Landry.

"I'll remember that pass more than any of the big ones I caught. Maybe it wasn't right in there but I should have caught it," said Drew Pearson.

"No, it didn't surprise me Dallas came back," said Redskin linebacker Chris Hanburger. "No, we didn't change defenses that much and didn't lay back. We tried to play the same way we normally play. Dallas just did a heckuva job. This is somewhat characteristic of the Cowboy–Redskin rivalry. We've come back before, too, though neither team has come from that far back."

Thanks to Clint Longley we did have another highlight to a dismal season. A lot of people said they were surprised the way he played. I really wasn't. It was no fluke. Clint has good, quick moves and a strong arm. We were a one quarterback team before he stepped in that Thanksgiving Day. Now the players have confidence in him, too. Clint is a guy who just doesn't seem to let anything bother him. I sometimes wish I were more that way. Last season was the first time since I joined the Cowboys that we weren't in the playoffs. It was depressing, but shortly after Christmas there was an experience which offset everything that had gone wrong during the season. This made me even happier than football could have.

An intercom system connects the waiting room to the delivery room at Presbyterian Hospital in Dallas. An expectant father can talk to the presiding doctor, hear what's happening.

Suddenly, Dr. Meek's voice came over the intercom. "Anchors Aweigh! It's a boy!" Somebody else yelled out. "You got a new flanker!" I was very excited but said, "Are you sure? Are you sure it's a boy?" They were sure. There was a new male member of the Staubach family, Jeffrey Roger, weighing eight pounds, seven ounces.

I'd been sitting in the waiting room, staring blankly at the Texas Tech–Vanderbilt Peach Bowl game on television. I had no idea what the score was or what was happening.

Naturally, we were very relieved the baby was all right and also happy it was a boy. Maybe now all the girls in my family can't gang up on me. We had been very worried. Marianne had suffered through one miscarriage and an inexplicable stillbirth. It had come as a surprise to us when we learned in the middle of 1974 that Marianne was pregnant. It was a very emotional thing for her to go through after what had happened the two previous times. It was in the back of our minds throughout the season that it might happen again. But once she passed the miscarriage stage we became very excited.

Dr. Meek said it would be a boy and people kept talking about us having a football player. Down deep we wanted a boy but our main concern was that baby be all right.

Jeffrey was born December 28, two weeks after our season had ended so abruptly in Oakland. Who said it was a bad year?

I was sitting in a meeting with the quarterbacks and receivers during training camp. There were about nine people in there and it occurred to me I was the *only* guy there who had been on the Super Bowl team. The Cowboys have gone through a big transition period but still remain competitive. It seems odd now with Hayes gone and Morton in New York. Dave Manders, our center, retired and so did Walt Garrison because he'd torn up a knee bulldogging at a rodeo exhibition.

Calvin Hill, a guy who joined the Cowboys the same year I did, still phones me from Hawaii but it's not the same.

And Bob Lilly has gone. Bob has his place in pro football history. He always personified the Cowboys and he was the only player I can remember whose contemporaries voiced admiration while watching him on films. He had the greatest respect of his peers of any player I've known.

But we have some new super stars in the making, such as our defensive ends Ed Jones and Harvey Martin. A lot of veterans said this club reminds them of the Cowboys in 1966, with a lot of good, young talent and yet it has more seasoned, proven veterans than that club. I believe, with this talent we'll be back in the Super Bowl in the near future.

My future in football excites me. The game still holds great intrigue for me and it still challenges me to do better, to keep improving. Certainly, I don't think I've done everything I can do yet. In fact, I believe my best years are ahead of me.

Right now my goal as far as competition is to go out on Sunday and try to be the best quarterback in the league. I've failed at times but I've also had some good days. But I'll never quit attempting to prove I'm the best, hoping this can help the team with the championship again.

We lost in the NFC playoffs two years in a row and we didn't make the playoffs the next season. But I don't look back on these things as negatively as I do constructively. A person can't keep negative feelings or give up on his goals and ideals when he has setbacks.

A lot of people got down on me in '74. I didn't have a good year but I've never been down before that I didn't fight back. People who are saying I don't have the ability anymore are wrong. I have the ability to compete with anybody. I'll devote everything in me to helping the Dallas Cowboys return to the Super Bowl! One thing ... I'll never stop trying.

U.S. NAVAL ACADEMY

1962
PASSING

Att.	Comp.	Yds.	Pct.	Int.	TDs
98	67	966	68.4	3	7

RUSHING

No.	Yds.	Avg.	TDs
85	265	3.1	7

1963

PASSING
(Regular Season)

Att.	Comp.	Yds.	Pct.	Int.	TDs
161	107	1,474	66.4	6	7
		(vs. Texas in Cotton Bowl)			
31	21*	228	67.7	1	0

RUSHING
(Regular Season)

No.	Yds.	Avg.	TDs
156	418	2.7	8
	(vs. Texas in Cotton Bowl)		
12	−47	−3.9	1

1964
PASSING

Att.	Comp.	Yds.	Pct.	Int.	TDs
204	119	1,131	58.3	10	4

No.	Yds.	Avg.	TDs
104	−1	–	2

DALLAS COWBOYS
1969
PASSING
(Regular Season)

Att.	Comp.	Yds.	Pct.	Int.	TDs
47	23	421	48.9	2	7

(Playoffs)
vs. Browns, NFL 1st Round

Att.	Comp.	Yds.	Pct.	Int.	TDs
5	4	44	80.0	0	1

RUSHING
(Regular Season)

No.	Yds.	Avg.	TDs
15	60	4.0	1

(Playoffs)
vs. Browns, NFL 1st Round

No.	Yds.	Avg.	TDs
3	22	7.3	0

1970

PASSING
(Regular Season)

Att.	Comp.	Yds.	Pct.	Int.	TDs
82	44	542	53.7	8	2

(Playoffs)

None

RUSHING
(Regular Season)

No.	Yds.	Avg.	TDs
27	221	8.2	0

(Playoffs)

None

PASSING
(Regular Season)**

Att.	Comp.	Yds.	Pct.	Int.	TDs
211	126	1,882	59.7	4	15

(Playoffs)
vs. Vikings, 1st Round NFC

| 14 | 10 | 99 | 71.4 | 0 | 1 |

vs. 49ers, NFC Finals

| 18 | 9 | 103 | 50.0 | 0 | 0 |

vs. Dolphins, Super Bowl VI***

| 19 | 12 | 119 | 63.2 | 0 | 2 |

RUSHING
(Regular Season)

No.	Yds.	Avg.	TDs
41	343	8.4	2

(Playoffs)
vs. Vikings, NFC 1st Round

| 2 | 2 | 1.0 | 0 |

vs. 49ers, NFC Finals

| 8 | 55 | 7.9 | 0 |

vs. Dolphins, Super Bowl VI***

| 5 | 18 | 3.6 | 0 |

1972
PASSING
(Regular Season)

Att.	Comp.	Yds.	Pct.	Int.	TDs
20	9	98	45.0	2	0

(Playoffs)
vs. 49ers, NFC 1st Round

| 20 | 12 | 172 | 60.0 | 0 | 2 |

vs. Redskins, NFC Finals

| 20 | 9 | 98 | 45.0 | 0 | 0 |

RUSHING
(Regular Season)

No.	Yds.	Avg.	TDs
6	45	7.5	0

(Playoffs)
vs. 49ers, NFC 1st Round

| 3 | 23 | 7.7 | 0 |

vs. Redskins, NFC Finals

| 5 | 59 | 11.8 | 0 |

1973
PASSING
(Regular Season)**

Att.	Comp.	Yds.	Pct.	Int.	TDs
286	179	2,426	62.6	15	23

(Playoffs)
vs. Rams, NFC 1st Round

| 16 | 8 | 180 | 50.0 | 2 | 2 |

vs. Vikings, NFC Finals

| 21 | 10 | 89 | 47.6 | 4 | 0 |

RUSHING
(Regular Season)

No.	Yds.	Avg.	TDs
46	250	5.4	3

(Playoffs)
vs. Rams, NFC 1st Round

| 4 | 30 | 7.5 | 0 |

vs. Vikings, NFC Finals

| 5 | 30 | 6.0 | 0 |

*—Cotton Bowl Classic record for number of completions.

**—Led National Football League.

***—Voted Most Valuable Player